VERT 10

HOW TO MAKE A JAPANESE HOUSE
日本の家の作り方

Cathelijne Nuijsink

nai010 publishers

CONTENTS

THEMATIC ESSAYS

FOREWORD TARO IGARASHI

ARCHITECTURE HISTORIAN, ASSOCIATE PROFESSOR TOHOKU UNIVERSITY

THE DEVELOPMENT OF POST-WAR HOUSING IN JAPAN WAS A PHENOMENON NOT SEEN ANYWHERE ELSE IN THE WORLD

There were a number of contributing factors, including the large number of homes that were burned down during the war; a government push for homeownership to stimulate the economy; growing anxiety among the middle class on their ability to purchase single-family homes amid a rapidly growing economy; the tendency to rebuild homes every 30 years (or what I call the 'Great Invisible Earthquake'); and the lack of high-quality urban residential complexes. As a result, many home construction firms sprang up, offering housing as a new type of product and giving architects more opportunities to create signature homes from a young age. Both Tadao Ando and Toyo Ito began their careers designing excellent small residences in the 1970s. Post-war Japan was an architectural testing ground from which were born numerous classics that refined the definition of residential architecture until it could not be refined any further. This, of course, did not happen overnight.
This book, as its title suggests, analyses the ways in which the modern Japanese home was created. It is not your typical coffee table book, simply showing picture after picture of unusually designed residences. Visuals on their own would only offer a sort of Orientalist pleasure at finding out what unique residences the Japanese people live in. That is not Nuijsink's intention. She wants to explain the background and process in which the modern Japanese home came into being, and what ideas and concepts lay behind their designs. Most notably, she has divided the content of the book between architects born in the 1950s (such as Kazuyo Sejima and Kengo Kuma), architects born in the 1960s (Manabu Chiba, Yoshiharu Tsukamoto), and architects born in the 1970s (Sou Fujimoto, Akihisa Hirata, Junya Ishigami), thus giving space to our youngest generation of architects before they have reached their full potential. There are also interviews with structural engineers and designers who have worked closely with them, in addition to critics, editors, producers and home construction firms to offer a multitude of perspectives on Japanese residential architecture.
There is surprisingly little published in Japan that offers such a wide perspective on modern Japanese homes. Perhaps it took someone from another country to actively seek out meaning behind the cityscapes that we Japanese have come to take for granted. I first met Cathelijne Nuijsink in Meguro, Tokyo. Initially, I attempted to speak in my rather poor English, but before I knew it, we were conversing in Japanese. Nuijsink has spent many years off and on in Japan and knows the country very well. It is this background that has allowed her to create a book that offers not superficial observations, but something meaningful for both Japanese and overseas readers. It is an important book that goes beyond Orientalism to help the rest of the world correctly understand the state of the modern Japanese home.

THE JAPANESE SINGLE-FAMILY HOME
A TYPOLOGY THAT MOVES WITH ITS TIME

Cathelijne Nuijsink

Worldwide, the typology of the single-family home has produced extraordinary statements about housing, but none of them can compete with the variety of innovations developed in Japan. Nowhere else in the world have so many architects built so many small and unique detached houses. The radical nature of the design, the minute scale of things, the limited building budgets, the extremely dense urban settings, the extraordinary living requirements of families, the excessive amount of building regulations and the relatively short lifespan of the structures make the detached Japanese residence a perfect laboratory for experimentation. In rapid succession, Japanese architects have been able to develop and introduce countless new ideas on housing, each reflecting the social, political and economic context of its specific time period.

MINUTE ON A LARGE SCALE
Why is the design of a detached house so dominant in the portfolio of a Japanese architect? Major commissions like large apartment blocks, office towers, museums, city halls, theatres and stations are primarily awarded to big construction firms because of the multidisciplinary character of such companies. Their handy combination of in-house engineers, architects, urban planners, landscape designers, and experts in traffic management, acoustics, lighting, and building physics means independent architects often miss the boat. They have to make do with the smaller projects that are left over. While their portfolios may feature only small homes with floor spaces of 100 m^2 or less, these architects approach each commission as a full-fledged project. Practically every Japanese architect starts his or her practice by designing a single-family home, and many continue to do so for the rest of their careers. Even well-established architects who have gone on to design larger buildings continue to design smaller dwellings 'because of the freedom, the speed of completion and the opportunity to experiment', as master architect Kengo Kuma (b. 1954) explains. Kuma himself is fond of using the small detached house as a test case for new ideas. Once a concept has been successfully implemented, he will re-use the idea on a larger scale every so often.

DOZENS OF CONSTRAINTS
If we are talking about extremely small homes in a context not comparable to cities in the Western world, what makes the Japanese house an interesting design assignment for the non-Japanese? First, Japanese architects work under the most extreme conditions. They have to deal with the strictest building regulations in the world, regulating the shape of the building envelope, the maximum building height and volume, earthquake prevention, a compulsory 50 cm distance from the neighbouring buildings, as well as sun exposure and sightlines. Even if they manage to come up with creative solutions under such challenging conditions, their design process has to be inspiring to others. Secondly, clients who commission an architect have often purchased an incredibly small and oddly shaped lot. High inheritance taxes often force the subsequent generation to subdivide the plot and sell the property. As a result, many large suburban properties have been subdivided into smaller plots in recent years, according to Yoshiharu Tsukamoto (b. 1965).[1] Used for mini-development projects, large properties have been turned into narrow strips, cul-de-sacs and flagpole lots.

Even when sold at a discount because of their awkward shape or unattractive location, these subdivided plots are still expensive because of the high price of land. As a result, any budget left over for the construction of a new home is very small. The houses are beautifully constructed as if they were high-end villas, but we are talking about *low-budget* houses. The average price of the houses presented in this book is 180,000 euros, which is still cheap, even in terms of the price per square metre of their limited floor space. None of these obstacles keep the architects from doing their job with passion. In fact, the many restrictions inspire the designers to get the maximum out of the project. Everything is done to transform an apparently uninhabitable plot of land into a comfortable place to live.

EXTRAORDINARY LIVING REQUIREMENTS

Unlike a rental apartment or house for sale that has to maintain its market value at a high level of comfort for a wide range of people, the single-family home in Japan is designed for one specific family. As it is unlikely to be inhabited by any family other than its initial occupants, architectural concepts can be taken to their extremes. Unusual features like a kitchen at an unorthodox height, a toilet as a separate volume off the main living space, a transparent bathroom in the middle of the living room, or a set of bouldering equipment lining the walls – requests unheard of in Europe – can be easily fulfilled in Japan. The short lifespan of buildings in Japan – an average of only 26 years in Tokyo – has resulted in a continual renewal of the urban setting and consequently a rapid implementation of new architectural ideas. As an incentive to new development, the depreciation of the value of a house is deductible from taxable income in Japan. Wooden houses, considered to have a lifespan of 20 years, can be completely written off in 20 years. A house built of concrete, with an expected lifespan of 30 years, can be written off in 30 years. Once a house has depreciated in value to zero, its owners can choose to continue living in it or tear it down and build a new one. By continuously building new structures, you can therefore obtain considerable tax advantages. Demolishing existing buildings and building new ones is also considered cheaper and easier than repairing old structures. 'Wood structures are prone to damage over time,' says ARUP engineer Ryota Kidokoro (b. 1976) to explain why the scrap and build mentality is still prevalent, especially in Tokyo. Besides the fact that the Japanese crave new things in all aspects of society, Kidokoro adds an architectural factor to the scrap mentality. 'Many agree that "normal" buildings designed from after the Second World War up to the 1990s are generally unpleasant – low ceilings, tiny rooms and cheap façades. These qualities are less accepted today.' In combination with their low-maintenance attitude, the Japanese are quite ready to empty a plot to make way for something new. Moreover, for many architects around the world, a tiny house would equal a short design phase. In Japan, more time and energy can be devoted to the design of a small single-family home, thanks to the commitment of students working part-time at architecture firms as part of their training or with the support of their mentor or *senpai.* The willingness of the Japanese to work until a certain level of satisfaction is reached, however long it takes, is also an advantage for the architect. In addition, the architects benefit from the fact that single-family homes, such as those described in this book, are all private commissions.

No unwanted interference or vision from a commercial developer disturbs the design process. A Japanese architect can therefore carry out a concept as clearly as possible through to the final completion of the building. When combined with a very high standard of execution – perhaps the best in the world – these single-family homes result in architectural concepts realized to perfection.

GENERATIONS OF ARCHITECTS

How to Make a Japanese House contains 21 interviews with 21 Japanese architects from three different generations, born in the 1950s, 1960s and 1970s. All of these encounters concentrate on one central question: 'How do the Japanese approach dwelling requirements?' – thereby offering insight into a series of unique design processes. Twelve interviews reveal the innovative design method of the latest generation of architects by featuring homes they have produced. Nine interviews with master architects place the designs of the latest architectural generation within the context of the historical development of Japanese housing. The selection of 21 architects is based on sustained interviews over the past six years, repeated site visits to newly built work, and the overall diversity of architectural ideas among the selected designers. Each home used to illustrate an interview represents a key project in the architect's portfolio, not only demonstrating an extremely innovative dwelling concept, but also providing an appropriate example of her or his design method. The design methodologies have been presented in interview style to allow the reader direct access, for once, to Japanese architects, in a very personal way. Critical monologues by Jun Aoki (b. 1956), Taro Igarashi (b. 1967), and Yoshiharu Tsukamoto (b. 1965) are complemented by five thematic essays that open up the mystery around the modern Japanese house and make it intelligible. Besides reporting on the state of the art of modern domestic architecture in Japan, this book also sheds light on different architectural generations. It shows the diversity of approaches to housing taken by three generations of Japanese architects. At the same time it explains what connects the architects within one generation and what makes each architect unique in his or her approach. This dual structure makes it clear that what we have here is not just a single type of architecture – modern Japanese architecture – but also an exposition of the way this design discipline is directly handed down, to wit: from *teacher* to *pupil*.

ZEITGEIST

Without an understanding of the traditional Japanese house, the cultural norms governing family relations and the restrictions on building in highly urbanized areas, it is not immediately apparent to Western eyes that these extremely small houses in Japan are comfortable places to live in. This book explains this siting, culture and *zeitgeist*, revealing that the power of a Japanese house has little to do with the rational, such as the number of square metres it encompasses, but everything to do with the spiritual. For example, economic and political forces have had a major impact on the evolution of the single-family home typology. After the Second World War, the American occupation forces imposed a new family ideology, based on equal rights for women, equal inheritance by all children, and a free choice of spouse and career. As a result, Japan embarked on a transition to a more Americanized nuclear family system. Subsequent shifts in family structure, such as married couples no longer wanting to live with their parents, were directly reflected in the planning of the urban dwelling. Post-war Japan experienced a period of rapid economic growth, which reached its peak during the so-called 'economic bubble' from 1986 to 1991. During this time, the Japan Housing Corporation encouraged the Westernization of Japanese society with the massive construction of prefabricated houses based on American models. Subsidized apartments designed according to the rational nLDK planning system, in which the 'n' stands for the number of rooms, the 'L' for the living area and the 'DK' for a combined dining room and kitchen became the new housing standard. The nLDK apartments were as rigid, uninspiring and repetitive as the open layout of traditional Japanese homes had been flexible. Economic prosperity resulted in the unbridled expansion of cities, and architects in the 1960s and 1970s responded to this by making the private sphere turn its back on the city. Homes isolated from the urban context were no longer the exception. There was a belief that closed concrete walls could protect the residents from the overcrowding and noise of the 'cruel' outside world. As a result, family life became a purely private matter, and a view of the sky was considered the only reliable factor in this context. After the asset price bubble burst in 1991, this negative stance towards the 'chaotic' city changed into a much more optimistic one. 'Whereas "Chaos" had been the ultimate paradigm for the postmodern city and Tokyo its prototype during the days of economic prosperity,' write Yoshiharu Tsukamoto and Jorge Almazán, architects adopted a more reflective outlook during the economic recession that followed, 'trying to go beyond the mere aesthetic contemplation of chaos and reveal the laws and processes that shaped the city'.[2] More and more people wanted to own a small plot in the expensive central parts of Tokyo, although this implied a very limited amount of floor space. Architects started to face the urban situation by highlighting the charms of neighbourhoods instead of only their problems. Through the design of a single-family home, designers and clients started to look for ways to re-create ties with the city. The single-family homes designed by architects from this period onwards represent a new relationship with the street, an exterior with a more open character, and an interior that is connected to the exterior without sacrificing the privacy of its occupants.

THE 1950S SPIRIT

The influence of a master on the formation of a student's architectural ideas is indispensable. New graduates have one master: their university professor. By the time they start their independent careers there is usually another: the architect they worked for immediately after graduation. This means we can roughly identify a new generation once every ten years. The oldest generation of architects featured in this book was born between 1950 and 1960 and is represented by Kengo Kuma, Kazuyo Sejima (b. 1956), Jun Aoki (b. 1956) and Kazuhiro Kojima (b. 1958). The architects of this generation all grew up with the ideals of the Modern Movement. They are all searching for ways to go beyond modernist ideals but admit it is difficult to completely liberate themselves. 'While those from the generation before us could talk about the city as a huge issue, my generation talks about concrete ideas for a particular client and site,' is how Aoki sums up the 'Fifties spirit'. Their clients, often older than the architects, are self-confident people who usually know what they want. They consider it the task of the architect to respond their requests, but allow them to put their own stamp on a project. 'Our thinking is not a kind of ideology, but more a fundamental thinking,' Aoki says to describe the difference with the older architects who addressed major issues such as the city as a whole. 'We don't strive for a big social change, but rather a slight change in attitude.'

THE 1960S SPIRIT

The generation of architects born in the 1960s started their practice during the economic heyday when everything was possible, or just after it when suddenly nothing was possible. During the years of prosperity, postmodernist buildings were the norm. During the crisis that followed, research instead of design became the main focus. Waiting for new design assignments, many architects formed teams and thoroughly investigated how to create a good relationship between the home and its surroundings. 'These unit groups are effectively organizations that are well-suited for survival in the post-bubble network society,' comments architecture critic Taro Igarashi on design firms like Mikan and Atelier Bow Wow. 'They have an extremely positive attitude towards the city, because they believe that reform and innovation begins with small things,' is how Igarashi explains the 'Sixties spirit'. The architects from this generation are represented in this book by Yoshiharu Tsukamoto (b. 1965), Manabu Chiba (b. 1960), Ryue Nishizawa (b. 1966), Akira Yoneda (b. 1959) and Katsuhiro Miyamoto (b. 1961). Compared to the elder generation of 'stiff-collar architects', this generation is 'notably casual, both in terms of its look and its start into the field', Igarashi says. As a result of their fieldwork and investigations, they discovered that the urban landscape could function as an incubator for new ideas,[3] and took advantage of the small size of sites in order to produce little houses with unique forms. 'I don't think we are so much reinforcing the status quo of Tokyo's landscape as looking forward to discovering what lies beyond,' explains Tsukamoto on how he addresses the city during a discussion with his contemporary Nishizawa and senior architect Riken Yamamoto (b. 1945) about his generation of architects.[4] 'This 1960s generation is very much influenced by the generation before me,' says Aoki, noting the skip of one generation. 'Because they also address the city, they have a more intimate dialogue with the generation born in the 1940s than the one born in the 1950s.' Although they are very much concerned with their clients' hobbies and individual lifestyles, when it comes to residential design the 1960s architects deal more with spatial issues. 'Of course I listen to the clients' requirements and respond to their requests, but the answer should be strong and able to apply to other clients or sites as well,' says Chiba in explaining the importance of a certain flexibility. 'My design attitude is how to make a skeleton for the urban fabric of Tokyo.'

THE 1970S SPIRIT

Due to economic hard times, design opportunities for the youngest generation of architects in this book, born roughly between 1970 and 1980, are limited to small-scale projects ranging from interiors, renovations, products, graphic design and small single-family homes. Nevertheless, they take the tiny projects very seriously. Their design methodology is flexible and multifaceted: not just applicable to small buildings but also suitable for developing products, interiors, bigger buildings. Their contribution to the discussion on the contemporary urban landscape lies in finding new ways to involve the family in urban life. Instead of withdrawing them from the city, architects propose new lifestyles that allow residents to reconnect with the urban context. What they have in common is their curiosity for little things happening immediately around them. By closely observing both location and clients, these architects arrive at phenomenal solutions. 'While the older generations of architects in Japan carry the status of a doctor or a judge in the eyes of their clients, the young generation of architects can be better described as life consultants,' architect and designer Naoki Terada explains. 'The young architects are of the same age as the clients, share similar interests and are really good in dealing with the highly detailed requests of their clients.' Architects and clients spend a lot of time together during the design process, casually drinking and eating together. Often a new friendship starts, something quite unlikely for the older generations. During these informal meetings, architects listen carefully to the minor issues of the family. Not surprisingly, this is when their clients' requests are truly understood by the architects. Suddenly the abiding love of the husband for his classic car emerges, or the secret that the female client is not good at cooking and consequently cannot arrange the fridge properly. Such a close relationship between client and architect often ensures a steady stream of work thanks to word-of-mouth publicity: a satisfied client will introduce the architect to his or her friends. In spite of the restrictions of the small plans (with footprints as small as 30 m^2) all designs have a liberating effect because their solutions focus on their three-dimensionality. The interiors emphasize a sense of grandeur rather than limitation. A remarkable thing in the era of rapid globalization is the locality that underpins their architectural concepts. Inspiration often comes from the immediate environment (the city), or from personal memories that still carry strong echoes of traditional Japanese culture. The young generation is very aware of the impact the Modern Movement had on the design of previous generations, but they look for solutions that gradually go beyond those of the modernists or elaborate completely new concepts based on modernist ideas.

A recent and recurring topic in the work of these young architects is the reinterpretation of nature. *Kisetsu*, the Japanese feeling for the four seasons, is still a prominent concept today. Architects realize that growing up in a world of concrete and plastic calls for solutions that go beyond the conventional idea of a garden, and they use nature as a metaphor for a new architectural language. Curiously enough, master architect Toyo Ito (b. 1941) takes a very critical view of the work of Japan's younger generation of architects. Having educated many now-renowned architects, such as Kazuyo Sejima (b. 1956), Makoto Yokomizo (b. 1962), Akihisa Hirata (b. 1971) and Hideyuki Nakayama (b. 1972), he believes most of the work currently being built in Japan is too white and abstract. 'I think that there is absolutely no future for architecture in the extension of twentieth-century-style pure abstraction,' he writes in an introduction to Sou Fujimoto's work.[5] 'The obsessive flatness and coolness of that kind of minimalistic refinement just leads to the loss of vivacious human sensibilities, and produces even more homogeneous, uninflected people.' Ito encourages young Japanese architects to go off in a completely different direction. By inviting young architects to collaborate, sitting on a jury for design competitions and through his own school, *ITO* (Initiative for Tomorrow's Opportunities in Architecture), he wants them to explore a way of architecture that 'can restore the primal relationship between people and nature'.

GLOBAL EXAMPLE

Despite its local inspirations and context-sensitive construction rules that do not apply outside Japan, the Japanese single-family home sets an example as a global design challenge. The largest developing countries in the world are currently undergoing a process of growing urbanization. Migration to the cities and the resulting shortage of space will force people to be satisfied with living in fewer square metres. In contrast to the high-end luxury villas most people can only dream of, the Japanese single-family home is a low-budget solution accessible to many. This book argues that the single-family home is not merely an example for building a similar assignment overseas. Built under the most extreme conditions and with a low budget, the design methodologies presented in this book offer solutions for the design process of any building typology, in any country. The lesson we can learn from Japanese architects is the ability to reduce things to their essentials, showing how the design of a single-family home can become a powerful mixture of spatial planning and top-notch structural design of limited size and budget while still leaving room for intuition and poetry.

1 K. Kitayama, Y. Tsukamoto and R. Nishizawa, *Tokyo Metabolizing* (Tokyo: TOTO Shuppan, 2010), 38-39.
2 Y. Tsukamoto and J. Almazán, 'Scrap and Build: Alternatives to the Corporate Redevelopment of Tokyo', *MONU Magazine* 4 (2006), 6.
3 Kitayama, Tsukamoto and Nishizawa, *Tokyo Metabolizing*, op. cit. (note 1), 11.
4 Y. Tsukamoto and R. Nishizawa, 'Discussing the Contemporary Urban Landscape', *The Japan Architect* 66 (2007), 10-13.
5 T. Ito, 'Theoretical and Sensorial Architecture: Sou Fujimoto's Radical Experiments', *2G Magazine* 50 (2009), 4-9.

THE 1950S GENERATION

SUBURBAN TOY HOUSE
Jun Aoki

STEEL TRAIN
Kengo Kuma

LEVELS OF COMPLEXITY
Kazuyo Sejima

UNDER THE CANOPY
Kazuhiro Kojima

SUBURBAN TOY HOUSE
Jun Aoki (Jun Aoki & Associates)

N is located in a typical Japanese new town and makes a reference to its immediate surroundings

Project name: N
Location: Yokohama, Kanagawa Prefecture
Year of completion: 2007
Clients: couple + two children
Special request: Let's try to make an *interesting* house together. If an extraordinary idea doesn't impose any inconvenience, the result could be fun
Site area: 165.00 m^2
Built area: 35.09 m^2
Total floor area: 127.39 m^2
Structure: reinforced concrete
Structural engineer: Kanebako Structural Engineers

ARCHITECT: JUN AOKI
Year of birth: 1956
Education: University of Tokyo, Tokyo
Work experience: Arata Isozaki (b. 1931)
Master: Kazuo Shinohara (1925-2006)

How do you go about designing a house for a client?
Jun Aoki: 'As architects, we know that every client is different. Clients who don't feel they're any different from other clients may have requirements that are very ambiguous or vague. Each design process starts with finding a coherent feeling about a house for a particular client. By visiting the site together with the client, we hope to add to the basic brief. The input from that visit helps us to pinpoint priorities and to form an initial design concept. In general, we create over 50 concepts for each house and eventually propose several options that satisfy the client's needs.'
What if the client's brief is simply too vague?
JA: 'I feel that all requests are based on personal experiences from childhood and that people cannot free themselves from returning to the past. For example, clients often request *tatami* rooms, but when we ask them to explain the need for a *tatami* room, they usually can't give a clear answer. What they really want, as we fully realize, is a place to relax or perhaps a room for guests. We often sigh when yet another client asks for a *tatami* room. We may decide to interpret a request for something specific, like a *tatami* room, by suggesting something more abstract. Our insights are usually correct, but not always, of course.'
What are the necessary ingredients for a house?
JA: 'A good house doesn't have to fulfil all requirements – just the basic ones that are high on the list of priorities. The function of a house is not permanent, because family members get older and children grow rapidly. It should be a very flexible space. If you design a singular solution that meets only the current requirements, in five years the house will no longer be convenient for the family. When we design a house, we give even the more specific elements a sense of adaptability. It can always be modified or renovated later.'
What is the most essential rule?
JA: 'The site is the most important factor, because it's usually the client who selects and buys the land, making the site not just a physical condition, but also a mental one. By visiting the site with the family we get a glimpse into the kind of lifestyle the clients foresee. When people choose to live in the heart of the city, which is very expensive, they typically picture a very unusual lifestyle. They ask for a house with a single purpose, such as a place to relax or to sleep. Take a historical example like the Tower House (1967), designed by Takamitsu Azuma (b. 1933), which is just around the corner from my office here in central Tokyo. Azuma said we don't need a living room, as the city itself is a living room. You can eat in restaurants in the neighbourhood instead of at home. You can meet your friends in the city and not at your house. Azuma's design ended up being

very small, almost like a staircase. But sites in the suburbs represent a more conventional lifestyle. Children can play outside here. The husband commutes to the centre of Tokyo every day to work and gets home late at night. N House is located in a suburban area, and the occupants wanted the feel of a conventional house.'

What role does the exterior of a house play in conveying the lifestyle of its residents?

JA: 'The exterior conveys a message about the occupants and how they feel about their surroundings. We can build a house as big as possible, with only a 50-cm setback from the property line. But this will make the house next door seem very oppressive, and there's no possibility for natural ventilation. It's essential to design with the client's attitude towards the surroundings in mind, especially with regard to the people living next door. The first thing we try to find out is how a client feels about relating to the neighbourhood. Choosing the space between the buildings, and the shape of that space, is one way to convey the message.'

Are you saying that the outside of a house expresses the client's opinion of the neighbourhood?

JA: 'It's not a deeply personal portrait, but it does reveal an attitude towards others. In my opinion a house should not be too unique; if it doesn't fit into its environment at all it appears to be egocentric. You live in a space because you like that place and thus should respect the area around you. The exterior should say that the family likes its surroundings.'

The context of N House is a typical new town.

JA: 'The new town is a highly specific type of community. We could call it "rootless space". The environment is not natural. It's composed of rational requirements and is a collection of signs. You can look at it as a landscape filled with "shortcake houses". In this country, the term "shortcake house" is used to express what the Japanese call a "cutie feeling". People living in the new town want a comfortable space. But "comfortable" is a mental requirement that draws inspiration from models, so to speak. For example, Amanresorts [luxury holiday resorts] claim to be places of relaxation, so people often try to imitate the "Amanresort look" in their homes. The same goes for lifestyles from other countries or even familiar colonial styles, all of which you'll find in our new towns.'

In designing N, you played with the shapes and materials used in conventional houses lining the streets of Japan's new towns. Please explain.

JA: 'We didn't set out to design an obviously unique house. Taking our cue from the surroundings, we gave the house a pitched roof and used the same materials as neighbouring houses for roof, walls and windows. Our roof even sports a chimney, although it has no function. The conventional house has brown or grey exterior walls, and white roofing materials are not available in Japan, so we had to buy dark shingles and paint them white with a silicone-resin emulsion.'

Do the neighbours see N as a misfit?

JA: 'The house is only slightly different. Passers-by may not notice that it's a different style from others in the vicinity, although now and then someone probably sees that the windows have square openings with asymmetric sashes, for example. On each side of the house an asymmetrically divided window has been rotated. And rather than having the drain run from the roof, bend towards the

The bedrooms represent the smallest of three different scaled spaces in the house

The large double-height living room located in the basement makes you feel tiny

Handmade railings are one of the architectural details that give the house a rich experience in contrast to cheap and artificial 'new town architecture'

building and continue straight down, we bent the drain away from the building and had it go up, just the reverse of what you'll find in an ordinary house. This house belongs to a different species. It's designed to be looked as if it wants to be part of a group but is unsuccessful. It communicates in another language – as though it were a toy house '

A toy house? Who plays with it?

JA: 'Every house in the new town is a toy to play with. That's the essence of the new town. But the expression of the house should be rich and natural, not artificial. That's why we didn't use cheap materials, which really would have turned it into a toy. We installed nutwood flooring, for example, a material with natural, rough patches that gives the house a sense of luxury.'

Was N the result of a set of rules? Or did it emerge from its situation?

JA: 'N wanted to obey the rules of its context, but – in line with our normal approach to design – we were not willing to abide by the laws of a standard code. The house did not rise from a tabula rasa. It's an interpretation of the surroundings. In Japan, contemporary designers like the idea of a tabula rasa; they like starting from zero. But I don't. I like changing the existing to create something new. Sometimes the change can be very small, but even a small change can make something happen.'

Tell us what it's like to be inside N.

JA: 'Roughly speaking, we prepared three kinds of spaces: a large-scale space in the basement, a small-scale space contained within the wooden volume, and a medium-scale space in the form of a terrace atop the living area. Think of Jonathan Swift's story *Gulliver's Travels*, which takes you to the country of giant men, where you feel your body changing size – as it does when you're in Arizona, for instance, a place that makes human beings seem very small. If you build a house whose spaces are all one scale, the body responds to only one scale. Walking around in this house, however, we're exposed to different scales and have different feelings.'

What do materials add to the experience?

JA: 'We make a distinction between the material and its application. The material itself is not as important as how it's positioned and what effect it produces. In the Aomori Museum of Art we used brick. But for Japanese people brick has a very heavy, Western feeling that I didn't want to convey, so we painted the brick white, creating a kind of optical illusion. People look at white and wonder what it is and what to think about it. It's hard for them to identify their reactions. In our Louis Vuitton projects we use transparent glass, but ordinarily we don't like communicating glass as glass. We want to express the transparency of glass – its immateriality. We've developed a treatment of glass that produces a non-reflective material with a translucent or matte quality.'

Can we call N an example of Robert Venturi and Denise Scott-Brown's 'decorated shed' – the basement being the shed and the upper floors the decoration?

JA: 'I assume N is neither a "duck" nor a "decorated shed". The house is outside this dichotomy. As Venturi said, architecture is a system of associations, a kind of message to the people. This message encompasses two ideas: meaning and media, the second of which conveys the first. Venturi believed in the existence of meaning. As for me, I don't think architecture should communicate meaning. I didn't try to give N meaning. If anything, I wanted it to confuse meaning. So in

1/2000

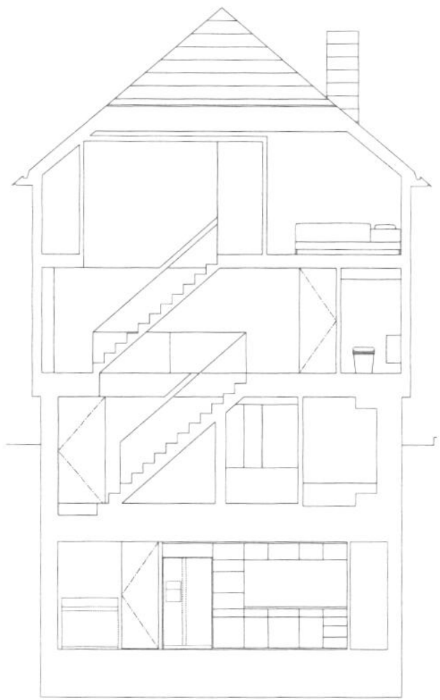

1/200

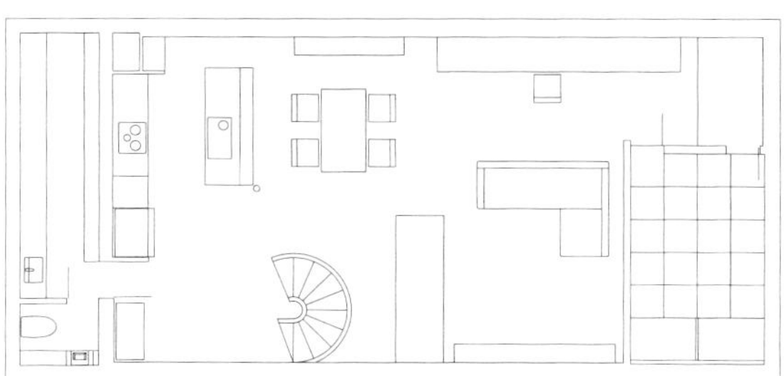

1/200

Square openings with assymetrically divided windows and white painted shingles betray that N behaves slighty different than a conventional new town house

answer to your question, N does not have the same purpose as the decorated shed.'

Recently, we've noted a renewed interest in a more pictorial representation on façades worldwide. Can we call your contribution to architecture 'iconic'?

JA: 'I find much of iconic architecture superficial – buildings made as decoration without any spatial contribution. It's difficult to adopt this method of design, because it's not the surface that interests us but a more complex relationship with various elements, not least the context. You can call N House a piece of meaningful iconic architecture, but only in the sense of overdone. And here the use of the term "overdone" suggests a very silent iconic architecture.'

'MAKING THE SITE IS NOT JUST A PHYSICAL CONDITION, BUT ALSO A MENTAL ONE'

JUN AOKI

STEEL TRAIN
Kengo Kuma (Kengo Kuma Architects & Associates)

The sturdy appearance of the house – made of 3.2-mm-thick moulded steel – evokes the image of a train parked on a side track

Project name: Steel House
Location: Tokyo
Year of completion: 2007
Clients: couple + two children
Clients' profession: university professor + tea master
Special request: A tearoom for tea ceremony classes and a display space for model trains
Site area: 202 m^2
Built area: 113 m^2
Total floor area: 265 m^2
Structure: steel + concrete
Structural engineer: Structural Design Office Ejiri

STEEL TRAIN

ARCHITECT: KENGO KUMA
Year of birth: 1954
Education: The University of Tokyo, Tokyo
Master: Yoshichika Uchida (b.1925)

You started your career during the economic bubble (1986-1991), a period in which real estate and stock prices greatly inflated. What was the zeitgeist of the architects, and what kinds of buildings were being produced?
Kengo Kuma: 'During this period of rapid economic growth, common people were suddenly able to find the joy of design and were really excited about getting something designed by a designer. Architects were really excited as well of course, because every kind of design or move was possible. I started my office in 1985, six years before the bubble burst. Although I was a beginner without any experience, I received large-scale commissions right away. I ended up designing a few postmodern buildings, which didn't leave me with a good reputation. The buildings became a symbol of the bubble era.'
What impact did the burst of the bubble have on your career?
KK: 'I suddenly couldn't find any projects in Tokyo and had to change the direction of the office drastically. My clients changed from rich bubble people in the Tokyo area to humble people from the countryside. After working on huge-scale projects at first, I was left with very small projects that didn't even make money. I wasn't happy with the situation at the time but now I believe experiencing the crisis was lucky for me. It was then that I learned to collaborate with local craftsmen. And because we weren't on a tight schedule, we could think up new variations of traditional details over and over again.'
You have experimented with a lot of materials, wood, glass, plastic and bamboo to name a few, in previous housing projects. Where does this curiosity about materials come from?
KK: 'In the quiet era, just after the bubble burst, I started studying traditional Japanese architecture again. The humility of traditional Japanese architecture perfectly fitted that time. Strangely enough, as a student at the University of Tokyo I wasn't at all interested in traditional Japanese architecture. I figured out it was because my professor didn't teach me the relationship between traditional architecture and contemporary architecture. Instead, he just taught me the frozen situation of traditional architecture. It was during the 1990s that I was able find a strong connection between the two. I found out that Japanese craftsmen are able to preserve the spirit of traditional design and that the essence of traditional Japanese architecture is deeply related to materials and details, something a professor can't teach you from textbooks – you have to experience it yourself.'
I can see a direct connection between your experiments in bamboo and wood and traditional Japanese architecture. But what about steel?
KK: 'Steel is also a material that is deeply related to craftsmanship. Although steel itself is kind of a global material, the way it is used depends on the local

culture. Japanese culture is very much craftsmanship-oriented. I selected the material of steel to experiment with details, like I did with the other houses. One of the intriguing things about steel is its pre-shape. It provides freedom and makes it possible to perforate the material.'

Can steel reflect the sensitivity of soft materials like washi paper, bamboo and wood, and other aspects of traditional Japanese architecture?

KK: 'With Steel House I want to show the beauty of shadow and natural light by showing the different layers of the façade. In the interior we combined the material of steel with that of plastic. Between the steel and plastic we inserted a transparent insulation material. Usually, architects hide the structure by covering it with an exterior material, but in Steel House I deliberately want to display the different layers of the façade. In traditional Japanese architecture the honesty of the structure was also very important and carpenters would always leave the structure visible, instead of covering it. It makes the project very different from, for example, modern Chinese architecture, where people appreciate the strong effect more.'

Nowadays you design huge-scale projects around the world. What role is left for small, detached Japanese houses in your portfolio?

KK: 'I like the design of small houses. Bigger projects require a lot of people, including developers and big contractors. It is very hard to strike a balance when so many different parties are involved. What's more, the schedule of large projects is very tight, so we're always being pushed. In a small house, we can still find the time to think deeply about details and in the process make the projects very experimental. To me, the typology of a small detached house is a perfect laboratory for developing new details and for studying new uses of materials. Those experiments are important to innovate on the large scale. If we didn't use these laboratories, we also wouldn't be able to produce designs as challenging as we are doing now.'

Steel House is a house for a friend of yours, a professor who loves model trains. What kind of house did he request?

KK: 'The only thing the client, a professor in computational design at the University of Tokyo, requested was a space for his collection of 10,000 model trains and a small table to make new models. As there were no requests concerning the spatial layout, I proposed a house with the dimensions of a train. The structure is a monocoque, exactly like that of a train.'

The house is designed like an interface between the family and the city. Why do you think it is important to invite people other than family members inside a private house?

KK: 'Traditionally, the Japanese used to live in close communication with their neighbours. Houses were not isolated, but physically and socially connected. It was after the Second World War that the American influence in Japan became very big and the country shifted in another direction. After the burst of the bubble in 1989, Japanese people realized that the foreign influence felt strange and started to feel sympathy for the compact, old-style Japanese city again. The baby-boomer generation in particular had been very much influenced by American culture, but now even they seem to prefer the atmosphere of the traditional Japanese city. Steel House is not just for the family: it is like a meeting space for the family and their guests. The owner deals with business contacts on a daily

The L-shaped steel box positioned atop of a concrete box naturally incorporates a 6-m height difference

The 23 windows in the steel walls allow for communication between the residents and the city

Lights incorporated inside the finishing create a ‘backlit wall’ that keeps the steel structure visible

basis, and receives them at home. His wife, a teacher of the traditional Japanese tea ceremony according to the Sou Hen Ryu School, receives her students in the tea ceremony room on the ground floor of the house. The roof terrace, 54.5 m^2, provides space for relaxed get-togethers with students and clients outside official business hours. Suspended above the compact urban landscape of densely connected houses, this terrace is like an opening to the city, virtually a part of the street itself.'

In contrast to the closed microcosm of houses built after the Second World War in Tokyo, Steel House wants to communicate with its surroundings. What is the dialogue?

KK: 'The location of Steel House is very unique, as it is defined by two narrow streets that cross at two different heights. The 6-m height differential is incorporated into the house as a natural phenomenon. The client believed the problem of this unusual site could only be solved with a distinctive kind of architecture. We designed an L-shaped steel box that contains the top two floors of the dwelling and positioned it atop a concrete basement. It's wedged between houses, the two streets and a stairway that connects the two streets for pedestrians. The sturdy appearance of the house – made of rough, moulded steel 3.2 mm thick – evokes the image of a train on a side track, which might be coupled to an engine and pulled away at any moment.'

A tactile quality of materials is usually not enough for you. You also like materials to change expression. What experiments did you do in Steel House?

KK: 'Steel can have many different faces and I wanted to show this diversity. The corrugated steel plates in the façade, for example, are for structural as well as decorative purposes. One of the qualities of corrugated steel is that you can make lots of openings. Steel House has no less than 23 windows and five doors that connect the house and the city. We studied the neighbouring houses, and each window in some way connects with a neighbour. Basically, we avoid a face-to-face meeting with the neighbours; it's more about an oblique connection with them. Inside, the structural plates are covered with a layer of urethane foam as insulation, as well as 40-mm hollow polycarbonate plating. Lighting was incorporated at floor level, so that we can see the curves of the steel plates through the polycarbonate and the insulation – not as a decorative motif, but as a reminder of the texture and the structural characteristics of the material. Insulation material is usually covered because people believe it is ugly. However, I like texture so we used a transparent sprayed polyethane insulation material.'

Hobbies seem to be the centre of this house. The main living space contains a cabinet where model trains can ride up and down.

KK: 'At first I thought that the client's model train collection would turn the house into a private museum. But after designing the layout, I found that the house is actually also a private museum for his wife. Happily, husband and wife respect each other's hobbies. The two routings through Steel House show this respect. In order to preserve the privacy of the family, the dwelling's circulation features a formal as well as an informal route. Students of the Japanese tea ceremony access the house via the entrance on the ground floor, where a traditional *mizuya*, a waiting room before the actual tea room, officially confirms their reception. At ordinary moments this entrance space is the setting for a game of table tennis.

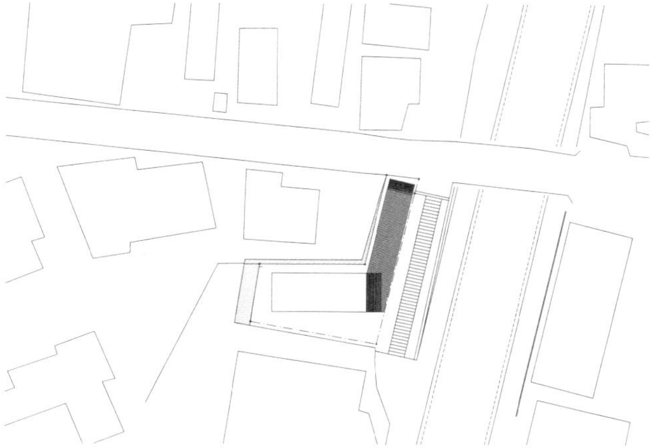

1/1000

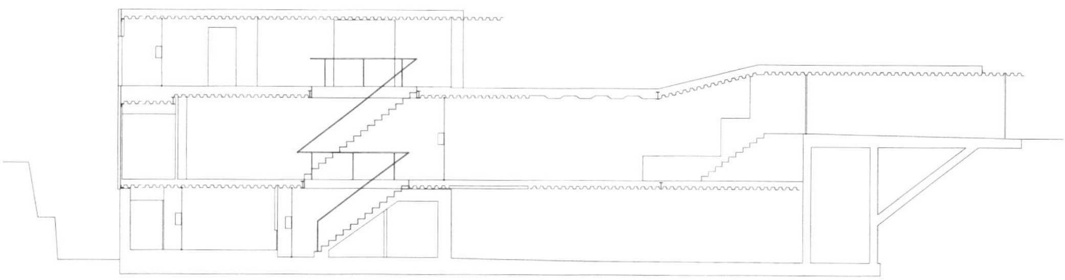

1/300

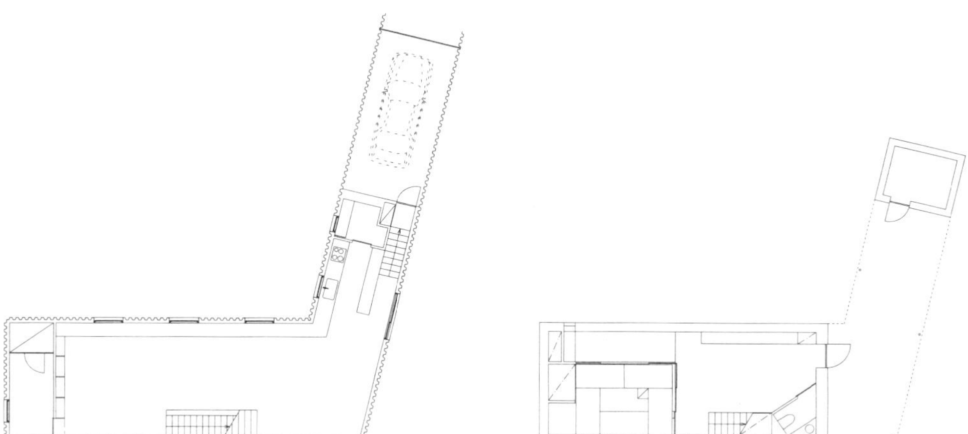

1/300

Bedrooms on the second floor are screened off from the hallway by soft curtains, rather than rigid interior walls

The living room contains a cabinet with 100 m of rails in which part of the extensive model train collection is permanently on display

The bare steel structure is finished with hollow polycarbonate plating and urethane foam to show the structural characteristics of steel in the interior

The informal entrance is situated on the level of the higher street. It is if two houses with two entrances are combined.'

It reminds me of an article you wrote entitled 'What the Paddock Will Look Like'. You mentioned that houses are only interesting when they have the power to involve society.

KK: 'The idea of the nuclear family is not a traditional Japanese concept, but one imported from the USA just after the Second World War. Before this, the Japanese family used to be very ambiguous. Families lived close to each other and shared many things. After the bubble burst, in the 1990s, the situation totally changed. A house became a place for leisure and hobby. At the same time the definition of the nuclear family became ambiguous again. Now multi-families consisting of different individuals share one house. On the other hand you have nuclear families where all family members come together in a one-room space. What I want to do in Steel House is show people that hobbies can be part of society. See it as a pleasure house that connects with the world outside. It shows that the typology of the single-family house still has its importance in society today, but in a completely different way.'

Is it actually quite natural for Japanese architects to now design houses that open up to the city?

KK: 'Yes, I would say we are going back to our roots.'

‘EXPERIENCING THE CRISIS WAS LUCKY FOR ME. IT WAS THEN THAT I LEARNED TO COLLABORATE WITH LOCAL CRAFTSMEN’

KENGO KUMA

LEVELS OF COMPLEXITY
Kazuyo Sejima (Kazuyo Sejima & Associates)

Curving walls as elegant as those of an obi – the sash of a kimono – wrap the exterior and interior of nine residential units in a complicated way

Project name: Okurayama Apartments
Location: Okurayama, Kanagawa Prefecture
Year of completion: 2008
Client: private individual
Special request: Long lifespan, no tall building
Site area: 457.77 m^2
Built area: 207.20 m^2
Total floor area: 553.11 m^2
Storeys: four
Units: 10
Structure: reinforced concrete
Structural engineer: SSC/Sasaki Structural Consultants

ARCHITECT: KAZUYO SEJIMA
Year of birth: 1956
Education: Japan Woman's University, Tokyo
Work experience: Toyo Ito & Associates
Master: Toyo Ito (b. 1941)

What's the difference between designing a single-family home on commission and designing apartments for unknown occupants?
Kazuyo Sejima: 'Apartment buildings house a wide range of residents. Even so, most developers want completely homogeneous buildings with identical apartments. That makes it very difficult to design owner-occupied apartments with a nice atmosphere. For example, when an architect suggests the use of natural wood, the developer might disagree on the grounds that anything made of real wood is unique, and that no two apartments would be exactly the same. Each variety of wood does have a particular grain, of course, but variations in the grain cannot be avoided. Designers appreciate such natural features, but developers have other concerns. They're afraid someone will comment on his or her apartment being different from the neighbour's.'
Please describe the type of apartment block most developers would build in a residential area like this one.
KS: 'Housing projects in Tokyo are usually located on small sites. A centrally positioned complex, rising amid a certain amount of greenery that normally reaches the building line, has a footprint of 50 or 60 per cent. Communal space includes stairs. Long rows of apartments are positioned to receive natural light from the south. I hate designing buildings like this, because they're ugly. In an ordinary apartment building in central Tokyo, each apartment functions independently. Most people hardly know their neighbours.'
In terms of layout and exterior form, Okurayama Apartments is everything but a standard Japanese apartment block. How did you refine the shape of the building volume from the first idea until the final construction?
KS: 'From the beginning I thought about two things. First of all, it is very hard to rent a space with a garden in Tokyo, so I thought about making small apartments with gardens. Recently many Japanese architects have been designing small housing projects, so-called 'designer mansions'. Basically, these apartment buildings feature double-height studios and look more designed because an architect is involved. The property of those sites is small, but the developer asks the architect to maximize the building volume. Automatically the architect will focus on the shape, the material or the interior design. Okurayama is slightly out of the centre of Tokyo, about 30 minutes by train from Shibuya. This time the client preferred *not* to opt for a maximum-sized building volume, leaving me space to make gardens. Less than half of the 450-m^2 site is occupied by building mass. It has a floor space ratio of 45 per cent, very low compared to other apartment buildings.
'Secondly, collective housing usually means several units that are put within one

volume. Instead, I want to think about the relationship between a housing block and its surroundings, while at the same time I want each apartment to have its own relationship with the surroundings. Every architect may have something to say about how to get a good relationship with the surroundings, but they always talk about the entire building volume. I want to bring character to each of the individual apartments, which is how I eventually arrived at this shape. The block can be read as nine apartments sharing one courtyard as well as nine individual courtyards, each belonging to a separate apartment.'

The curves make it very sculptural. How did you make sure it didn't become an object in the city?

KS: 'The first idea of three courtyards cut out of the rectangular volume displays a very closed character towards the neighbourhood. Making cuts in the exterior façade as well, I felt, would already improve the connection between the building and its surroundings. However, at this stage the one-volume idea was still stronger than the idea of the individual unit. Thinking about continuity, I located the entrances of all nine apartments on the ground floor. Moreover, I experimented with a big garden on the ground floor instead of filling it entirely (except for the entrances) with interior space. It was a bit of a pity not to use the ground floor at all, so I moved the volumes up and down: some apartments touch the ground and others do not. In this way the apartments could get an own private garden space on the ground floor or a private terrace on the rooftop. The final design is thus a mixture of the first and second idea. The rectangular perimeter of the building is simply defined by the site after accounting for a 2-m setback, as I wanted to plant some trees between the building and the street.'

Is Okurayama Apartments a statement against the current state of housing in Japan?

KS: 'People seem to feel more comfortable with a life in the interior space as they spend more and more time inside, while at the same time they try to wipe away any dirt from outside. I know this is because when the interior space is cut off from the outdoor environment it is easy to get control over it. If you were to open a window, they would suddenly feel very uncomfortable with cold air and sound entering. It is a bit scary to me that people can only feel comfortable in such a closed space, because you do not necessary have to think about other people's behaviour in this way. In Okurayama Apartments I deliberately put loose soil in the garden instead of a perfect pavement. Japanese people are getting too afraid to even touch soil. I want to make a place, an apartment, where people can feel more open towards the city and where there is a better relationship with the surroundings, while remaining comfortable. This comfort might sometimes be disturbed by wind or dirt, as I rather want them to feel or find the comfort of the place. If a space is completely closed or fenced off, it is not necessary to claim territory. But isn't it much nicer to see some kind of communication happening, for example residents telling "intruders" on their territory not to touch or enter further as it is their private domain? Up to a certain point it might not be a problem having no clear fenced boundary, but if someone intrudes too far on a private domain, the residents simply communicate that it is their place.'

What is the difference in the atmosphere of the gardens in your earlier project of Seijo Town Houses (apartments for sale) and those of Okurayama Apartments (apartments for rent)?

The complex shape of the residential block ensures that each apartment has its own character and relation with the surroundings

Large windows seamlessly connect the interior life with the outdoors

A 3-m-wide public path through the entire site and four curved private courtyards facing the street make the ground floor a curious mixture of semi-public and semi-private outdoor space

KS: 'I believe that close proximity to greenery and soil is essential to good living, especially in a place like Tokyo, where people forget what it's like to be in touch with nature. Soil is something that should literally enter – and even dirty – the house. Seijo Town Houses is situated in a very low-density area. The footprint of my building is only 40 per cent. By spreading greenery accross the site we've not only given residents more freedom, but also connected dwellings to the outdoors and anticipated contact among residents. I tried to bring out the special character of the location. Some of the communal space "belongs" to your neighbour, while at other places it's as though you, as a resident, get part of that communal space back. Most importantly, I tried to make a good living environment for different families in one complex. Although the entire site is fenced for security reasons, I tried to establish a relationship between the garden and the neighbourhood. The atmosphere I feel around Okurayama Apartments is that it is about the movement of the air and about soil. The soil is more spread out than in Seijo Town Houses, as not only the gardens but also the terraces are finished with black soil. Okurayama Apartments also shows there are actually no problems with security even though it is not fenced, as people simply use the roads along the building block. Curiously enough, it is elderly people who show interest in this openness of the block, while young people just walk by.'

What did you achieve with the curved walls, something you couldn't find with the straight walls of Seijo Town Houses?

KS: 'This time I wanted a better mixture of light. In Seijo Town Houses the walls are flat, so one side of a façade either gets light or is dark because it lies in the shadow. When making curves the sunlight radiates in gradations, giving a better mixture between the interior garden and the surroundings. As Seijo Town Houses are for sale, the units required three bedrooms. But using a curve to divide space into smaller parts to make the required rooms would produce rooms difficult to use in terms of layout. The units in Okurayama Apartments are only half the size or less than those in Seijo Town Houses – basically one-room studios. Because the studios are long, curves can divide the space more easily. For furnishing reasons, we took care to give each studio two straight walls, except the centre one, which only has curved walls.'

What happens in the outdoor space between the units?

KS: 'According to the regulations we had to make a 3-m path through the entire site connecting with the street. I made three curved garden spaces, each facing the road. In this way I created a public street, semi-public gardens for all nine residents and more private gardens, not exactly closed but extending further inside the site. I hope that the people living here will arrange the gardens themselves, as well as the space in front of their entrance. This behaviour should affect those who buy an independent house in the neighbourhood, with owners adding some trees next to their own doors or in front of their house. In this way, gradually the nine residents will create an entire environment.'

What was your biggest surprise during the whole design process?

KS: 'The final shape of the volume was the biggest astonishment, as until now my projects were somehow easy to describe after completion. Although the process is long, the final form always seems a very simple one, and normally I can explain why this shape or why this structure was the result. With Okurayama Apartments, the shape was easy to understand until the first stage, as it was

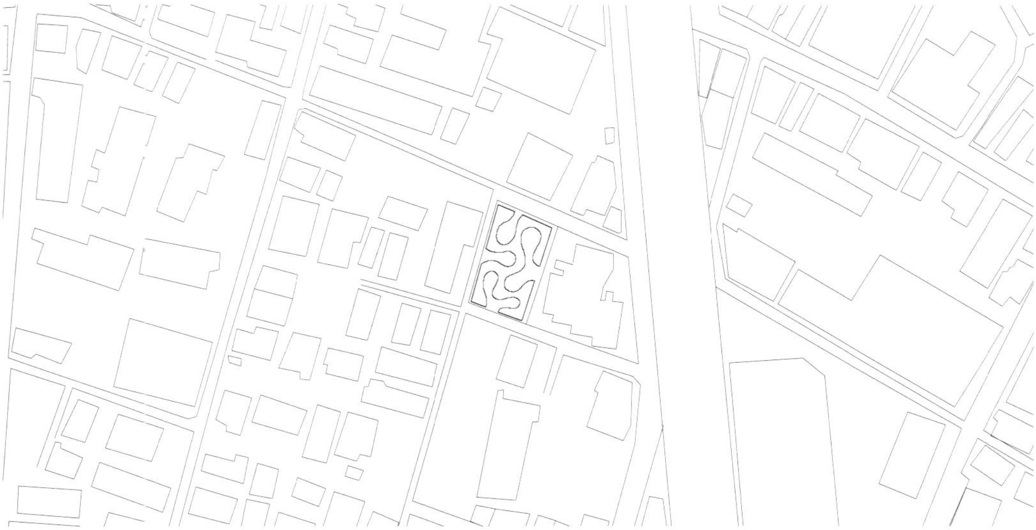

1/2000

1/300

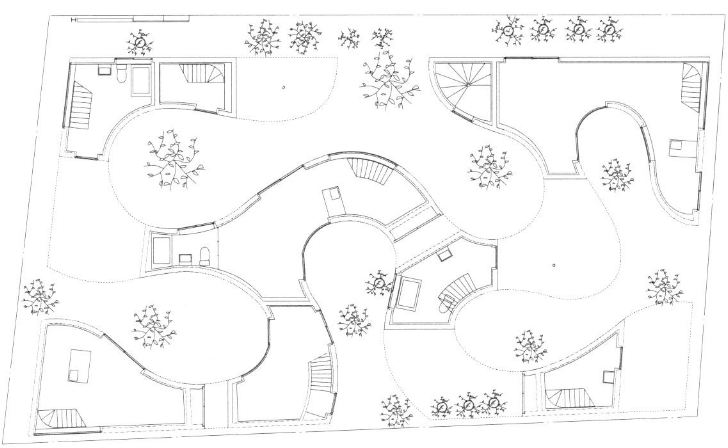

1/300

To make the curved apartments easier to furnish, each studio is provided with two straight walls

one block with nine units that accommodated a courtyard by raising the volume on *pilotis*. However, this volume was too closed: it blocked air flow within the courtyard. The final volume of Okurayama Apartments is very hard to describe in terms of structure or shape, as some parts have been moved up and some down. Small details, like the relationship of a higher or lower volume with the neighbours is what determined the final shape of the building. Surprisingly, it is the most complex one I have made so far, as it doesn't look straightforward at first sight.'

In what way does this project give you some food for thought for future projects?

KS: 'If I were allowed to use more money, I would have thought more about the structure. Using a steel structure with all those curves wouldn't have produced a very beautiful effect, so we opted for concrete. However, concrete needs more thickness and therefore shows heaviness. This was not a low-budget project – rather mid-range in terms of cost. Still, if I had been able to I would have liked to develop a new structure that was a mixture of concrete and steel or something else that would allow for more thinness. Recently, I have been thinking about the physical weight of a building, more than the context or the materials. Let me explain. The site of this project is very close to the station. In Japan a station area is naturally surrounded by bigger commercial buildings while behind these commercial areas we suddenly have small-scale housing. The context is a contrasting mixture that is hard to describe, but to me it is the distance and the density, together with the programme, that conveys the impression of the real weight of the area. Looking at the area from this standpoint, the concrete we used now feels a bit too heavy for its surroundings.'

‘IT IS A BIT SCARY TO ME THAT PEOPLE CAN ONLY FEEL COMFORTABLE IN A CLOSED SPACE’

KAZUYO SEJIMA

UNDER THE CANOPY
Kazuhiro Kojima (CAt/ Coelacanth and Associates Tokyo)

Located on a calm site next to a fruit tree orchard, it was possible to design a house with four glass façades

Project Name: Sunken House
Location: Odawara City, Kanagawa Prefecture
Year of Completion: 2010
Clients: couple + one child
Clients' Profession: office worker
Special Request: The possibility to hide stuff in some kind of storage, a house in which to live a simple life, a roofed parking space for the vintage car
Site Area: 270.67 m^2
Built Area: 86.50 m^2
Total Floor Area: 91.42 m^2
Structure: wood
Structural Engineer: Jun Sato Structural Engineers

ARCHITECT: KAZUHIRO KOJIMA
Year of birth: 1958
Education: Kyoto University, Kyoto, University of Tokyo, Tokyo
Master: Hiroshi Hara (b. 1936)

You were fortunate enough to study architecture under Professor Hiroshi Hara (b. 1936) at the University of Tokyo. How did he influence your way of thinking about architecture?
Kazuhiro Kojima: 'Hara taught me how to look at the world and how to understand the world. He extensively researched many villages around the world together with Riken Yamamoto (b. 1945) and other students. By getting acquainted with different cultures, sites and people, Hara obtained his own strong logic. This is a very essential quality when you have to deal with clients.'
I am sure you did comparable studies of small villages in Hara's laboratory. What kind of design methodology did you eventually develop out of those studies?
KK: 'At the very beginning of my career in 1986, I had this idea of shrinking Tokyo by making the city denser. My designs turned out to be very complicated, and apartment buildings started to look like small complex villages in themselves, similar to the ones we researched. Key projects in my portfolio, like Kobe Factory/Komatsu Forklift (1991) and Utase Elementary School (1995) in Chiba, eventually changed my design approach. From those projects onward, I started to consider a design from the existing activities rather than form.'
Is this how the idea of the Space Blocks came into existence?
KK: 'The system of Basic Space Block (BSB) is a design tool that can generate complicated three-dimensional spaces in an easy way. It was first applied in the project *Space Block Kamishinjo* (1998). BSB is a system of spatial blocks consisting of three to five extremely small, interconnected cubes. By not dividing the insides of the cubes that are connected, we produced a combination of fluid spaces within a square section. The BSB units make a sequence and blend in with the surrounding townscape, creating architecture with an indistinguishable outline. Most small apartments in Japan tend to be designed by plan or based on the layout of the rooms. However, we put a combination of cubic blocks (Basic Space Blocks) into small apartments, so we could recognize rooms as solid space. Residents will have a much richer experience.'
Did the idea of simplifying a complicated space emerge because Tokyo is a city with an incredible visual complexity?
KK: 'I admit that I prefer the visual image of cities like Venice, Paris and Manhattan to that of Tokyo. However, the experience of living in Tokyo is very exciting, because it has many gap spaces and different sceneries. Life in Tokyo is like a small trip with many different experiences. Every day another one! This kind of excitement derives from the complicated city structure of Tokyo itself, which for outsiders seems to have no urban control at all. While 20 years ago I incorporated the shape of Tokyo more directly into my designs, I now prefer to think about the continuation into my design of urban experience and activities already taking place.'

You used to talk a lot about a classification of spaces into 'white' and 'black'. Isn't that an outdated concept?
KK: 'Of course, the reality is that a space is not just merely black or white. We mainly use the black/white concept to communicate with the client or with ordinary people. Especially when designing schools, the main typology in the portfolio of our office, C +A, the given program is always completely black. In that case, we consider that half of the space can become white and turn into a space where a variety of activities can happen. White space doesn't mean universal, but space where people can come up with the function themselves. If the meaning of all parts of a building is already decided and people cannot decide anything, it makes for a very rigid situation. I don't like such uncomfortable spaces.'
Does this mean that white includes all kind of ambiguous grey tones?
KK: 'Once we can have 50 per cent black in our projects and the other 50 per cent any kind of grey or white to allow possibilities, I will be satisfied.'
How do you translate this concept into housing projects?
KK: 'Clients for private houses have so many requirements about the kitchen, the bathroom, the bedroom, and so forth. If you have a large house, let's say 500 m^2, you don't need the idea of black and white, because you can easily include all the wishes of the client. But when talking about a small Japanese house, the entire house will become nothing but black if we include all those demands directly. What we do instead is to tell our clients that we will incorporate all the requirements, despite the fact that 50 per cent of the house will be kept white. We solve the problem of the limited square metres by thinking about how we can shrink many issues into a small space and show them different solutions. We never tell the clients that they should stop having wishes.'
What was the starting point of Sunken House, a 90-m^2 house located in Odawara?
KK: 'The cityscape in Japan, as a rule, changes rapidly. The site of Sunken House is an exception. On two sides it faces a kaki fruit forest that is protected by law. Therefore, the surroundings are rather calm and continuous. Because many trees surround the house, we didn't experience as tight a situation as we would when building in the centre of Tokyo. We had the rare opportunity of designing a house with four glass façades. The proposed lifestyle is one that is very connected with the exterior. We sank the floor level of the entire house 70 cm, so that the residents feel they are living under the kaki trees.'
How would you like to see the residents communicate with the neighbours?
KK: 'The kaki forest doesn't belong to the residents of Sunken House. It is the owner of the kaki forest, an old lady, who is seeking a new way of communication. When she comes to pick the kaki fruits, she freely enters the grounds and communicates directly with the residents because of the unusual openness of Sunken House. But although the house is setting a nice example, I am afraid the other people in this neighbourhood are not so keen on opening their own house to the city.'
Is it perhaps too much of a luxury glass villa set in the forest?
KK: 'No, the total budget of this project was extremely low! So low that we couldn't believe we would be able to construct a single-family house. To be precise, the total budget of the house was about 155,000 euros. In comparison, young Japanese architects usually build a single-family house with a budget of around 230,000 euros. Nevertheless I wouldn't say it became a poor project after all! How to produce a space with the material is an important factor.'

A small annex on top of the house provide the residents with a little space to retreat to, from which they can enjoy the kaki fruit trees from a different angle

With the sliding doors open, the bathroom becomes one with the adjacent 'rooms'

An original partition system using sliding doors flexibly divides the square floorplan into anything from one to nine 'rooms'

A thick 'wall' around the inner core of the house hides the toilet, storage space, the washing machine and the refrigerator

What were the key issues for the clients?
KK: 'The clients are a young couple, a "salaryman" and a housewife. They asked for a master bedroom and two children's bedrooms and at the same time they requested a very open house. She added the request that she wanted to be able to store many things out of sight. But with a small budget it is impossible to design a big house with separate rooms. In the end we came up with an original partition system. By moving the white panels the residents can divide the house into nine spaces as they like. Usually, in daytime the residents prefer to keep the sliding doors completely open, making it a one-room space. At night, they create bedrooms by closing some of the sliding panels. We solved the storage problem inside a thick wall. It contains closet space, the television, and the toilet. If you simply divide the activities in a house into daytime and night-time, it is very easy to talk about black and white. But in the case of Sunken House there are many kinds of grey gradations. Only when all the sliding doors are closed to create bedrooms can we speak of a division in black and white. The layout possibilities of the house are endless. If one is using the space, it is still possible for others to use the house in a flexible way. And even when the wall is used as storage space or for facilities, people can still use it as a shortcut.'
What is the innovation in this house?
KK: 'The section, showing the sunken space, is very important. We intentionally turned the common U-shaped foundation upside down so the house sinks 70 centimetres in the ground. In this way the lower part of the ceiling aligns with the trees, which gives you the feeling of being *under* the kaki trees. Although the house was made with a universal and conventional wooden framework structure, there is a sense of a much wider space extending towards the outside, as we concentrated most of the support in the centre of the house, while the rest is held up by thin white columns. The strange box on top of the house looks as if it is separate from the main house, like a small annex. It is a special room in case one of the residents wants to withdraw for a little while from the rest of the family. The floor of this annex room is made of a lattice screen. Natural light comes through into the central part of the living room underneath.
How can a transparent floor provide privacy? Are you perhaps talking about a mental privacy, instead of a physical one?
KK: 'The family consists of only a mother, father and one child, so they don't require privacy in an isolated way, completely closed off from each other. The top room just gives them a change from everyday life. The view from upstairs is completely different from that from the house itself. While in daily life the residents linger underneath the trees, upstairs they feel as if they are on top of the trees. From here they can enjoy a far-reaching view over the forest and the surrounding houses. If the couple get really angry at each other one day, I guess one of them will go for a walk outside.'
Do you feel you made the daily life of the clients happier with this house?
KK: 'The clients used to live in a standard rental apartment. In Sunken House, they feel very free, including in relation to the surroundings. They told me that they have many possibilities for arranging their life.'
In what sense did you create a new environment here?
KK: 'Recently, we have been talking about the concept of fluidity, including elements like windows, light, water, sounds and activities. Activities are fluid.

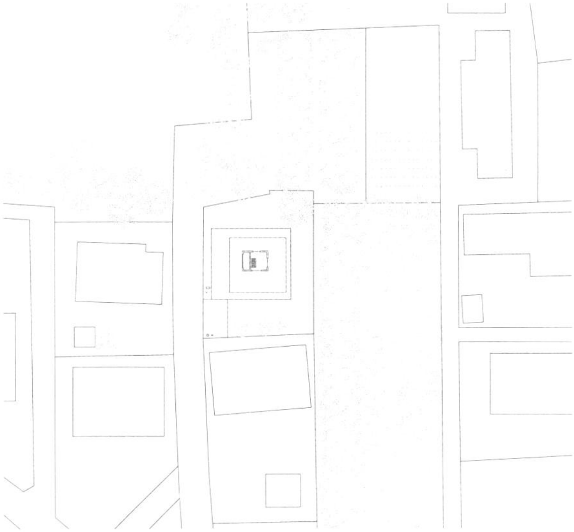

1/1000

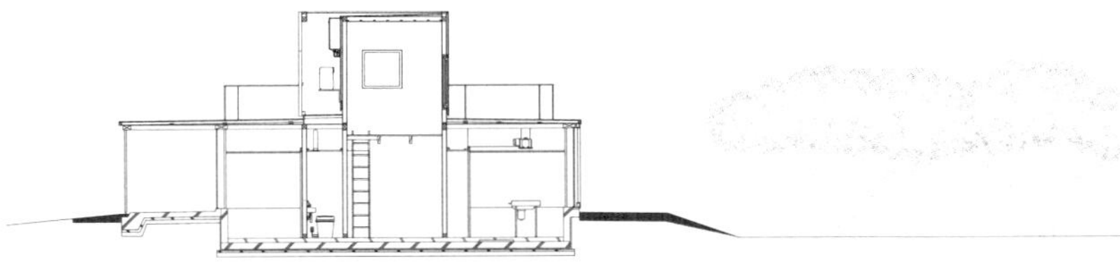

1/300

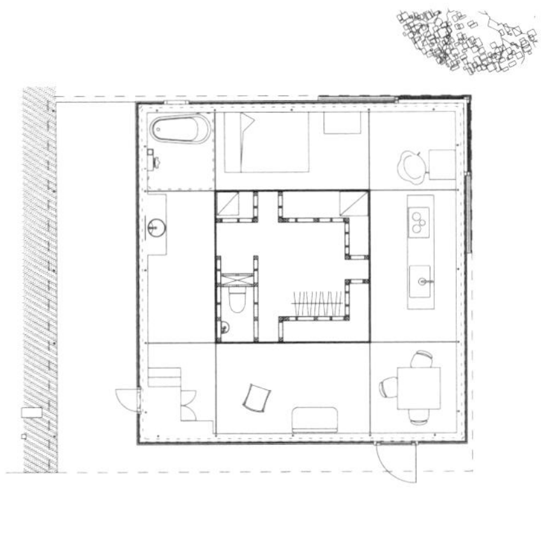

1/300

The house sinks 70 cm in the ground, which gives you the feeling of being under the kaki fruit trees

Designing architecture means setting the direction of the flow. When designing a small private house, we also think a lot about the flow in the surroundings. In this case, it is about how to share the kaki forest, how to deal with shadow and how to control the visibility. Almost all parts of the house are visible to passers-by. Gradually, the behaviour of the surrounding people will change, something we also consider fluid.'

While designing this house, did you come up with an idea you would like to research in your next housing project?

KK: 'At the moment I am interested in *al fresco* or what I consider semi-outdoor space. In Sunken House, almost all parts are interior space, but I like the idea of residents being able to live more outdoors as well. In Jetty Cabin (2007), a single-family house in the shape of a ship, I designed a semi-outdoor space underneath a cantilevered structure. Passers-by feel as though they are between inside and outside. At the same time, the cantilevered wooden deck facing the street is a great outdoor space for open-air parties for the residents. Many neighbours walk pass the cantilevered wooden deck. I like it when people naturally start to gather on the road and talk with the people on the deck.'

Sunken House is very open to the city. Is this possible because the surrounding houses are still very closed?

KK: 'A traditional Japanese house consists of 90 to 95 per cent white space and 5 to 10 per cent black. This is because of the flexible use of the *tatami* space. The built-in closet and the *butsudan,* a small Buddhist altar in Japanese homes to commemorate deceased family members, are the only fixed elements in a traditional Japanese house, and therefore its only black spaces. The Japanese are traditionally very flexible in changing the function of a space. With a foldable futon mattress instead of a bed, an undefined room covered with *tatami* mats can change into a bedroom in an instant. When the mattresses are replaced by a low table the very same space transforms into a dining room. It was only in the 1960s that Japanese people were introduced to the Western notion of privacy. Nowadays, young Japanese people especially have a curiosity for new types of living. I believe that if you design one part of the house very closed, for example an underground bedroom, the other part of the house can be extremely open.'

‘ONCE WE CAN HAVE 50 PER CENT BLACK IN OUR PROJECTS AND THE OTHER 50 PER CENT ANY KIND OF GREY OR WHITE TO ALLOW POSSIBILITIES, I WILL BE SATISFIED’

FOUR ARCHITECTURAL GENERATIONS
Monologue by Yoshiharu Tsukamoto

I would like to talk about the trends in twentieth-century houses in Tokyo and specifically about the fourth-generation house, the house built after the year 2000. Tokyo's first suburban developments in the 1920s produced the first contemporary Japanese house. As the average life span of a single-family house in Tokyo is 26 to 30 years, we can distinguish four generation cycles, which started in 1923, 1949, 1975 and 2001, respectively. Theoretically, we have thus experienced three generations of houses in Tokyo. Inevitably, architects today are designing a fourth-generation house. This continuous cycle of housing generations in Tokyo is quite unique compared to other megacities. Fashion, for example, has a really short cycle of only six months or a year. Infrastructure, on the other hand, has a long-time scale of 100 years. The Tokyo house provides an intermediate time scale, between commercial, fashion, social activities and infrastructure. By embedding a 26-year regeneration frequency within the residential areas, we can begin to observe a variety of building behaviours in Tokyo according to specific generations.

During the post-war period, Japan rapidly produced a consumer society. The construction of detached single-family houses not only articulated the difference between a nuclear family and an extended family, but also separated the individual from the family. It introduced private rooms using the so-called nLDK system, a format indicating the number of rooms plus letter designators indicating the presence of common areas: Living, Dining and Kitchen. Instead of equipment and furniture for one room (common in the traditional Japanese house) each room in the modern single-family house needed a television, a radio, a table, a bed and a chair. This really accelerated Japanese domestic demand. The flip side of this legacy is that the single-family house became solely for the family. The modern Japanese house has also undergone many changes. Since the 1970s, it is fully equipped with air-conditioning, which is used constantly, while the curtains are habitually closed. And the houses stand closer to each other than ever before, because all plots have been subdivided. All these facts mean the Japanese single-family house has become intolerant. The task of today's architects designing fourth-generation houses is to escape from this spiral of intolerance and create a better relationship between people through architecture. To achieve this objective, a house should include certain spaces that accept people from outside the family. We can achieve this by integrating other functions such as an office space, a workshop, a café or a shop, and inviting in those who are not members of the family. Secondly, more opportunities for the residents to spend time outside in a quasi-exterior space can be provided, for example by introducing a loggia or a balcony. When people become familiar with spending time in a semi-outdoor space, communication between residents and pedestrians will take place. Thirdly, the typical gap spaces between two detached houses could be redefined. We can invent new uses for these spaces, for example as a light chamber or balcony.

To understand the dynamics of Tokyo, and the meaning of a single small house in the context of a megacity, it is not enough to study only the urban form. You need to study the rhythm and time scale of the city as well. We summarized those investigations in our book *Behaviorology.*[1] Only when we study behaviour can we sense a time scale. Within one building we distinguish three kinds of behaviour. One is the behaviour of human beings. It is about the relationship between the posture of human users and furniture, for example. Second is the behaviour of natural elements, such as light, heat, wind and humidity. These elements involve with the micro-phenomena of physics, which arise outside and eventually infiltrate buildings. Third is the behaviour of buildings as observed in the larger context of a city. We investigate the vocabulary a group of buildings shares on a particular site, without overlooking its retroactive quality as well as its inherent flexibility. The range between the architectural languages is what could be called the behaviour of buildings.

To investigate behaviour, we need a certain time scale. For example, the behaviour of human beings, including the acts of waking up, eating, drinking, going to the toilet, working, resting, eating, going to bed and waking up again, need to be observed over one day. Social behaviour, including activities such as going to school or the office and a weekend off, needs at least one week. To find out about the microclimate inside a house, you might need only three hours, from 9 a.m. to noon. To observe the changes in the behaviour of buildings in the city you need at least 50 or even 100 years, so behaviour relates to typology. In places where buildings share a certain set of characteristics, a streetscape hierarchy is produced. If you carefully look around a Tokyo residential area, you will discover that several different generations of houses exist next to each other. Although the details may be different, it will be easy to identify the first generation, the second and the third. The changes in generations show in fact the different kinds of behaviour of a building in the city. Architectural design can synthesize all different behaviours in one entity. By trying to understand those behaviours, we can transform the existing behaviour in a more humorous way.

One of the most obvious building behaviours I discovered during my research on residential neighbourhoods in Tokyo is the Urban Village. The Urban Village describes a residential neighbourhood surrounded by ten-storey fireproof buildings along the main street – the Fire Prevention Access configuration. The rows of fireproof buildings prevent fires from spreading to the neighbouring blocks and keep the main street safer for evacuation. At the same time it provides Tokyo with a distinctive urban configuration. Buildings within the firewall are kept very low in height. They face narrow, winding streets with almost no traffic. Once you leave this block, you are in the middle of the city with ten-storey buildings and shops. The second phenomenon I discovered is what I call *subdivurban*. The first generation of suburban developments in Tokyo, like Denenchofu and Okusawa in the 1920s, started 10 km from the city centre. Because the city has expanded, however, these suburban areas are now located in the midst of the city. There is much pressure on these areas, because the price of land became extremely high under the condition of high inheritance taxes. While the first houses in the suburban residential neighbourhoods totalled 240 m^2, the land soon became unaffordable for ordinary employees to inherit whole. This has accelerated the subdivision of property in order to pay inheritance taxes. The initial concept of those residential neighbourhoods has thus been transformed. A third phenomenon I discovered is *commerzidence*. Cat Street, a well-known shopping street famous for its hip youth-oriented fashion shows and cafés, is the most

typical example in Tokyo. In this small street commercial activities interact with the structure of a residential area. This is an urban pattern that Tokyo residents really like, combining shopping with working and living, all in one place. Typically for a *commerzidence*, the buildings are small and in keeping with the scale of the urban space. We do not find any chain stores or big companies in such areas. All the buildings are maintained by small capital, and customers know the owner personally. This kind of urban typology was never planned; it has always emerged during a transformation of a residential neighbourhood by means of commerce. A good example of *commerzidence* in Tokyo used to be the area around Nakameguro Station, an area that was discovered by young people in the 1990s, and one of the centres until 2006 or 2007. Nowadays the centre of *commerzidence* is moving towards the west side of Tokyo, around Ookayama.
Architects from older generations tried to turn the house into a microcosm in an attempt to criticize modernism. Modernism focused on a fantasy of creating super-transparency between the inside and outside. Architecture had to be universal and functional. I cannot learn from the modernist approach anymore but simply being opposed to modernism is also passé. I would rather find the solution in architectural intelligence: a common creativity embedded in the architectural language of a building. It is similar to the kind of intelligence still found in Italian palazzos, Parisian apartments or Kyoto's old *machiya* (old wooden town houses). An architect is not somebody who just designs a building but also somebody who thinks about the social framework of architectural production and urban creation. This framework must be investigated in order to discover how to see the city, how to understand the city, and most importantly, how to activate the city. The challenges left in Tokyo for our generation of architects definitely lies in the design of public space. We have too many buildings in Tokyo, but there are still many undefined spaces. Look at all the non-organized interstitial spaces between buildings, streets and front yards. With public space I don't mean the kind of public space in buildings owned by the government. We should design public space that appears in different venues. I can imagine it could even extend into privately owned buildings like single-family houses.

1 Atelier Bow-Wow, *The Architectures of Atelier Bow-Wow: Behaviorology* (New York: Rizzoli, 2010).

THE 1960S GENERATION

KALEIDOSCOPIC VIEWS
Manabu Chiba

ACTIVATING THE GAPS
Yoshiharu Tsukamoto

VOID IN A VOID
Akira Yoneda

CURVES FOR PRIVACY
Katsuhiro Miyamoto

COMMUNITY SPHERES
Ryue Nishizawa

KALEIDOSCOPIC VIEWS
Manabu Chiba (Chiba Manabu Architects)

The unappealing setting and the proximity of the neighbours became the theme of this small apartment building

Project Name: Studio Gotenyama
Location: Shinagawa-ku, Tokyo
Date of Completion: 2006
Client: Artec co., ltd
Special Request: A product clearly designed by Manabu Chiba. The general producer of this project is related to an art museum, so he wanted the building to be one of his masterpieces
Residents: three individuals/couples
Site Area: 131.40 m^2
Built Area: 80.28 m^2
Total Floor Area: 277.35 m^2
Maximum Building Height: 11.30 m
Storeys: four
Units: three (rental)
Structure: box frame type reinforced concrete
Structural Engineer: Kanebo Structural Engineers

ARCHITECT: MANABU CHIBA
Year of Birth: 1960
Education: The University of Tokyo, Tokyo
Work experience: Nihon Sekkei Inc.
Master: Hisao Koyama (b. 1937)

What can you as an architect contribute to the design of the urban landscape?
Manabu Chiba: 'I recently talked with landscape architects who spoke about the sculptor Robert Alwein. Alwein listed four definitions for a sculpture. First, he talks about "site dominant". In this case the sculpture is made without thinking of the setting of the sculpture. In fact, the sculptor doesn't care whether the sculpture is a garden or a museum. The second concept is "site adjusted". The sculptor thinks about the kind of location in which the sculpture is going to be placed, for example a station plaza or a garden. The third concept is well known and is "site specific": the artist has visited the site and thinks about a sculpture that really fits. But according to Alwein, there should be a fourth definition, namely "site generated". Once the sculpture is placed on the site, the meaning of the site becomes clear. By making the sculpture you gradually discover the context and aspects of the site that were unknown. Compared to this, "site specific" is actually a very passive concept. Alwein's explanation of "site generated" describes my ideas on architectural design very well. In Tokyo, it is really hard to explain the context. Some say it is chaos, while others say the chaos is its beauty. I still believe we should look for a context. Tokyo's context is hidden, and you have to discover it each time you create architecture.'
What is the context of Studio Gotenyama?
MC: 'The site is typical Tokyo, a dense mixture of modern high-rise towers and old two-storey or three-storey wooden structures behind them. There is little sunlight and limited views. It is easy to say that this is not a good environment for living. But if we take this attitude we will always have to repeat the scrap-and-build methodology, immediately destroying everything that is not good. Tokyo has many aspects we never discovered before. At the Gotenyama site I wanted to design a building that can rebuild the charm of that area.'
What did you discover about the site?
MC: 'The distance between the neighbouring buildings and the site is a mere 1 m, so I concentrated on the boundary design and the relationship between the interior space and the very dense exterior environment. The first discovery was the effect of putting depth in the windows. I created deep window frames – between 700 mm and 1000 mm – all around the apartments. Sitting at a window you have a direct connection with the outdoors. On the other hand, because of the depth, you can easily hide yourself and find privacy as you move through the apartment.'
It's nice way of thinking about privacy, but not enough to make a positive statement towards the ugly environment.
MC: 'Yes, that's why I came up with the idea of cladding the inside of the windows

with reflective stainless steel. The steel gives interesting reflections, like a kaleidoscope. The reflections provide more detail about the micro-landscape on the site. The deep window controls the privacy, but at the same time it reveals a very unique living condition by reflecting the micro-environments found between buildings. The reflections give you a little bit of illusionary scenery.'

At first you made a thick and defensive wall. Then it seems you softened the wall again by punching it full of holes.

MC: 'A design process is always full of contradictions. People want to protect themselves and at the same time communicate with each other. Living very close to each other in a very dense urban environment like Tokyo, it's difficult to find a good balance between privacy and community. So people usually just take the easy way out and shut out the neighbours for the sake of their own privacy. Because there is not an extremely nice view from this site and the apartments are located close to a noisy thoroughfare, I started off with a thick boundary to protect the residents from the environment. Inside this boundary, in the perimeter of the house, I put all the facilities such as storage, toilet, bathroom and kitchen. But by merely enclosing the private space with a thick wall we get a kind of 1960s attitude. From the 1960s onward we experienced rapid economic growth in Japan, and the cities expanded at tremendous speed. Architects naturally responded to this situation by closing off the living environments from the chaotic urban environment. Tadao Ando's Row House in Sumiyoshi (1976), a small two-storey concrete house cast on site, is an icon of this era. The house is completely separated from the neighbours and Ando used the sky as the only reliable context in the city. I respect Ando's solution a lot, considering the *zeitgeist* of that period. But as times are changing, I would like my buildings to express a different attitude towards the city. After I made this thick protective wall, I started to think about opening it again by means of windows and establishing a connection between the interior and the exterior. The holes in the very thick wall make for an ambiguous boundary condition.'

This is a small apartment building with rental units. What is the difference with a single-family house?

MC: 'When designing a private residence, I know the clients and their way of life. Still, I always try to stay away from lifestyle. To me, architecture is an extension of the topography or the urban fabric. If an architectural space can repeat or exaggerate the charm of the site it will be a nice place to live for anybody, not just for one particular family or lifestyle. Studio Gotenyama contains three apartments for rent, one on each floor. As I didn't know who was going to live there I made the space very flexible. Flexible space doesn't mean universal space. Flexibility is people figuring out for themselves how to use a space. For example, when children visit a vacant lot, they just use the existing topography as a playground. That kind of dialogue between topography and human activities is something we can always find. If I can make a residence or housing complex as an extension of the urban topography by means of architectural space, then anybody can live there or enjoy discovering how to use the space.'

Do you feel limited in your design if you don't know the clients?

MC: 'Basically, people are not so different the world over. My attitude is about how to design a skeleton in the urban fabric of Tokyo. How much you design as an architect and how much the owners design as residents – that is what I call a

Window frames set in an extra-thick wall (containing storage and facilities) provide the residents with some distance from the neighbours

The window frames are clad with stainless steel on the inside, which reflects the abominable view like a kaleidoscope

To soften the defensive attitude of the façade, Manabu Chiba punched openings in the circular plan apartments

creative space. The needs of clients may differ on a detailed level, but in the end they all request some kind of privacy and a connection with other people at the same time.'

So how do you achieve a common level of comfort?

MC: 'People feel relaxed when entering an open space, but feel scared going into a dark or invisible space. This is a universal phenomenon. Children, for example, always tend to enter closed spaces or niches. The built-in closet space in a traditional Japanese house is the perfect playground for children because it feels like a protected space for them. On the other hand, children also like very large, open spaces to run around in. When I talk about flexibility, I'm not talking about a standardized use of a space. I'm talking about land form and topography, rather than the square metres or the amount of rooms. When I design I try to respond to that level of use or equipment of facility.'

What can we learn about Japanese flexibility?

MC: 'Making rooms and corridors can solve a lot of architectural problems in a very simple way, because you can easily provide privacy. But this way of thinking is too black and white. When my clients request privacy, I am sure they also mean they want some sort of connection with other members of the family or their surroundings. You cannot resolve such conflicting requirements by just making a door that opens and closes. That is too meagre a connection, like zero and one. A wall or a door works functionally, but not mentally. With the door closed, the connection is completely gone. I prefer making one continuous space that contains private space as well as connective space.'

What kind of space do you have in mind when talking about connective space?

MC: 'Imagine you are going to the forest for a picnic. The best spot in which to eat outdoors will never be the same spot children choose to play. Adults will pick a lovely tree to sit underneath to eat. Children who want to play will move to a place that is more open. Human beings are always reacting to a space. The forest is an interesting example, as it is a continuous space but at the same time a place that you can hide in.'

How can a natural forest be translated into architecture?

MC: 'Natural phenomena like the difference in light conditions outside could already form a kind of separation between the family members. Even the movement of a tree outside that is reflected inside the house is useful as a mediator. If we consider natural phenomena or time as an alternative to walls, we can establish both a connection and separation, and make very delicate levels of distance.'

In your opinion the layout of a Western house is too rational. Do Japanese architects design more poetic housing plans?

MC: 'Because we have four distinctive seasons in Japan, our culture knows many ways of appreciating nature. We can enjoy the same tree in a completely different manner throughout the year. The changes in natural conditions have provided the Japanese with a delicate sense for even subtle changes in their environment. Take the traditional Japanese Zen garden Ryoanji in Kyoto. It is a rock garden, but we Japanese can imagine an entire sea by just looking at stones. This kind of attitude is very strong in Japan.'

Where are the natural phenomena when we talk about the concrete jungle of Tokyo?

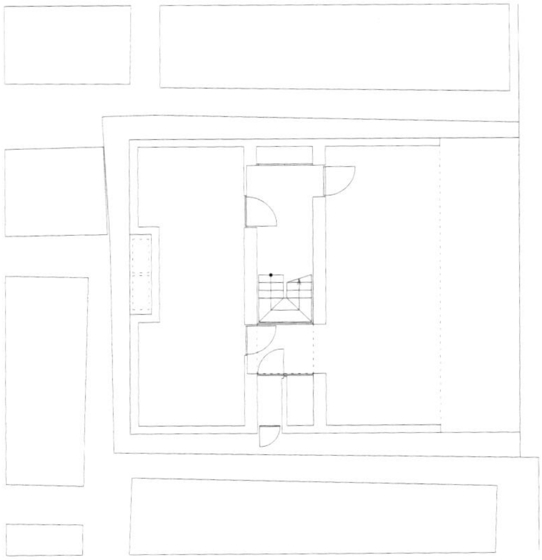

1/160

1/200

1/200

Depressing views humouriously turn into illusionary scenery once reflected in the window frames

MC: 'Tokyo itself is like a forest. Every day we experience different trees, new buildings and new activities. The entire figure may seem the same, but on the smaller scale there are subtle differences. Think of the humidity, the change of seasons, or the dryness in wintertime. Tokyo may not be a natural forest, but activities are always happening here, just like in a forest.'

What subtle changes did you make the residents of Studio Gotenyama aware of?

MC: 'There is a really ugly wall behind the apartment building, and also a not so beautiful tree. Why not consider the tree a nice bonsai tree, or think of the tree as a micro-garden inside the urban fabric? Although you are looking at an ugly tree, with a subtle treatment of the windows, as done in Studio Gotenyama, you can turn it into something beautiful. With a bit of imagination, it even looks like you are inside a big, gorgeous garden. Perhaps this is something Japanese. Anything small, in temples, shrines, gardens, can turn into something extremely nice.'

Is the smallness of things and buildings the potential of Tokyo?

MC: 'Recently developers have been building a lot of high-rise buildings in Tokyo. It is a disaster because the scale exceeds that of normal apartment complexes in the city. Tokyo apartment blocks are really small compared to European standards. While in Europe you have one city block filled with one apartment building, in Tokyo that same city block contains many different buildings of a smaller scale. It is this small scale that activates the city and gives Tokyo the image of a forest. If Tokyo can remain a forest, with each tree changing individually, some trees dying, some new trees growing, it can continue to be a very exciting but stable environment.'

‘IF AN ARCHITECTURAL SPACE CAN REPEAT OR EXAGGERATE THE CHARM OF THE SITE, IT WILL BE A NICE PLACE TO LIVE FOR ANYBODY’

MANABU CHIBA

ACTIVATING THE GAPS
Yoshiharu Tsukamoto (Atelier Bow-Wow)

The access alley planted with trees has become a little garden to look at for the neighbours' house

Project Name: House & Atelier Bow-Wow
Location: Shinjuku-ku, Tokyo
Year of Completion: 2005
Clients: Yoshiharu Tsukamoto and Momoyo Kaijima
Special Request: A house and office like a semi-public building
Residents: architect couple
Site Area: 109.03 m^2
Built Area: 60.94 m^2
Total Floor Area: 218.67 m^2
Maximum Building Height: 9.94 m
Programme: private house + office
Storeys: four (B1-3F)
Structure: steel frame with reinforced concrete basement
Structural Engineer: Structural Design Office Oak Inc.

House & Atelier Bow-Wow sits on a flag-shaped site crowded by buildings on all sides and can only be accessed from the main street by means of a narrow path

ARCHITECT: YOSHIHARU TSUKAMOTO
Year of Birth: 1965
Education: Tokyo Institute of Technology, Tokyo
Master: Kazunari Sakamoto (b. 1943)

The single-family house is a major component of Tokyo City. Why do you favour the small scale instead of the large-scale developments recently going on in Tokyo?
Yoshiharu Tsukamoto: 'Tokyo is a city of small property ownership and detached houses. To give you an idea, Tokyo has more than 1.8 million different real estate owners, 1.7 million are private. Tokyo's urban structure is characterized by the huge scale gap between the mega business development and small independent houses. Since the land ownership is really segregated, the single-family house plays an extremely important role in the urban structure. I am interested in a new sense of order; an emergent spatial development by the accumulation of small elements rather than an implication of order on the big scale. The single-family house is also interesting because we are still able to discuss the rationale "Why do we build?".'
Ideally the individual house forms a link between the city and its residents. Why have most houses in Tokyo lost this connection?
YT: 'One reason is that the properties in Tokyo became smaller and smaller over the past decades due to the subdivision of land. By now, detached houses have lost their gardens and semi-covered thresholds. The windows have become much smaller as well, and are usually shut off by curtains. The result is very introvert houses. In addition, the relationship between neighbours is not so much respected these days. In early days, people used to share a lot of things in their own neighbourhood. But nowadays we hardly share with the community anymore. People are living in an abstract social system where there is no autonomy of community space.'
Is it a big problem that people opt for individuality instead of a community-based life?
YT: 'One of the most shocking things in Japan today is that single elderly people die alone in their houses and are not discovered for months. Many people say it is because of the lack of solidarity among people. But I believe it is also a spatial problem. Since the houses are so introverted, we don't know what's really happening inside of the house from the outside. People value a house based on the level of privacy. But the problem is that the spatial translation of privacy is very poor and it easily falls into an enclosed, protective gesture. I think privacy does not have to mean enclosed and introvert. A house can have different faces in one. For example, one part of the house could be very open, while other parts are more closed-off. That is the reason I like to introduce loggia spaces, especially in a mega-city like Tokyo. Loggias enable residents to spend time outside the house, while passers-by are able to check if the residents are all right. It also gives another dimension to the detached family house, a place that today is purely for the family members.'

The property of House & Atelier, your private home and the studio of Atelier Bow-Wow, is a typical flagpole-shaped site. The common solution for such limited space is to simply erect closed walls. What is your alternative?
YT: 'The flagpole-shaped site is a form of site fragmentation often found in Tokyo. This kind of site is wide to the rear, closely surrounded by buildings on all sides and only connected to the road by a very narrow strip of land. Because the building can hardly be seen from the street, it provides a sense of living within the building block. When starting the design of House & Atelier, we observed the surrounding conditions and found limited openness towards the south and the narrow alley, and a proximity towards the neighbour's walls. We chose the building volume that follows the building code, and tested the spatial articulation inside the volume to find a better framework for utilizing the maximum volume. The volume is 10 m high and almost 2 m below ground, giving us 12 m in height. Initially, we divided the entire volume into two: the upper part for our private house and the lower part for the atelier, with a 1.4-m-high storey in between for storage purposes. In this proposal there was an exterior staircase, which provided independent access to the living part from outside. But we rejected the scheme because the relationship between living and working was too fixed in our eyes. If the scheme assumes that living and working should be disconnected, then it is better to build them separately on different sites. On the contrary, we were interested in seeing how living and working can mingle and transform our behaviour in the building in an appropriate way. The final scheme we came up with has only one entrance and the interior spaces are vertically connected from bottom to top, from common work area to private living space.'
How do you bring life into flagpole-shaped sites?
YT: 'Each building in Japan is independent, and adjacent buildings do not share walls. Because of this, gap spaces arise between buildings. Gap spaces, without name and shape, exist everywhere in the city and carry a strong significance. Although they are regarded as a by-product of construction costumes in Japan, the existence of gap spaces should give feedback to the design intentions.'
In what way is House & Atelier redefining the gap space?
YT: 'We examined the use of gap spaces as part of the exterior living space, providing its users more opportunities to spend time outdoors. It is very important that each house has some explicit exterior spaces where people can communicate across the street, the garden or a gap space. It is not necessary for people to actually talk. Just a bow or exchanging smiles might be enough to reconstruct the solidarity among people. We shouldn't forget the vegetation that enriches gap spaces in an unexpected way. In House & Atelier, we planted three trees in a very tight gap space on the northern side of the house. One of them, a Paulownia tree, is now 10 m high and nicely provides shade on our balcony.
The exterior of the building, with its unusual slants and projections, responds to the surroundings, which seems to have an impact on the interior as well.
YT: 'Following the building regulations, the exterior wall slants inwards. Segmented floors, larger than the stair landings, float inside the building volume. Central columns also incline, follow the edge of floors on the first and third storeys, and affect the behaviour of the people inside.'
It seems landings and stairs, and not 'rooms', fulfil the primary functions in this building. What relationships did you create inside?

A large window in the living room (left) is one solution for the unused gaps between buildings in Tokyo; it allows natural sunlight – bounced off the next-door neighbours' exterior wall – into the interior

YT: 'This house contains landings, floors and stairs that vary in size. The objects occupying those landings, floors and stairs give them their character. The disposition of different objects from the living and work area on separate floors create a spatial continuity inside the building. It is a space that doesn't appear autonomously. It constantly changes your perception, while at the same time incorporating the gap space adjacent to the building.'

You took the visual openness very literally. House & Atelier Bow-Wow features a floor-to-ceiling window in a very unexpected place of the living room, directly facing the neighbour's walls.

YT: 'House & Atelier introduces visual openness by making large openings towards the neighbour's walls. The large window manifests that our living room is part of the surroundings. It reframes the exterior wall of the adjacent building as wallpaper. We wanted to define this floor between living and working like a plaza in the city where different activities can happen simultaneously.'

How do you deal with the two programmes – a private home and an office – in one building?

YT: 'The solution is space-time-sharing. During weekends the entire building becomes a big house for two people. During weekdays the office extends its territory into two-thirds of the building. What is important is that the building is inhabited 24 hours a day and very efficient in terms of energy saving.'

It means that the line between the office and your private home is constantly shifting?

YT: 'Yes. This is what we like to do.'

A flagpole-shaped site means minimum sunlight and poor ventilation. What actions did you undertake to make the most out of those inferior conditions?

YT: 'Normally the exterior unit of an air-conditioner exhausts heat into the gap space between buildings during the entire summer. It discourages people from opening the windows to get a breeze in the house. In order to escape from this negative situation, we installed a geo-thermal system using well water for heat storage. This system exchanges the heat with well water from 40 m underground, water that is a constant 15 degrees throughout the year. The production of hot water in winter and cool water in summer starting from water with a temperature of 15 degrees can significantly reduce energy consumption compared to normal air-conditioning. The radiator you see in the centre of the building allows hot and cold water to run through the entire building.'

The building was completed in 2005. Have you already noticed improvements in the neighbourhood?

YT: 'Recently, the neighbours that border our alley started to renovate their house. Before that, their windows were always closed on the side of our alley but nowadays they open this window. It seemed they don't find us so aggressive anymore but have recognized we are disciplined. Our access route alley has become a little garden for them.'

What else can architects contribute to the neighbourhood with the design of a small single-family house?

YT: 'Although the house is for specific residents, it can also be positioned in the genealogy of housing types. Japanese architects of our generation are designing the fourth-generation house. The detached house type initially appeared in the 1920s during the first suburban development. As the average life span of

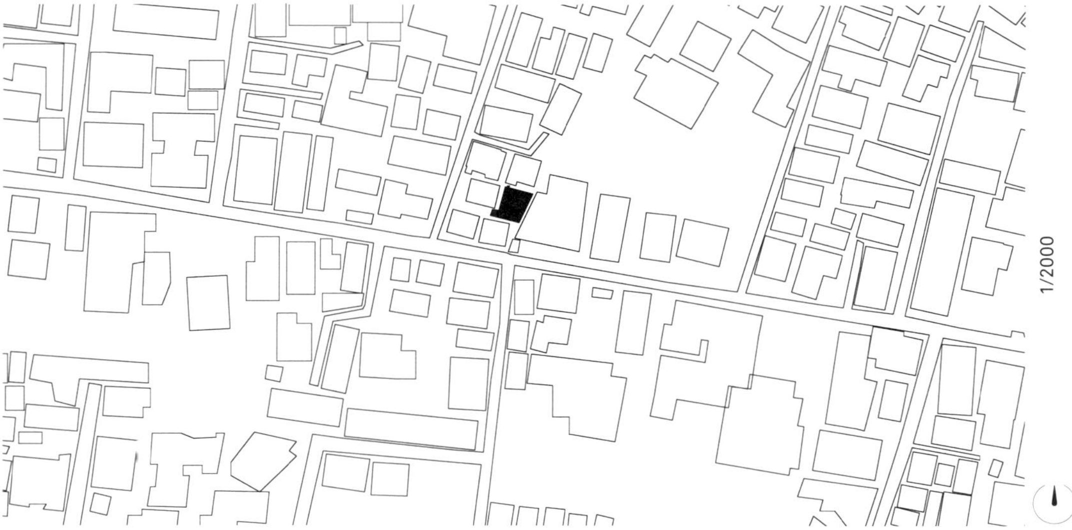

1/2000

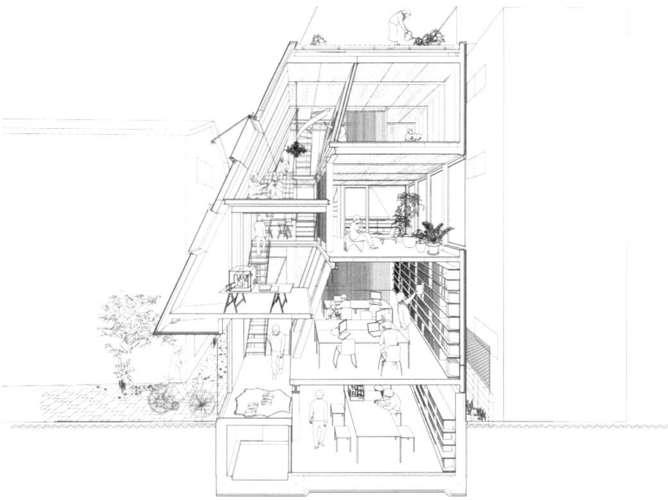

1/200

1/200

The boundary between the private house on the top floors and the office space on the lower levels is permeable and shifts according to the time

A long white heating and cooling radiator as part of a geothermal heating system runs vertically through the entire building, eliminating the use of artificial climate controle

The rooftop terrace provides a view of central Tokyo and is used for private gatherings, discussions with architects and other guests as well as an occasional staff party

Providing an exterior space as simple as a balcony or small terrace can significantly change the residents' lifestyle, allowing them to spend time outside the house

Japanese homes is less than 30 years, the buildings have been regenerated at least twice during the last 90 years, and now we're starting the fourth-generation houses. Each generation is based on its time. The difference is obvious. The transformation of the house during the twentieth century, observed from the first to the third generation, can be summed up in that house properties became smaller, and houses became purely for family, and houses lost outside space for socializing. In short, the house became intolerant and ungenerous. Architects can question these tendencies and show a new framework for creating better living conditions through typological proposals. The house genealogy is quite important in terms of the cityscape: a random disposition of different house generations. Solidarity through architectural production was totally forgotten. This deeply affects the state of community today.'

Can you summarize the dialogue between House & Atelier and the surroundings?

YT: 'House & Atelier is a typical fourth-generation house, and with that a direct critique of the previous generation of houses built in the twentieth century.

My intention was to make the house more generous in the following ways: by reintroducing the space where non-family members can stay naturally, by providing covered exterior space in order to give inhabitants more opportunities to spend time outside the house and by redefining the gap space in order to extend the concept of living territory to the physical surrounding of houses. The quality of the surroundings, surely a part of the city, should be reconsidered every time we construct a new house. This is the most fundamental way to improve Tokyo, a city made of houses.'

‘PRIVACY DOES NOT HAVE TO MEAN ENCLOSED OR INTROVERT. A HOUSE CAN HAVE DIFFERENT FACES IN ONE’

YOSHIHARU TSUKAMOTO

VOID IN A VOID
Akira Yoneda (Architecton)

The pipe-screened translucent building volume inserted into the semi-enclosed site acts like a void inside another void

Project Name: Hojo
Location: Shibuya-ku, Tokyo
Year of Completion: 2009
Client: Dr Yasuaki Oeda
Special Request: A retreat in the midst of the city and a pool for his beloved dog
Site Area: 101.94 m^2
Built Area: 55.12 m^2
Total Floor Area: 92.67 m^2
Maximum Building Height: 6.86 m
Stories: two
Structure: steel + reinforced concrete
Structural Engineer: Yasutaka Konishi

VOID IN A VOID

ARCHITECT: AKIRA YONEDA
Year of Birth: 1959
Education: University of Tokyo, Tokyo, Harvard GSD, Cambridge
Work Experience: Takenaka Corporation
Masters: Tatsuya Hirobe (b. 1932), Tadao Ando (b. 1941)

What is the first thing you do when you visit an empty site?
Akira Yoneda: 'A void space or empty lot should be read as a positive territory. Once you start putting architecture on that plot like a solid mass, the space around the site will become nothing but negative. Architects should look for a building that expands positively across the boundaries and can actually enliven the space between the house and the neighbouring houses. Making the house as an expansion. This fundamental dialogue comes from Gestalt theory.'
Why did you develop a design theory based on Gestalt?
AY: 'In Gestalt theory a perceptual pattern or structure is seen as possessing qualities as a whole that cannot be described merely as a sum of its parts. In other words, the notion of a good form is introduced by the unification of elements that relate to each other. Traditional environmental design in Japan transforms such contrast in continuity, but the unification is based on the contrast between figure and ground. The Japanese used to combine a house not only with artificial landscape elements, like gazebos, gates, steps or fences, but also with natural landscape elements like ponds, rivers, mounds, trees, stones and sand into a total environment. At the same time Japanese environmental design differentiates the scale, the distance and the viewpoints in its totality. Hojo is a tiny project without any solid walls, like a void in a void. The loose and weak boundary of the house can effectively perceive the subtle changes in the surroundings. It defines the territory physically and at the same time sensitively communicates with an area far away. The existing low wall on the site border defines the garden territory and simultaneously includes the scenery in the distance in a way that is similar to *shakkei*, a typical Japanese landscape concept.'
A membrane roof, pipe screens and the openness give the house a very temporary character, almost like camping in Tokyo.
AY: 'The mode of this house relates to the temporality found in traditional Japanese architecture. Traditionally, buildings in Japan were constructed with a wooden modular frame system. This frame could easily be taken apart, removed and reconstructed at another site. It is a system that allows for quick modification and reproduction. While Western culture aims to protect humans from nature, Japanese culture is open to nature and accepts the ephemeral transition around it. The client for Hojo, a doctor working in Tokyo but living permanently in the suburbs, drops by this house from time to time to enjoy the daily and seasonal changes.'
A weekend retreat in the middle of Tokyo. What makes you think we can relax better inside Tokyo than in the suburbs?
Traditionally, the Japanese have lived in densely populated areas, often in wooden

town houses called *machiya*. Accordingly, they introduced small retreats into those urban dwellings: micro-courtyard gardens marked by greenery. These settings eventually provided a place for the Japanese tea ceremony and gave rise to the notion of *sichu no sankyo*, which means "a cottage with a small garden in the midst of an urban context". Hojo is a modern descendant of this tradition. The *machiya* shows that the Japanese can interpret even a small garden as a high form of nature. The Japanese are in a way a very imaginative people. We can see small things and interpret them as vast and big!'

The openness of Hojo gives the impression that the client and the architect were very indifferent to its neighbours. Is that true?

AY: 'Although a lot of foreigners live in this area, the owner of Hojo is Japanese and hopes that his neighbours understand Japanese values. The very thin screen is a very Japanese example of an imaginary boundary. Once you cross this imaginary boundary, people will notice and somehow apologize for the violation. Hojo has a weak boundary made of pipes, which screens and defines the site physically and at the same time expands it in a sensuous way. A low wall around the site in traditional Japanese architecture has a similar effect. It defines the garden while simultaneously including the scenery in the distance. Hojo is just a temporary abode, so that the idea of openness is not so crucial for the neighbours who are living there permanently. In the most ideal situation, the owner will start planting trees in the near future that will work as an extra screen, and with that contribute to a positive environment.'

Would you say this is a typical Tokyo house?

AY: 'Spending little time in your house is something typical for modern people, not only in Tokyo but also in other metropolises. Urban people are used to living in public spaces or a café, as it is so convenient nowadays to go anywhere. The necessary elements to call a house a house are historically already limited in Japan. A traditional Japanese house is a very neutral space, the size of 6-jo or 8-jo (9.18 or 12.24 m^2) with very few specified rooms or functions. Occasionally, people arrange the neutral room into a setting for dinners or guests. Now, about 50 years after the Japanese government introduced functional apartment buildings based on an American typology, Japanese architects are starting to realize that small spaces become even more limited when they are subdivided into smaller rooms, Western-style. They realize that for the Japanese it is not necessary to divide a small living space into specified, individual rooms to have a comfortable life.'

Do you give the spaces in your floor plans names?

AY: 'The term "storage" doesn't carry any additional requirements in Japan, so after architects provide the required 1LDK – a living room, a kitchen, a dining room and one bedroom – we tend to call all other spaces storage. With that, we leave it up to the clients to do what they want with the space. To avoid a 1LDK apartment become a rigid building, creating many "storage spaces" is a common solution among architects and is even recognized by Japanese officials. The regulations state that all rooms inside a 1LDK apartment have to have a window for ventilation. But even officials realize that you can't always put in a window when buildings are set so close to one another!'

Do your clients often come up with strange requirements?

AY: 'Recently, clients have become more familiar with architecture themselves and enjoy having a unique solution for their house. Actually, it is not the

The thin structure made of steel columns gives the house a floating feeling

The house makes use of a geothermal heating system in which the dog's pool functions as a waterbasin connected to the underground well

The interior scenery is based on a mechanism of differentiation in distances which refers to shakkei (borrowed scenery), a technique used in traditional Japanese landscape design

requirements that are strange, but the situations! Often the client cannot imagine the right solution for his or her own lifestyle. That is why they ask architects to come up with a solution. In general, it is a client's dream to make the plot, however the conditions, into his or her own kingdom. In Japan, dreams belong to the clients. They don't want to make them into a public showcase but prefer to put them into a small space, their house, and keep them for themselves. Only people who have the luck to have a really big living space are willing to share.'

What is the gap between dreams and reality?

AY: 'I try to include all the dreams of the client in one design. In reality you have limitations because of the physical dimensions, but as I said, clients have a lot of imagination. If you can realize all those dreams on a small plot, the clients will expand their dreams to a suitable size by themselves, using their own imagination. Even a tight space can become as wide as the universe! In verbal statements dreams are so huge, but once I draw them into the small limitations the clients can understand the limitations of the plot. Sometimes they are disappointed when they realize how small their plot is. But when this happens, I start to expand their dreams again. The power of Hojo doesn't stop at the plot's boundaries.'

Could you construct the project as you wanted?

AY: 'The construction costs were calculated to be twice as high as the original budget, so we had to shrink the size of the original design. But the accomplishment of the house in a physical way was the most important thing. We architects are often asked to include a *tokonoma* [a built-in recessed space in a Japanese-style reception room, in which items for artistic appreciation are displayed] and *washitasu*, a Japanese-style room with *tatami* mats, but there are people who don't even know the original use or size of these spaces anymore. A *tokonoma* was originally the size of one *tatami* mat, 1.53 m^2, though nowadays people are satisfied with a smaller version, 30 x 30 cm for instance, enough to display some flowers.'

You mean Japanese clients can easily be satisfied with smallness?

AY: 'Usually "the big accepts the small", which is physically true. The reverse phrase "the small accepts the big" is not so common, but spiritually we recognize that kind of affordability. For example, a *furoshiki*, a small Japanese traditional square wrapping cloth, can be used in multiple ways. In the same way, in the Japanese mind a very small tea ceremony room can contain the vast atmosphere of the cosmos. Even the Imperial Palace in Kyoto is not a big, overwhelming, gorgeous building but actually a very simple and mainly wooden structure, not so different from common people's houses.'

Talking about structures, your projects always deal with a complicated construction. Why this interest?

AY: 'A structure is very important in defining the quality of a space. The human perception immediately recognizes the quality of a space, even before realizing the exact details. Once you enter a space, the structure should be immediately clear, or at least you should be able to feel the presence of the structure, its scale and its dimensions. When you enter a big church you cannot immediately grasp the structure, but we can feel the atmosphere of the space created by the unique structure. This is a very essential issue for me.'

What do we feel when entering Hojo?

AY: 'The structure is a slanted system, not rigid at all. From the redundancy of the

1/2000

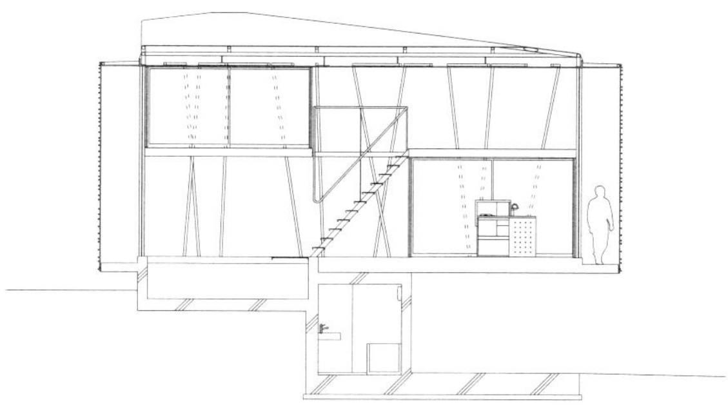

1/200

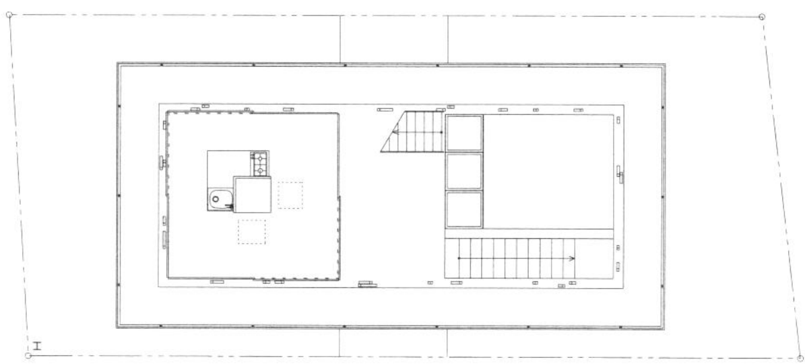

1/200

Hojo has tried to reconfigure a traditional small Japanese spatial unit into today's urban environment, both physically and spiritually

The light steel structure, pipe screen and membrane roof are archored to a concrete basement, which contains the entrance and the bathroom

The membrane roof gives the house a temporaral and tent-like character

structure you can feel openness, a floating feeling. Visitors might not directly understand the structural system, but they will understand that it is the small, slender columns that make the floors float. If I had used a very rigid structure with big and straight columns, the structure would be immediately clear to anybody but obviously would not contribute the same casual and light feeling.'

Should all void spaces in Tokyo be filled with floating structures?

AY: 'Void spaces can be seen as vital elements in the city. We architects should reinterpret negative void spaces into positive, public ones. I predict that in the future architects will be mediating more between the large and small scale.

The Japanese notion of imagination can also be applied to public space. People can easily expand a small public space into a big one. A small bonsai tree can be considered a huge tree, while a small gap between houses can be interpreted as a big, green forest. The principle of borrowed scenery, *shakkei*, is one solution. It could evoke a new relationship between an object and its environment, extending a space further. Although *shakkei* is an old Japanese concept, I see possibilities to use this in contemporary Tokyo on the scale of the city.'

‘ONCE YOU START PUTTING ARCHITECTURE ON A PLOT LIKE A SOLID MASS THE SPACE AROUND THE SITE WILL BECOME NOTHING BUT NEGATIVE’

AKIRA YONEDA

CURVES FOR PRIVACY
Katsuhiro Miyamoto (KMAA)

A clover-shaped steel wall divides the interior into a communual living and semi-private study and bedroom spaces

Project Name: Clover House
Location: Nishinomiya, Hyogo Prefecture
Year of Completion: 2006
Clients: father + two sons
Special request: To dwell in a ruin
Site Area: 117.44 m^2
Built Area: 46.95 m^2
Total Floor Area: 76.19 m^2
Maximum Building Height: 5.71 m
Storeys: two (B1F + 1F)
Structure: steel plate, steel frame, reinforced concrete
Structural Engineer: Masaichi Taguchi(TAPS)

A 4-m height difference in the site made it necessary to dig into the ground and 'bury' the house

CURVES FOR PRIVACY

ARCHITECT: KATSUHIRO MIYAMOTO
Year of Birth: 1961
Education: University of Tokyo, Tokyo
Master: Seibun Suzuki (b. 1927)

Based in Hyogo Prefecture, do you feel any difference from your Tokyo colleagues?
Katsuhiro Miyamoto: 'My office is based in Takarazuka, a small city near Kobe that is located on active faults. The earth can rise from the ground and turn any site into a mountain. The places I work always happen to have a special topography. When I design architecture, there is always this strong relationship between the earth and the building. When I talk with my contemporaries in Tokyo, I don't feel any difference. Our methods are very similar. Yoshiharu Tsukamoto, for example, talks about environment. Environment for him means the circumstances around architecture. Every element around architecture is the result of designing. This way of making architecture is almost the same as my approach. The architects of my generation tend to have a sensitivity towards the city. While older generations of architects used to design only the site, our generation always thinks beyond the plot borders. Designing a new house feels like making an addition to a city.'
Tell me about your interest in topography.
KM: 'Clover House is a clear example of architecture that has to do with the topography. It is a very small house built on an extremely low budget. The cost of excavating the site took one-third of the budget. The steel plates used took another third. It was an extraordinary balance of costs, as we could only use one-third for architecture, the rest was all for the foundation. The client wanted a house like a ruin. This inspired me to come up with the idea of living in the basement. He was thrilled by the idea of doing so.'
What other requests did he have?
KM: 'Just before the start of the project, the client's wife suddenly died. In response to this, he asked for a new house that would cheer him up. We started digging the ground and the house began to make a reference to *kikkobaka*, turtle cemeteries found on the Okinawa Islands. Many families gather in front of those graves once a year, eating and drinking together. Of course, a cemetery is not considered a happy space in Japan either. However, the sense of living with deceased but beloved people is very common. Every house in Japan has a *butsudan*, a small pavilion commemorating deceased family members. Clover House is a modern interpretation of the traditional *butsudan*. Both the main space of Clover House and the front yard of a *kikkobaka* are surrounded by curved walls. One of the wave-shaped walls in the dining area of Clover House contains the *butsudan*. The family eat and drinks in front of it, like people in Okinawa gather in the front yard of their ancestor's *kikkobaka*. Living with the dead was not the concept of the house, but after the construction was completed, both the client and I saw similarities with this kind of graveyard, in that people are living in front of the memories of the dead.'

Was this a particularly difficult site?
KM: 'When the client was looking for a site, he found this very steep site. It was very cheap precisely because it didn't have any parking space. Making a parking space would be very expensive on this heavily sloped site – the height differential is almost 4 m – so the client asked for a discount. At first we started digging a carport. But when it was completed, the client saw the potential of living in this excavated space. He pictured himself living in the carport, together with his car. But we gave up this idea and parked the car somewhere else. Most difficult in terms of construction was how to solve the strong soil pressure. We had to make a strong retaining wall in a curved shape. Eventually, we chose three clover shapes. The client, around 40, and his 5- and 13-year-old sons would each get their own clover as private territory. Although we chose curved sheets against soil pressure, eventually we had to change the construction system. The clover shape could resist the soil pressure but not prevent the house from sliding. Although we used the weight of concrete behind the curved steel plates, the distinctive shape of the clover itself remained and we used it to resolve the planning.'
What about the privacy in this house?
KM: 'A curved wall is very convenient. Wherever you are, you can see what is happening. Behind each alcove is a private space that I call a box. The father's own private box is the kitchen. The two sons used theirs as their own study space. So, all three family members have a very private box and a semi-private alcove. Although it is a very small house, the residents can carefully choose their privacy. But, well, there are only three men in the house, and no women.'
Where do they sleep?
KM: 'Each family member has his own tiny sleeping space on the loft level, the actual ground level. They climb up to the loft with a ladder. The big loft is open, and the family members can communicate with each other when they are standing. But as soon as they lie down, they cannot see each other anymore because the curved wall acts as a partition screen. From outside, people cannot look into the bedroom spaces, as the floor is elevated.'
What do the clients like best about this house?
KM: 'Many features in this house are always changing. For example, on a very sunny day, the sun is reflected on the curved white walls. At such moments, you cannot sense the scale of the house anymore as its depth is modified.'
Does Clover House add anything to the neighbourhood?
KM: 'Usually, a residential building is a concrete box on top of a site with a space to park the car next to it. In the case of Clover House, we didn't add any extra volume to the site because we excavated. You could call the house a pocket, a void in the middle of a residential area. Making a good void is a contribution to a dense neighbourhood. In the future, the client of Clover House would like to have an exhibition space or other event inside Clover House. The walls at the entrance are curved in a Baroque style to welcome the visitors. In other words, the hall of Clover House can become an expansion of the public street.'
And the pocket was topped off with a roof?
KM: 'For the architectural concept we didn't need a roof, but it was necessary to protect the residents. We decided on a very thin roof. Seen from a certain angle, the intervention really looks very light, like a floating roof. When seeing this image, I suddenly realized why the client told me at the very beginning that he wanted

The top floor loft sits on the actual ground level and contains 2.70 m-high semi-private sleeping spaces located between the 'clover leaves', accessed by a ladder

The clover-shaped division wall fluidly extends in the exterior to give the entrance a sense of grandeur

1/400

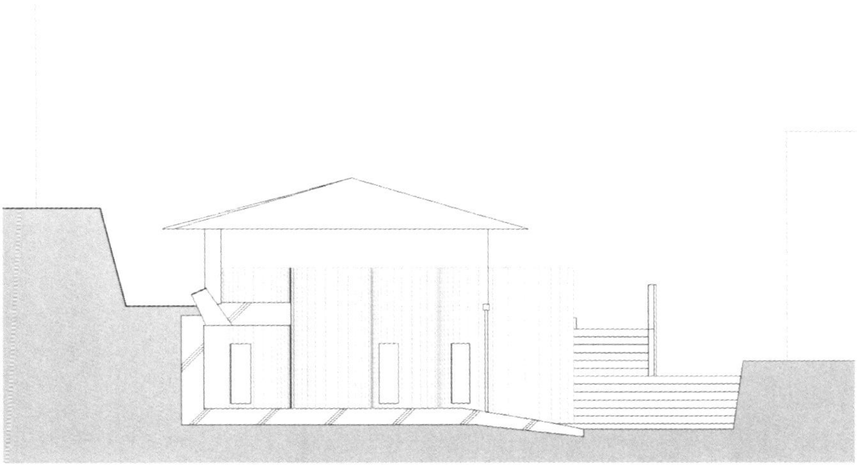

1/200

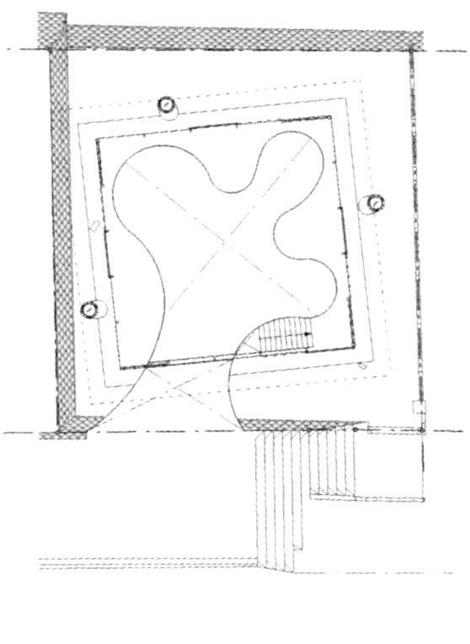

1/300

to live in a ruin. Although I didn't understand at that time what he was talking about, I understood when the house was completed. A ruin is an already existing structure. My client was just looking for a place that looked as if it had been there for a long time.'

Did you propose a new lifestyle to the family?
KM: 'Yes, their way of living certainly changed. Right after the completion of the house, the family felt like members of the same sports club. The situation in the house was perhaps not always tidy and they felt a little confused, but totally happy together. The client recently remarried. His new wife and her son also moved in. So now the five of them are sharing this house. The situation didn't change much, though. The new wife and son naturally joined the club as if they were new members of the sports club. As the only female person in the house, the wife is like the housemother in a dormitory.'

How did they redefine the space with two extra members? KM: 'One of the private boxes is now used as the main bedroom for the parents. One private box contains a new double-decker bed for the father's two sons. The wife's son sleeps in the loft.'

This means that this 72-m² house is very flexible? KM: 'It is not the house that is flexible, but the family members who are flexible! When the two new family members joined, we thought about adding an extra volume to the house, like an annex or changing the roof into a volume. In the end we didn't perform any changes. The client preferred to keep on living in the house as it was.'

Does the form of Clover House substantiate the residents' way of living? KM: 'Usually you start with a function and a function leads to a certain shape. But in this project the relationship between form and function is reversed. We first created the clover shape, and after that we divided the functions. After we agreed on the clover shape, we started to think about how to live in this form. For privacy, we added some closed boxes behind the waved walls. Then we wondered where to make the bedroom space. The client is super-flexible and that is the power of the project. Usually a client does not know what he wants, so I like to respond by first putting a structure on the site. It is similar to the concept of *bricolage*, making creative and resourceful use of whatever materials are at hand. I would say Clover House pays homage to the existing topography.'

‘I LIKE TO RESPOND BY FIRST PUTTING A STRUCTURE ON THE SITE, SIMILAR TO THE CONCEPT OF *BRICOLAGE*’

COMMUNITY SPHERES
Ryue Nishizawa (Office of Ryue Nishizawa)

Rather than building one massive structure, a solution was found in designing the apartments as small blocks, a concept that fits the openmindedness of the site

Project Name: Moriyama House
Location: Ota-ku, Tokyo
Date of Completion: 2005
Client: Mr Moriyama
Site Area: 290.02 m^2
Built Area: 130.06 m^2
Total Floor Area: 263.08 m^2
Maximum Building Height: 7.82 m
Units: variable (1-6)
Storeys: variable (B1F-3F)
Structure: steel plate
Structural Engineer: Structured Environment

ARCHITECT: RYUE NISHIZAWA
Year of Birth: 1966
Education: Yokohama National University, Yokohama
Master: no statement

Moriyama House is located in a typical Tokyo residential neighbourhood. What is the charm of this area?
Ryue Nishizawa: 'The beautiful thing is that each community in Tokyo has its own history. Suburban neighbourhoods were only created after the Second World War, and are therefore not so very old. They used to be rice fields that developed into new towns because there was a shortage of places to live. Kamata, the area where Moriyama House is located, originates from the late 1940s, which means the community is around 60 years old. Mr Moriyama, the owner of Moriyama House, was born on this property together with his friend who now lives 10 m away. In Kamata, people still maintain a traditional lifestyle. Gardens and public alleyways, the *roji*, are part of people's daily life. They grow plants along the street and use the alleyways as small pocket parks where kids can run around. It is a very beautiful way of using a town. Nowadays, almost all streets in Tokyo are covered with asphalt and allow for a very specific programme only. I can't feel freedom on the streets of Tokyo anymore. If you spontaneously want to picnic on the street for lunch with a friend, you will have policemen coming up to you saying that the street is not a place to sit and enjoy yourself. In Kamata, people still maintain the original way of using a city. Some *roji* are still unpaved and not used for serious traffic, but used for growing plants or as public space.'
Nowadays a lot of roji in Tokyo have lost their original meaning. The result is a strange distance between the houses without any communication. Why does this distance feel strange?
RN: 'Although not many people use the *roji* anymore, I am not too negative. Cats, for example, still can really appreciate those spaces. The positive point for people is that we still have in-between spaces between neighbouring houses, which give the neighbourhood a feeling of transparency. We used to have row houses in Tokyo, *nagaya*, a traditional form of urban housing in Japan with long narrow houses closely connected to each other along a communal street. Small, detached houses give a complete different feeling to the city. You feel daylight coming from all sides, which gives a very light feeling to a city.'
Moriyama House didn't start with a mere copying of the typical urban structure. It seems you added a little more space between the volumes than the width of a roji. What was the starting point of the design?
RN: 'My purpose is not to represent the old society. I wanted to create something more fundamental than just copying a structure. I was looking for architecture that could be used for community life again and about in-between spaces to use as *roji*. Moriyama House doesn't want to limit the programme. It allows the freedom to start thinking about the function or programme. People

coming to the house can imagine for themselves how to use the buildings. It could as easily be a kindergarten, a group home or a school.'

You dismantled the housing programme and distributed the boxes over the site. The ten independent volumes, scattered across the site, host six housing units at the moment. How did you decide on the exact size and place of the volumes?

RN: 'I didn't want to repeat the size of the neighbouring houses, as that wouldn't be interesting. But if I made Moriyama House into one big building, it would turn out really huge for this area. That's why I broke the big volume into several pieces. Each house is therefore really small, but they are not the same. All have different proportions. The programme of each box and the connections between the boxes is also different. If I had given every box the same layout and proportion, the project would have looked like an army camp! I created diversity, designing some boxes as rooms, some as houses and some as a machine room or a doghouse. Because the boxes have different shapes, different openings and different connections to the gardens, very different things appear in this landscape. It is filled with a little bit of the same feeling, but at the same time is a little bit confusing.'

So the scale is a very important aspect in this project?

RN: 'Yes. I tried to make all volumes different, but there is one thing that all of the volumes share, and that is smallness. There is no such thing as bigness inside this plot. If I had failed in making good smallness, it would have been my death sentence as an architect! Walking on the streets of Tokyo, you see so many bad examples of smallness. Look at very small apartment rooms where people shut the window with a translucent, very ugly type of glass and a very bad curtain. I don't like that at all. Although nobody tells you to do anything about those kinds of in-between spaces, I decided to do so.'

The small urban scale within the mega-city is a character unique to Tokyo. Do you share my affection for Tokyo's urban smallness?

RN: 'A city is where you can have many different kinds of scales in the same place. The combination of a very big river, a very big park and a skyscraper, like the city structure of New York, gives a very great feeling. However, smallness has another advantage that people in a big skyscraper cannot have. If you live in a tiny Tokyo apartment you don't have to move around to get something, as everything is within arm's reach. It is like you are sitting in a car – nothing that you cannot reach. How great! Besides a very flexible space, smallness also provides a very intimate feeling, something a big park or big river cannot do.'

Does the landscape you created with Moriyama House contain signs of intimate relationships?

RN: 'Just after the Second World War, the Japanese government started to provide very repetitive public housing without any difference among the units. At that time, the composition of families was also almost the same, consisting of a young couple with 3 or 4 children with the wife staying at home and the husband working in the city. The floor plans of that time reflected that every family could live the same way, but be independent because the apartments were divided from each other by means of strong thick concrete walls. In Moriyama House, there is a very different relationship among its residents. It shows a much more contemporary relationship among urban people: the residents are equally close and equally far away. They don't share too much with each other, but on the other hand they are

From within the apartments one can always sense the entire community and its common exterior space

not disconnected like they were in the "microcosmic" houses designed in Japan after the war.'

The key person of Moriyama House is the owner, Mr Moriyama. Although he might someday use all the buildings himself, he now rents out five of the units. The reason why this small community seems to work so well is because Mr Moriyama is the person who binds all the residents together. What kind of life does he lead? RN: 'Moriyama is a very childlike, open person. He actually didn't appreciate windows at all and lived in a very dark house for 50 years. He used to shut all his windows as well as the *amado*, wooden shutters in front of his windows, to create a dark room so he would have lots of wall space to store his great collection of movies, music and books. When he visited my studio to commission the design of his house, he asked for a really enclosed one with no windows. However, my idea was the total opposite.'

Why did he accept your radical proposal?

RN: 'Moriyama is really open to things new. He has the ability to learn what he doesn't know yet. That is why he loves Moriyama House. One of his great new hobbies, for example, is planting flowers outside and inside the house. Another occasion in which he showed how open-minded he is was during a sudden visit by some rather rude Italians. They unexpectedly opened the windows of Moriyama's apartment to say hello. This is definitely not something you should do in a Tokyo neighbourhood! However, Mr Moriyama was nevertheless kind enough to invite the people into his house.'

Does Mr Moriyama have special criteria for selecting new residents of Moriyama House?

RN: 'When Moriyama House was completed he asked me to find people who could live here. I chose the very first residents among friends and acquaintances: an actor, magazine editors and a young architect. Moriyama instantly agreed. Actually, I don't think he's said no to any newcomers since then. But I am sure that, according to him, people who want to live here must be very positive towards the use of the space. If people want to live in a standard one-room apartment, they'd better move into a typical developer's mansion building.'

All volumes are punctured by rather large windows. How do the residents find their own privacy?

RN: 'Everybody says Moriyama House is really open, but in reality more than 80 per cent of the envelope is steel panel construction. Windows account for only 20 per cent of the façade, which is not that open compared to a regular Japanese house. The difference is that I made a really big window in important places, which gives the impression that the apartments are very open. For example, I made one really big opening on the top floor of the tower, Moriyama's bathroom. This is one of the first things people encounter when approaching Moriyama House. After 5 p.m., when the residents start turning on their lights, you feel the presence of the people. But you can't in fact see the residents directly. In my opinion, Moriyama House is not that open. When designing this project I had the feeling that I wanted to create privacy through means other than a wall. There are many ways to create comfort. To me, privacy is a kind of atmosphere that you can create by using architecture, the garden, the street and furniture.'

Moriyama House is a new, independent environment within an existing

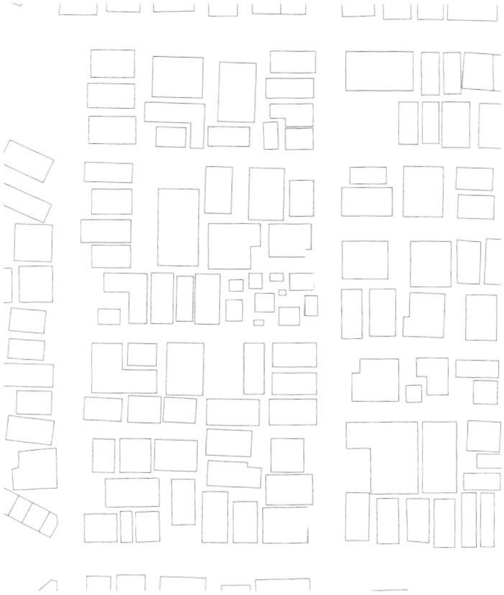

1/2000

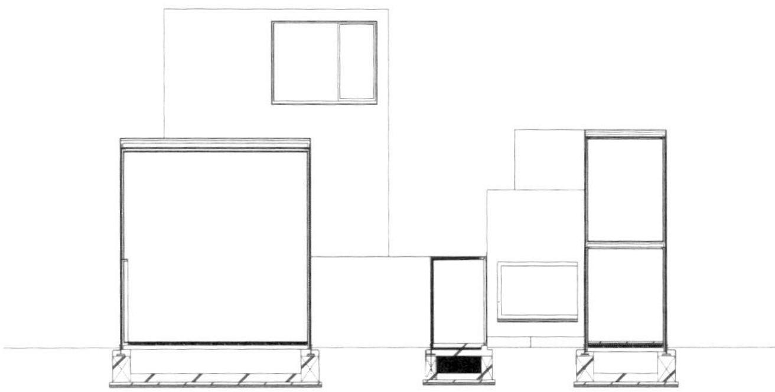

1/200

1/200

The spaces between the apartments and annexes can be used as semi-private gardens, for an open lifestyle between the different residents

Although the programme is broken up into pieces, there is a strong unity between the individual architectural structures, similar of spirit to the existing residential neighbourhood

Big openings in the structures give the entire apartment complex a breezy feel

neighbourhood but without any walls. Do the residents feel part of one communal garden, or can they feel individuality?
RN: 'The territory inside the plotlines of Moriyama House is communal, but not well defined. Each owner can create his or her own border to show what is communal and what is private. I didn't give them any strong walls to divide the communal garden, as the residents can naturally make a series of connected semi-private gardens. What I wanted to establish with this project is a relationship that doesn't have any centre. Inside the plot, you can create your own centre even when you are living at the edge. In that case the edge suddenly becomes the centre. Think of the feeling when you are living on the border of two neighbourhoods that are connected. It is the authorities who decided on the political borders, but people themselves don't feel those borders. Neighbours go beyond political borders. This neighbourly feeling is a spatial concept of Moriyama House that you don't notice immediately. By living here for a while, say one or perhaps five years, the spatial concept is gradually felt.'
Moriyama House was completed in 2005. What has been the impact of this project on the Kamata neighbourhood so far?
RN: 'There are many different people that appreciate the architecture. For example, there is this woman who uses the grounds of Moriyama House as a shortcut to run from A to B. She understands the concept! There are also different cat communities in this neighbourhood who all go through it. They understand the concept of transparency. Another woman living next door often brings Moriyama the newspaper to say hello. Before, in order to say hello, she would have to go out of a gate, enter the street and open another gate. Now, it has become so easy to say hello. I hope Moriyama House will give some lightness to the city. If I had presented one big house containing all the units, it would give nothing but shadow to the city.'
What does the atmosphere among the white volumes of Moriyama House have in common with the traditional atmosphere in the old-style roji?
RN: 'Both *roji* and the in-between spaces are not spaces defined by the government. People living around a *roji* decide how to use it. In this sense they are the same. But there is also a big difference. A *roji* has a historical layer. Many different people used to share a *roji* as a communal territory where everybody knows everything. Young Japanese people nowadays dislike *roji*, because they can't find any privacy. They associate this with having no future and that is why they move out of the inner city. Many *roji* have disappeared since the Second World War. I am concerned that people have become very disconnected from each other.'
How do you see people becoming more connected again in the future?
RN: 'During the past 50 years Tokyo has grown too much. Tokyo has an aging society. The population is shrinking and more and more houses are being abandoned. I believe people will start to show interest in the local community again, and move from the city to the province. In the last 50 years, Tokyo residents were content to live without appreciating the local community and without privacy. But from now on a very different situation will prevail. People will start to think about what kind of connections they want to create in their living environment. I don't want to merely create architecture, but rather a contemporary city space. I wanted to make an atmosphere, a total environment of architecture, city, garden and many other things in one. Instead of putting up a

fence around the plot, I opted for a comfortable continuity throughout the house, the garden and the *roji* and the city, like one gradual movement.'

It sounds like you want to go back to the good old days of the Edo period.

RN: 'No, it is not about going back in time. We must look to the future. But we can learn from the past by bringing something of it into the future in a very contemporary way. Moriyama House creates the future. It shows a new way of living. Although it doesn't give a very concrete example, it provides a starting point for thinking about the use of a house. I often go into the city and collect things I appreciate. Then I think about how I can use those impressions, not in a historical way, but in a contemporary way. It is something that every architect must do.'

'IF I HAD FAILED IN MAKING GOOD SMALLNESS, IT WOULD HAVE BEEN MY DEATH SENTENCE AS AN ARCHITECT'

FROM RIPPLES TO WAVES
Monologue by Taro Igarashi

Post-Bubble
Each time a new generation of architects in Japan emerges they change their attitude, and sometimes this attitude is completely opposite to that of the previous generation. For example, the three latest generations we can distinguish in Japan are the bubble generation, the post-bubble generation and the 1970s generation. The post-bubble generation includes students baptized by the bubble economy. After the burst of the asset price bubble in 1991, they wanted to start their own career. But because the ladder was removed, it wasn't easy for them to survive. A lot of architects grouped into units, like Atelier Bow-Wow and Mikan. The unit-groups were effective organizations to survive the post-bubble network society. As there were no longer clear 'establishments' and 'powers' to resist, the architects of the post-bubble generation began to build from the familiar and ordinary. Their point of departure was to reveal reality in the awkward slits in the banal and unremarkable day-to-day life. Having little work, they started to do fieldwork in the city. Atelier Bow-Wow did the *Made in Tokyo* project; Manabu Chiba researched void spaces in the city, while Katsuhiro Miyamoto looked at the slope, the land topography and infrastructure prior to his design. Although Tsukamoto and Chiba are more into urban topography, and Miyamoto more into the historical and regional, they share the same survey technique. Ryue Nishizawa was still very young when he started SANAA with Kazuyo Sejima, so he didn't have time to do the fieldwork exercises like Tsukamoto and Chiba. But Nishizawa also developed an interesting point of view on the environment. All architects born in the 1960s have an extremely positive attitude towards the city. This is because they believe that reform and innovation begins with small things. They don't design strong architectural forms because they depend on outer conditions.

1970s generation
There was a rise in cool individual types among the 1970s generation. While the unit-groups of the 1960s generation did not assert their individuality, the 1970s generation consists of architects with character and great talent. However, the tendency of architects to avoid creating strong powerful spaces continues. There are now more architects coming from foreign offices or apprenticeship relationships – Toyo Ito, SANAA, Jun Aoki and Kengo Kuma, to name a few. Finally, more are working seriously with computers and making active use of the web. Sou Fujimoto and Junya Ishigami are both attempting to grasp a new principle. Instead of constructing their architecture from observational fieldwork in the city as characteristically done by Atelier Bow-Wow and Mikan, Fujimoto and Ishigami attempt to communicate the principle of their architecture before explaining the external conditions of a site. A similar attitude is recognizable in the work of Akihisa Hirata, who creates spaces with twisted topologies.
From the 1990s onward, postmodernist modes of form-making have lost popularity in the architectural world and we see a gradual return to modernism. The common technique of creating complex spaces while still maintaining conceptual clarity through formal simplicity is utilized by architects like Jun Igarashi and Go Hasegawa. Neither strictly functionalist nor fictional, they

define their architecture through a soft formalism. The unit-groups of the 1960s generation, in contrast, intentionally avoided expressing conceptual clarity to achieve a sense of ambiguity.

Japanese architects have always had many opportunities to practice their design in housing projects. After the 1990s, architects were unlucky and unable to obtain bigger projects anymore. Young architects nowadays have to continue their career designing houses. That is why this generation considers interior design, installations and renovations as real architecture projects. But the advantage of small commissions is that they can innovate a lot. The keywords that fit this generation best are 'principle' and 'phenomena'. We cannot clearly explain the character of the spaces the 1970s generation has designed, because of the phenomena occurring inside this space.

Many new generations appeared from Toyo Ito's office and the influence is still continuing. For example, Junya Ishigami (b. 1974) worked at Kazuyo Sejima & Associates, Sejima (b. 1956) worked for Toyo Ito (b. 1941) and Ito worked for Kiyonori Kikutake (1928-2011), the architect of Metabolism. We can even trace a fourth-generation line starting with Maki Onishi (b. 1983). Toyo Ito supports the young generation, but he also complains about that their design in too subtle, focusing on too many little details. To start designing overseas you need to be much stronger. Ito provided the catchphrase 'the ripple-architects in Japan's doldrums' for the cover of Takashi Nakazaki's book, *A Softly Connected Society – The Condition of New Spaces Seen in 31 Architects* (Nikkan Kensetsu Tsushin Shinbunsha, 2006). Sou Fujimoto, Junya Ishigami, Jun Igarashi and Akihisa Hirata are all included in this book. While this can be taken as a harsh remark from Ito towards the young generation of architects, surely he has a point. Fumihiko Maki (b. 1928) once named Kunihiko Hayakawa (b. 1941), Takefumi Aida (b. 1937), Itsuko Hasegawa (b. 1941), Yuzuru Tominaga (b. 1943) and Kazuhiro Ishii (b. 1944) the 'bandits of a peaceful age'. Maki's comment was directed more generally at the postmodern generation of architects born in the 1940s, which of course also included Ito. With this remark, Ito commented on the amateurish attitude of the younger generation architects in a similar way Maki once did on his generation, and called the 1970s generation 'bandits'. But those who were once bandits themselves, Tadao Ando (b. 1941), Toyo Ito (b. 1941) and Riken Yamamoto (b. 1945), now enjoy worldwide fame and have designed large-scale projects all over the world. The 'bandits' turned into 'ripple-architects', and so will the 'peaceful age' change into 'doldrums'. We shall watch closely to see which architects will step forth from the ripples to generate big waves.

We often use the word 'Galapagos' for Japanese products. The Galapagos Islands, part of Ecuador, are very isolated from the rest of the world. Here we can find very interesting and unique creatures developing independently. Sometimes I feel Japan is like the Galapagos Islands. Japanese architects design in such a refined and very detailed way that it is not always easy for foreigners to understand. The interest of the 1970s generation of Japanese architects, for example, is very local. Ideas circle among the architects. Very Galapagos. They all talk about modernism as 'past' and about the need to innovate. To me, Sou Fujimoto, Akihisa Hirata and Junya Ishigami are the ones who changed the most basic rules of architectural design. Fujimoto, for example, showed a new variation on Le Corbusier's Domino model. Ishigami is one of the most extreme ones, as he tries to float structures.

There are many talented young architects based in Tokyo, but there aren't many masterpieces being built yet. If those young architects were given the opportunity to design bigger projects, they might be able to develop a kind of sightseeing spot in Tokyo. Although for the architectural scene even a tiny house can be a masterpiece, Tokyo needs large building to have impact. Moriyama Apartments, designed by Ryue Nishizawa, is one of the most important housing projects of the 1960s generation in Japan. That innovative project could be realized because its scale is not big. But good small-scale projects like Moriyama House can become 'Long Tail bestsellers'. Think of the 'Long Tail effect' of book orders at amazon.com. 'Long Tails' are the niche books that account for a large share of Amazon's total sales. People still buy these books many years after they were first published. It works the same with those small housing projects. Tokyo is so big and has so many people that when it is only possible to work on the small scale, architects should aim to create interesting 'Long Tail' projects. Bestsellers in Japan are still the prefabricated houses designed by a commercial house-building company. To have successful projects overseas, with considerable less quality in construction than in Japan, young Japanese architects will need a very strong concept. Fujimoto's projects have a chance of succeeding abroad. Some other architects' designs are so sensitive that it will be very hard to realize the same quality overseas.

THE 1970S GENERATION

NESTED BOXES
Sou Fujimoto

MOUNTAINOUS LANDSCAPE
Akihisa Hirata

TWO UNIFIED VIEWS
Kumiko Inui

HEAVENLY STATE
Jun Igarashi

FRIENDLY NOD
Takei Nabeshima Architects (TNA)

A VIOLIN INSIDE A ROCK
Mount Fuji Architects

ALLEYWAY LIVING
Suppose Design Office (Makoto Tanijiri)

LIVELY BALCONIES
Go Hasegawa

EMPTY HOUSE
Hideyuki Nakayama

UNREACHABLE SPACE
Yuko Nagayama

TRANSPARENT SCENERIES
Junya Ishigami

RULER OF THE SITE
Ryuji Nakamura

NESTED BOXES
Sou Fujimoto (Sou Fujimoto Architects)

Covered by a huge 7.5-m-high box, the house looks like a ruin of an ancient structure

Project Name: House N
Location: Oita, Oita Prefecture
Year of Completion: 2008
Client: Couple in their sixties
Special Requests: Husband: A stylish, but not luxurious house. Rooms with plenty of air. Wife: Multiple routes, entrances and exits
Site Area: 236.57 m^2
Built Area: 150.57 m^2
Total Floor Area: 85.51 m^2
Building Height: 7.54 m
Storeys: one
Structure: reinforced concrete
Structural Engineer: Jun Sato Structural Engineers

NESTED BOXES

ARCHITECT: SOU FUJIMOTO
Year of Birth: 1971
Education: University of Tokyo, Tokyo
Master: not relevant

You invented an artificial and cave-like scheme as an alternative to Le Corbusier's Domino system.
Sou Fujimoto: 'In Le Corbusier's Domino system all elements (slabs, columns and stairs) are clearly distinguishable. They have their own, well-prepared function and are combined logically with each other. In my system, the slabs are slabs but at the same time chairs, steps or shelves. It's an undefined structure that can be used at will. The function only becomes clear after people respond to the space. My structure invites and inspires people to behave freely. Because every person responds in a different way, the function or meaning will always be different. Modernist thinking is too simple. If you rigidly divide inside and outside, you completely miss out on the richness of all gradations in between.'
Several of your earlier housing projects are cave-like. What do you find so appealing in this quality?
SF: 'I make a distinction between a nest and a cave. For me, a nest is a functional space, assembled with a certain purpose. A cave, however, is something that's already there: an existing space people can find a use for. The cave-like space is richer and has more possibilities for use. I ask myself whether it's possible to create an artificial cave in an architectural form. Once people live in it, the cave will gradually become a nest.'
By reinterpreting basic elements like clouds, mountains, caves or forests, you developed a new point of view on architecture.
SF: 'Recently, I have become interested in old solutions to present-day questions, rather than inventing new solutions. A long time ago, the house and the forest were mixed entities. Of course, a house was a house, but the forest used to be a place for people to live in. City and forest were interdependent. In the modern-day world they're completely separated. Thinking about this is extremely interesting. It's a primitive line of thought, but studying those old living conditions can create something completely new for the future.'
How do you turn those references into architecture?
SF: 'When I talk about the cave or a forest, it is not a real cave or real forest but a landscape that inspires people to behave according to that landscape. It is a space not well-prepared for people but a field of complexity where people can find their own meanings and own functions in their own ways. I already developed a few methods to create such complexity, for example by means of randomness, stacking or using layered spaces. Dividing the elements into small pieces and assembling them independently into a network can result in a method to create new architecture. Stacking, for example, is a very simple process, but how to stack is open. It can create unexpected space or surprising accidents.'
Most people dream of simply having a single-family house with a garden.

Your 'House N' in Oita, on Kyushu Island, goes beyond that dream. Why this experiment?
SF: 'The first idea for this house came from the fact that the site is rather large, compared to a Tokyo site. Japanese people – like people in most other countries – wish to have a garden with their house. I like to turn this common wish into a richer experience. A city is a city, and a house is a house; that is a rather boring concept. When you open the door, you are immediately stuck inside the house. I think that a much richer gradation of spaces is possible. Over the years, I have been trying to make in-between situations – part garden, part house, part city – in various ways. The box-in-a-box system I used in House N is one of the simplest ideas.'
So what exactly was your intention?
SF: 'First of all, I wanted to propose a new prototype for a house with a garden in the city, with a contradiction built into it: it has a garden that seems to be both inside and outside. Secondly, I tried to create something that is back-to-basics. I made a garden, covered by a huge box that resembles a ruin of an ancient structure. Only walls are left and the window frames hold no glass. It makes for a very dreamlike garden. But the garden is not only a garden. When inside the house many layers surround us, and the garden is one of those layers. Through the openings we can see the garden, but also the sky and the not-so-attractive old houses of the neighbours. The garden, the neighbours and the sky contain an equal hierarchy. Compare it with the effect of *shakkei* (borrowed scenery) used in the arrangement of a traditional Japanese garden. In House N each layer works like *shakkei*. That's why we feel depth.'
The three nested shells connect with the city in a different way than the plotlines do. What is the impact of this house on its surroundings?
SF: 'The white box is very different from the traditional two-storey wooden houses of the neighbours, so it doesn't look like a house at all. It is more like an empty space. From the street people can peek through the biggest box and see the sky. It feels as if the volume has suddenly landed in the neighbourhood. But after we planted the trees, the neighbours were very surprised that the volume didn't feel as strong anymore. It had become park-like. This is a result of the balance between open and closed. From outside, the inner shell looks very small. Inside, we can feel the atmosphere from the street.'
I spotted the bathroom in the outer shell. How do you make sure the house functions well?
SF: 'Programme-wise, the inner shell is not the most private one. The smallest shell contains a living room and a dining room, the middle shell has a bedroom and a guestroom, while the bathroom, for example, is located in the outer shell. It is not about hierarchy. It is about creating various kinds of spaces by using those shells. With the abundant combinations of those openings and layers we can create many kinds of distances and connections. The bathroom is located in the outer shell, but at the back of the house. From here we can only see the outer walls of the gardens and thus the residents are protected.'
Have passers-by ever misunderstood the boundary lines of the private domain and trespassed onto private territory?
SF: 'That mistake could generate a very interesting city landscape! In this case, however, it didn't happen, as the site is almost square and the street is very much a street. Passers-by naturally stay outside the plot limits, but friends of the

Rather than thinking in terms of ‘house’ and ‘city’ as two radical opposites, the box in a box system allows for an indefinite number of gradations between interior and exterior

clients can communicate through the layers while the clients are still inside. The "fence" is not an ordinary boundary in this house. It is spatially more developed. It is a transparent kind of fence, like a territory where people can walk in and out but where it is clear where the limits are. I don't want the residents to expose their whole life to the city. That wouldn't make a good house. I protect their privacy but at the same time open the house up to the city. There could have been one more shell one size bigger in this design. In that case the street would be included in the shell, which would perhaps have created more confusion.'

How do the current owners, a retired couple with their dog, handle this place without strict boundaries?

SF: 'At first, the male client requested a division between the bedroom and the living area, as his wife receives lots of friends who chat very loudly. After moving in he didn't need it anymore. He could find a place of his own, hidden to some extent from others, by simply moving himself. And if the chatting gets to be too much for him, he can always escape to the garden! It is a space that inspires residents to linger and where people can act and walk freely. Sunlight comes and goes, cutting through all these layers and openings. When exposed directly to the sun, a space becomes very bright, but one can easily move to another area, according to the weather and differences in brightness. The layers and openings provide the clients with different areas inside.'

Kazuyo Sejima and Ryue Nishizawa love to use gardens in their housing projects. What makes your gardens different from their idea of making a garden?

SF: 'For example, House A, designed by Ryue Nishizawa, has a garden inside the house. When I visited the project and entered the garden room the skylight was open and the atmosphere was filled with outside air. However, as soon as Nishizawa closed the skylight, I felt the air flow stop. At that moment you realize you are indeed just inside. The situation of the light and the condition of the space may be the same, but when we shut the windows, the flow of the air changes completely. Experiencing this contrast so clearly was amazing. I like to make a more straightforward outdoor garden, though completely different from an ordinary outdoor garden. I am very interested in the traditional Japanese garden, as it is like a universe containing a field of variety. To me, that kind of garden is like "architecture with no roof". Take Kyoto's Ginkaku Temple, my favourite. It looks very chaotic, but inside the garden we realize that it is a field containing many relationships. The architecture of House N is not solid but soft. It is not easy to say if something is far away or close by, because of the various distances and depths.'

What quality are you trying to add to the current housing stock in Japan with your innovative housing designs?

SF: 'I would like to create a house like the city of Tokyo, not a Tokyo house. A house that is complicated and confusing in its inside-outside relation, but well-functioning as a house to live in. I'm influenced by the city of Tokyo, not only in this house but also in my other projects. Tokyo is half artificial and half natural. While it is made up of artificial things, the experience is rather natural in the sense that it is a jungle. It acts as a very crowded, small-scale city that goes on and on. With every step you take you're confronted with new views. Streets in Tokyo feel like interiors. Although my house designs are always completely new, I like that distinctive quality of the city to return.'

Would you say that with this house you created a little Tokyo in Oita?

1/1000

1/200

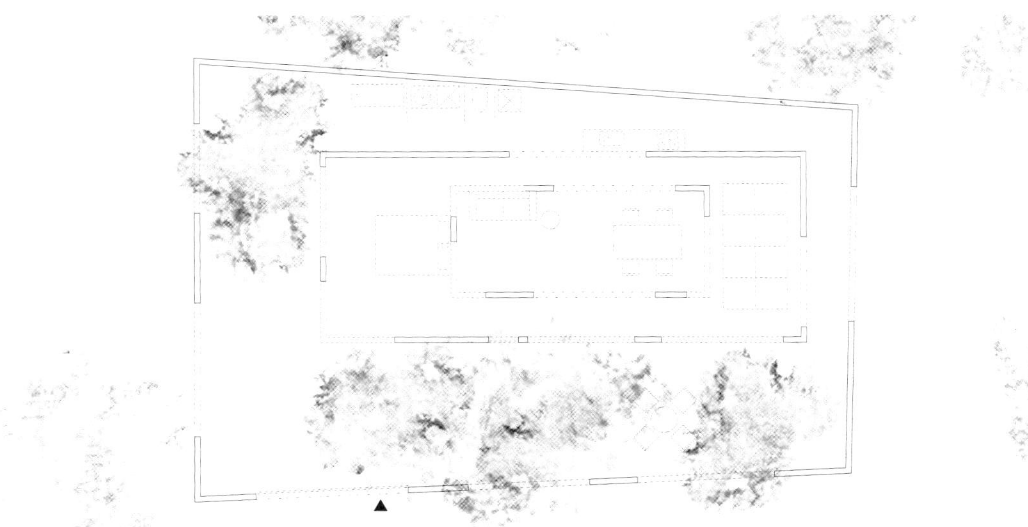

1/200

The outermost of the three shells covers the entire site and creates a soft transition from the street to the covered semi-indoor garden

SF: 'A good point of Tokyo is the crowded city that is like a soft cloud, mixing emptiness with density. The basic box-in-a-box system that organizes House N has something in common with the organization of Tokyo. When designing the house, I didn't intend to export Tokyo to the city of Oita, but just the feeling of this cloud. We could easily put the same kind of house in Tokyo, and I think it would even have a better impact. If I have a chance, I would make another kind of House N in Tokyo with rather strangely shaped shells or even with four or five shells.'

What kind of variations on elemental concepts are you going to surprise us with in your upcoming projects?

SF: 'I am very interested in making something between natural and artificial things. While in the twentieth century we had to simplify things in order to get control over them, in the twenty-first century we can handle more complex situations because we have computers. Artificial architecture is getting closer to nature. If I can combine nature and architecture I can create a space where people behave more challengingly. My long-term outlook on architecture is to extend the barriers of artificial architecture, so that it touches the natural.'

It is very exciting to enter your house, but I can imagine that it is not always easy to convince clients about the inconveniences.

SF: 'Our projects might look strange, but they are actually all about very fundamental things. We think about what a really good place to live in is, and in what way people can live in a more three-dimensional way. We come up with a very joyful idea that we propose to our clients. Usually the client can easily understand that the house contains fundamental issues and that it will be pleasant to live in. If clients want a really ordinary house, they'd better ask another architect . . .'

Why all these efforts to change?

SF: 'A house should be a rich experience, not only for the clients but also for other people. It contains openness but at the same time protection. This kind of duality between openness and privacy is a very fundamental feeling, and should also inspire other people.'

‘IF YOU RIGIDLY DIVIDE INSIDE AND OUTSIDE, YOU COMPLETELY MISS OUT ON THE RICHNESS OF ALL GRADATIONS IN BETWEEN’

SOU FUJIMOTO

MOUNTAINOUS ROOF LANDSCAPE
Akihisa Hirata (HAO)

The shape of the residential complex derives from the natural undulating terrain, and forms a small topography within a larger one made of small roofs

Project Name: Alp
Location: Kita-ku, Tokyo
Year of Completion: 2010
Client: couple in their thirties
Special Request: A (rental) dance studio in the basement
Site Area: 294.0 m^2
Built Area: 161.9 m^2
Total Floor Area: 499.00 m^2
Building Height: 9.65 m
Storeys: four (B1F-3F)
Units: 12
Structure: reinforced concrete
Structural Engineer: Takashi Manda

The roofscape of alp resembles a mountain ridge

MOUNTAINOUS ROOF LANDSCAPE

ARCHITECT: AKIHISA HIRATA
Year of Birth: 1971
Education: Kyoto University, Kyoto
Work Experience: Toyo Ito
Masters: Kiyoshi Sey Takeyama (b. 1954), Toyo Ito (b. 1941)

Toyo Ito is Japan's master of innovation. Did you discover his secret during the eight years you worked for him?
Akihisa Hirata: 'There were a lot of discussions between Ito and the staff about the development of ideas, but he showed no interest in talking about anything that wasn't directly related to actually making something. What I learned from him is the need to maintain a strong focus in order to reach a goal. What's more, Ito is very good at switching between reality and imagination, which enables him to realize a desired programme in an innovative way. If you concentrate only on the limits imposed by reality, you may be able to realize a project, but it simply won't be interesting. When you get carried away by imagination, you can't implement your idea. Only by going slightly beyond the physical boundaries – by integrating the concept with technologies and users' demands – can you produce something new and interesting.'
Did you always follow the master's lead without exception?
AH: 'After about three years, I contemplated a slight shift away from Ito's ideas – as a means of developing the work we were doing then. For example, while working on the Bruges Pavilion in Belgium, Ito advised us to make something similar to the first sketch of Sendai Mediatheque: a slab supported by a light structure. But I didn't want to make a carbon copy of an existing design, so I proposed new solutions in line with Ito's work. We ended up with a structure of aluminium honeycombs. By covering only the necessary parts, it started to look like lace. Flatness, which seemed important to Ito at that time, was associated with the idea of continuous space, the central dogma of modern architecture. I'd rather make something that's not flat.'
As the head of your own firm, Hirata Akihisa Office (HAO), where do your interests lie?
AH: 'I wonder if it is possible to make architecture that resembles living things. Life has its own generating principles and thus a strong basis for continuation. At the same time, life is fragile. The aim of modernism is to make a homogeneous space independent of its surroundings. To get beyond this style of architecture, we need to come up with a new principle.'
What kind of principle are you thinking of?
AH: 'I always use the example of a tree. People feel very comfortable sitting beneath a tree. The tree, however, didn't assume a comforting shape by thinking of people. Its shape derives from the practical need for a maximum surface area for photosynthesis. As a result, people see this shape as both interesting and comfortable. To make architecture that resembles the relationship between people and trees, you need generating principles. In the same way that someone

chooses a spot beneath a tree as a pleasant environment, an architect can choose and develop generating principles. Although spaces that are defined in this way are not controlled by human activities, they can still provide people with comfort and stimulate creativity.'

And this theory differs from Ito's . . .

AH: 'The comparison between us reminds me of the famous discussion between Newton and Leibniz. While Newton argued for the existence of absolute, motionless space, Leibniz claimed that space exists not on its own but as a relationship between things. I believe that Ito's use of modern glass boxes subscribes to Newton's way of thinking. I am drawn much more strongly to Leibniz's argument, as it contains the possibility of making architecture like a living being. Ito often cuts off the generating form along the perimeter of a building to create rectangular glass surfaces. He does this, in my opinion, because he uses a generating rule that has no ability to create an outer shape. I find it much more interesting to look for a generating principle that leads to a building that seems to be "growing" from a given environment – like a living thing that develops when you put it in a certain environment.'

How do you establish a principle?

AH: 'Our surroundings provide us with meaningful forms. Without reducing their meanings, we can liberate these forms with the use of principles. Take a roof, for example. The similarity between mountains and the pitched roofs of a residential area lies in the efficiency of water drainage. To me, a generating principle is a kind of seed for a project. Each design starts with the selection of a seed and with a search for similarities with nature. Next, we make a lot of quick study models using clay, foam or CAD. With these we can accurately define the geometry of the building in question.'

It seems that, as a result of such studies, most of your buildings feature pleated spaces.

AH: 'I am not trying to avoid simple boxes as an end in itself, but curved objects have curved lines and pleated objects have pleated lines. These are shapes that create unique relationships. Pleated surfaces, for example, allow for a variety of alcoves, but they can also produce one continuous space.'

You like to draw inspiration from the Tokyo urban landscape by looking at it from a bird-eye's perspective, don't you?

AH: 'When we look at Tokyo from above, it looks like a living being. I get especially intrigued by West Tokyo, since innumerable buildings tangle into the original pleated topography and create the current topographical condition. I believe that the cityscape created by these pleats holds elements that recall an animal instinct.'

What kind of discoveries have you made so far?

AH: 'Alp Apartments has a roof shaped very much like a mountainous landscape. I imagined residents living in a similar geographical environment. Inside the 12 apartments people constantly feel the uneven walls. A semi-private corridor running through the building volume seems to have been swallowed by the earth.'

Alp contains apartments for rent. Could you be completely free in the design?

AH: 'Designing rental apartments usually means designing a rather standard interior. In the case of Alp, however, we were able to make randomly angled walls

The line of the mountain valley penetrates deep inside the building volume to create a semi-private street-like corridor

The building volume is made with the idea of a living thing 'growing' in a given environment

All 12 individual apartments are unique but share the organic integrity of irregularly shaped walls

and stairs. Each tenant can have a different spatial experience because of the irregularly shaped walls and the different light phenomena. They can feel the exterior shape of the building form inside. The apartment block is in this case related to the surrounding environment, as if it were a cityscape of mountains. Even inside, the tenants can feel a relation with the city.'

Are there possibilities for innovating the programme of housing in an apartment block, like we can with a single-family house?

AH: '*What* we can innovate is different. In the case of a single-family house, the architects can design everything, including the kitchen. We can create the internal relationships, the way to live, as well as the relationship with the exterior. In an apartment building we can create a new relationship between the different apartments as well as a relationship between the entire building block and the surroundings. It is about how to connect the outer shape (total idea) to the city, so tenants feel where they are living. See it as a relation between the big world and their own private world. The impact of a single-family house tends to be smaller than an apartment building. You can propose a way of living, which directly affects the family. In an apartment building you can add urban elements like a semi-private street.'

If you were to design a single-family house, what would it be about?

AH: 'My keyword now is "fermented". I would like to cause the house to change through the action of living substances. With that, I want people's way of living to be more closely connected with nature. I am not talking about a rigid, limited space but a mixed one. "Fermented" refers not so much to changing the way of building, but to the relationships between rooms and interior and exterior. The Japanese master of modernist architecture, Kunio Maekawa (1905-1986), an heir to Le Corbusier (1887-1965), has the same opinion. He said that architecture history has a tendency to decrease the area of the part in a plan that is coloured black. If we develop this process further, we could imagine architecture where the space is divided by a modern skin that is all stirred and mixed. I am thinking of architecture that holds a system of extending areas similar to fermented bread dough that holds air and becomes a larger volume. My architecture presents the image of mixing the air of the interior with that of the exterior.'

What happens when you combine one or more generating principles?

AH: 'Tree-ness House, an apartment block, is a good example of that. Although the project is situated in a very dense part of Tokyo, the client requested a large amount of floor space. I found the solution to the problem in the hierarchical structure of a tree, whose different parts are loosely defined by branches, leaves and open areas. In my architecture, I also like to create open areas that are not defined by the envelope or enclosed by walls. In designing Tree-ness House, I stacked various boxes and made openings, producing diverse relationships between inside and out, which I enhanced with greenery. The building is covered in plants. Many in-between areas that actually belong to the exterior feel very much like an interior space. The result is as ambiguous as the spot beneath the branches of a tree. I think this kind of architecture can improve a city. Imagine a wide array of three-dimensional gardens hanging in the sky. Tokyo would be really green!'

And part of that revelation is the need to make new architecture?

AH: 'It's not important to make a new shape per se. I want to explore the relations

1/1400

1/400

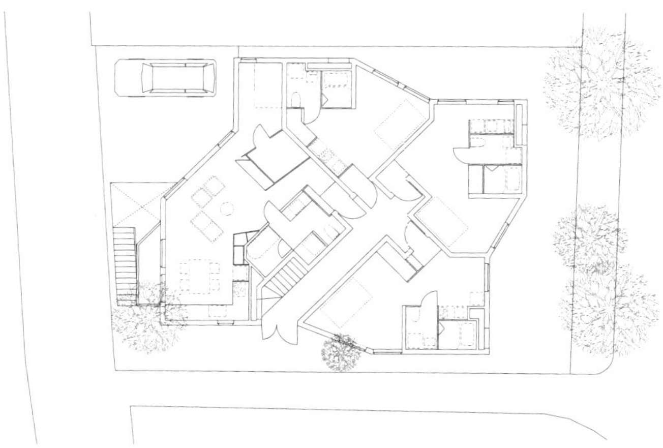

1/300

The roof line is always present inside the interior, whereas residents can make a mental connection between the entire building and their own private life

between things we take for granted by using new principles. Life is defined by species, and species are always looking for new ways of living in order to survive. My approach to architecture is a natural instinct.'

‘I WONDER IF IT IS POSSIBLE TO MAKE ARCHITECTURE THAT RESEMBLES LIVING THINGS’

AKIHISA HIRATA

UNIFYING TWO VIEWS
Kumiko Inui (Office of Kumiko Inui)

The small apartment tower contains one 20-m² apartment per floor that is arranged around a 5 m² central staircase core. From the exterior one can not tell if the building is one single residence or a housing complex

Project Name: Apartment I
Location: Shibuya-ku, Tokyo
Year of Completion: 2007
Client: EARLY AGE CO., LTD
Special Request: Add special value to an unpopular site by using creativity and imagination
Residents: various
Site Area: 48.44 m^2
Built Area: 25.74 m^2
Total Floor Area: 127.57 m^2
Building Height: 11.50 m
Storeys: five (B1F – 4F)
Units: five
Structure: reinforced concrete
Structural Engineer: Space and Structure Engineering Workshop

The floor plans vary between O-shaped and U-shaped mirror-reflected apartments to bring the center of daily life to the most appropriate position according to the surroundings

UNIFYING TWO VIEWS

ARCHITECT: KUMIKO INUI
Year of Birth: 1969
Education: Tokyo University of the Arts, Tokyo
Yale School of Architecture, New Haven
Masters: Yoshihiro Masko (b 1940), Kijo Rokkaku (b. 1941), Jun Aoki (b. 1956)

Since 2000 you have run your own practice. Why does your work focus on discovering the order or disorder surrounding Tokyo residents' daily lives?
Kumiko Inui: 'Daily life in Japan is disorderly. Look around Tokyo, there's no order to be found! The city consists of different designs, heights and people. Even the attitudes of young and old people are completely different. When I design a building I don't want to ignore the surroundings – I want to think about them and capture the disorder.'
Does the variety of the urban vernacular stimulate your desire to meticulously observe and understand the sites of your projects?
KI: 'My ideas come from my love of observation. If you carefully look at Tokyo's urban landscape you notice a strange mixture of small houses next to big apartment blocks. And the inner landscape of apartments is chaotic due to the small floor space of each unit. In Apartment I, I compare two kinds of chaos – inside and outside – and observe them simultaneously. For example, if an apartment is clean and beautiful, the landscape outside is considered horrible. If the landscape outside is beautiful, the interior feels awful. In this project I erased the division between inside and outside and used the small size of the apartments to help create an equal situation. Because of the narrowness of the interior space – the maximum width is 1.80 m and the minimum only 0.75 m – there is a great interior brightness during the daytime. I intentionally made the interiors of the apartments as bright as the exterior, creating the illusion that the two landscapes have identical illumination. Adding the element of furniture into this artificial singular landscape makes the belongings look as if they are placed in the foreground of the overall chaotic urban backdrop.'
How else are you able to manipulate people's perception of spaces?
KI: 'The use of colour is a major factor when attempting to deceive perceptions. In the boutique for Jurgen Lehl's apparel brand in Marunouchi, for example, I made a space that appears to be illuminated by coloured lights. The blue room looks like it is lit by a blue light, the red room looks as though it is lit by a red light and so on and so forth. However, if you look carefully, you will notice that the room is not what is seems. I have implemented simple visual trickery: there are no coloured lights that illuminate the rooms. It is the gradation of the colours; the floor is painted the darkest and the ceiling the brightest. Walking inside this shop makes you feel a little bit drunk. For a retail space it is essential to make the customer happier when inside the store than when he or she is outside on the street. So, another goal of mine in creating a gorgeous happy space was to slightly confuse people, but only enough that the

customers gradually embrace the comfort once inside the store. The evolution of emotions is critical and colour was the key in this instance.'

Is the disruption of normal perception your unique point?

KI: 'For Apartment I we tried to create the right interior. The space for each tenant is very small, only 20 m^2. We thought a tenant would never be able to keep his space tidy with so few square metres. The interior would be always messy. We wanted to be positive about this reality. When designing this interior landscape, we found out that the landscape in the exterior is also messy. We thought it was great that both inside and outside are messy. If the brightness of the interior and the brightness of the exterior is equal, we can create one Gestalt, and take those things as one situation. The boundary between interior and exterior is gone, and we see one unified landscape.'

Do people outside expect a messy interior?

KI: 'Before we started this apartment, we researched the average studio apartment in Tokyo and found out that it usualy faces the same direction, has a repetitive balcony, and its window size is always the same. The neighbours living opposite can be seen by the occupants. The neighbours behind this kind of apartments also feel bad because they are always ignored by the occupants. The occupants themselves are also unhappy, because the exterior of the apartment already tells from the outside that the interior is very small. The occupant exposes his life to the city, which also feels bad. So lots of people around this apartment start to feel very unhappy. We don't like this situation, so we tried to create a different stance. In Apartment I, every occupant faces a different direction. The neighbours feel better and the occupants feel better, as their lives are not exposed.'

Their lives are not exposed? But everything is visible!

KI: 'Yes, but only parts of their lives are exposed. From the exterior, it becomes difficult to even comprehend that you are looking at a housing complex. To make the conditions more interesting all functions are scattered along the perimeter so that the structure appears as if it were a single residence.'

Is exposure part of a typical Tokyo lifestyle?

KI: 'Housing policy in Japan uses the American system as a model. In the USA a lot of people also purchase a single-family house, and even poor people own a detached house. After the Second World War, the Japanese government tried to follow that policy and that is why we see so many single-family houses in Japan. The big difference between the USA and Japan is the site of the lot. So although it is based on the same layout system, the result is very different. We've been making miniaturized versions of American houses.'

Can you avoid the system?

KI: 'Actually, we Japanese architects are enjoying this mistake and trying to make it better. We observe the landscape around the houses very carefully. We can treat the small world as a nice thing. We mix the interior and exterior world in a more complex way. In America, indoor and outdoor are separated; the landscape around the house is very simple. The design of the house is always dominated by the family's demands, kind of boring. A Japanese house is more complex, as we have to think about the family's demands and about how the interior relates to the exterior landscape.'

How do you imagine Tokyo in the future? Will the number of Apartment I's grow exponentially?

A room is at most 1.80 m wide, smaller then the 2.10 m ceiling height, which makes a room as bright as the exterior

Living in a narrow space with the core wall in the back is seen as a cozy form of residing in a one-room apartment in the midst of the city

1/1000

1/200

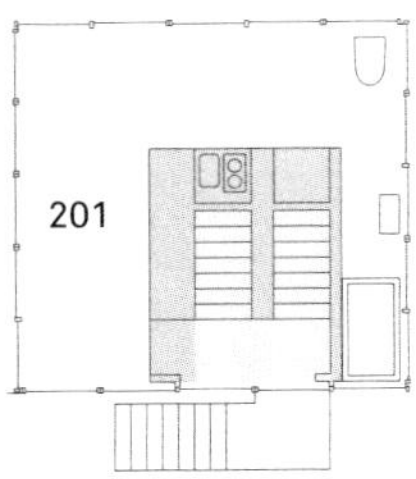

1/200

KI: 'I feel that more and more young Japanese people now share a positive attitude towards the landscape. Japanese people currently in their sixties tried to protect themselves very much. We became more open minded and tried to enjoy our lives more than previous generations. Opening your life to the outside world is the most rational way to enjoy life. I think that life can be shared by a lot of young Japanese people. Gradually, they also want to live in a new-style house.'

Why do you think the young generation can easily open their minds?

KI: 'I feel that through the Internet, young people try to form relationships with others. They demand a bond. That is very new for us. Before we always focused on personal activity. Young people don't buy a lot of personal items like cars, clothes and gadgets anymore, because now they are paying money to create a bond. In the last five years, people have been paying for services to connect them. They are tired of being a selfish, individual person.'

How does this affect architecture?

KI: 'Now a lot of people are interested in common space, rather than in individual space. I think that influences our way of designing architecture.

Does your personality relate to your designs?

KI: 'I have two different personalities: one personality is very strict, serious and honest and my other half is like a joker, somebody who loves humour. That humour is apparent in all the façade designs I have created. At first I wasn't interested in brand designs at all, but the early commissions in my practice, for Dior and Louis Vuitton, made me start to think about brand designs, forcing me to become that humorous person.'

So there is always a touch of humour in your designs?

KI: 'I have this contradiction inside me. I'm interested in rational things. The common space issue, for example, is a very rational thing. At the same time, I like the fantasy world. Architecture, especially housing design, has to have some fantasy. Nowadays, a lot of people don't want this amount of fantasy inside their house. They believe in the typical fantasy, the typical lifestyle with very little variety. Even in the designers' apartment you find a typical style: concrete walls, a big window and a big space with nothing more than a designer-style chair. I don't think this is nice. I wish a lot of people would demand their lifestyle by intuition. I want to make houses for these unique people. That's my dream.'

Do your dreams also come from abroad?

KI: 'Of course we study the work of foreign architects. But we also know that we cannot directly import this information but have to adjust it to our situation. After the Second World War many master architects tried to import the modernist theory, but at the same time they invented a new Japanese situation. Our generation is still much influenced by this situation. We learned the basic attitude of how to import ideas from abroad from our master architects.'

What is the point of analysing international building typologies as a reference?

KI: 'I'm interested in foreign projects because of the roots of how the project is created. What inspired those architects? I am not interested in just copying a foreign project into our situation, but since we are living in the same age, I feel that our generation of architects in Japan can share some things with those abroad.'

What form of design deception can we expect from you in the future?

KI: 'I am interested in thinking about thresholds. They strongly relate to the human sense because they exist as the boundary between two conditions. For example, after continuous contact with cold water, the sensation of cold changes to a sensation of pain. Sensations like cold and pain do not seem to have much to do with each other. However, they can approach each other until they almost meet. I want to translate this idea in order to design a semi-outdoor interior place. But not simply one that merely separates the indoors from the outdoors. I asked myself what the minimum requirement is for people to understand that they are in an indoor environment and what the minimum requirement is for them to feel like they are outside. In this way, I can arrive at an outdoor-like interior that could not have been imagined had I simply tried to think of a place where indoor and outdoor meet.'

'I DON'T WANT TO IGNORE THE SURROUNDINGS – I WANT TO THINK ABOUT THEM AND CAPTURE THE DISORDER'

HEAVENLY STATE
Jun Igarashi (Jun Igarashi Architects)

The house is designed as a self-contained volume in a configuration of 14 rectangular volumes that vary in height from 3.50 to 8.95 m. Skylights are the only contact with the outdoors

Project Name: House M
Location: Asahikawa, Hokkaido Prefecture
Year of Completion: 2009
Client: couple
Site Area: 267.76 m²
Built Area: 155.23 m²
Total Floor Area: 185.04 m²
Building Height: 3.20 - 8.95 m
Maximum Building Height: 8.95 m
Storeys: two
Structure: timber frame
Structural Engineer: Daisuke Hasegawa & Partners

ARCHITECT: JUN IGARASHI
Year of Birth: 1970
Education: Hokkaido Institute of Technology, Sapporo
Master: not relevant

Contrary to Tokyo's young architects, you seem to have a rather negative view of the Japanese city. Are your houses introvert to shut out the cold exterior environment, or also because you think the surroundings are not that beautiful?
Jun Igarashi: 'It is related to both. The conditions in Hokkaido Prefecture are different, so the outcome cannot be the same as that of architects in Tokyo. Winters are very cold up here, which means that you almost unconsciously deal with the "state" of a place. You have to design for the cold, otherwise living becomes very unpleasant. On the other hand, I don't have any aversion to the city. Rather, I feel a strange gap between architectural ideas from architects who live in the city and mine. I don't think I have a negative view. A city is attractive because it is chaotic. Because we cannot predict what is going to happen, the city stays attractive. If a city does not metabolize like a living creature every day, it will die. I'm not interested in making a small response to the city. Architects are usually interested in problems close to their own personal environment. Such thoughts are always caught up when you work in the city, unless the situation is projected objectively.'
Houses designed to protect the human body from the bitter cold of winter on Hokkaido require special means of dealing with the forbidding natural environment. How do you resolve such problems?
JI: 'The ideal "state" or primordial place of comfort for human beings I am looking for in architecture is making a pleasant and comfortable space. I think that this depends neither on the era nor on the trend; it is the space for primary human senses. My main concern is the performance of the insulation, the quality of the air and the heating facilities. By designing those three things I can make a stable hydrothermal (temperature and humidity) environment inside each house. Insulation, air and heat are the primary elements of architecture that make a house in Hokkaido comfortable. With the spatial layout of a house you can amplify this comfort. For example, because of the extreme cold in Hokkaido, it is a rule to sink a house 60 cm into the ground. Usually this space is just filled with concrete. But by using this 60 cm, I can, for example, make a really high living space.'
In what sense are your house designs different from the closed-off domains Japanese architects used to make in the 1960s, 1970s and 1980s?
JI: 'The houses in my portfolio are almost all located in small cities in Hokkaido and inevitably the result of a response to the surrounding environment. If the view surrounding the house is nice, I make sure the residents can see it. But I have no intention of making a direct connection with the surroundings, as privacy is the most important issue for me. Although your neighbours are located far from your own house in the countryside, everybody knows everybody. Having familiar people around might be convenient in some ways, but in terms of privacy it is not. To me

those closed-off houses that were built in Japan between the 1960s and 1980s were a mere spatial representation of the architect's thinking.'

Your main architectural interests are light and shadow. Why is House M an apt example?

JI: 'Light is a universal theme in architecture and always involved in the most important amenities a client requests. In House M I judged from the circumstances that there was no need to make openings in the walls of the house. Instead of windows, the house receives natural light through different skylights in the roof. I carefully thought about the light conditions. When you stand close to a large glass window, light can be very strong and very violent. But how about looking at this strong light from the back of the room? Strong light can be softened and diffused by means of depth or distance. The same idea is used in House M through the use of skylights. Because all the rooms have very high ceilings and there is a certain distance between the person and the light source, the light we experience at ground level is a comfortable, soft light. Each of the 18 rooms in House M has this kind of manipulation of the light conditions.'

Light and shadow are features of traditional Japanese architecture. Are you talking about a similar interest?

JI: 'Yes, my architecture and the concept of light stems from the traditional Japanese spatial element of *engawa*. You can compare the diffuse light quality in House M with that of an *engawa*, a floor extension at one side of a Japanese-style house facing the garden. A traditional *engawa* has many different functions. In this case I focused on the function of influencing the quality of the light. The concept of diffused light in traditional Japanese architecture is captured as an in-between space and is created by the floor, the ceiling and the depth. Instead of direct light, I opted for a softer variant: reflected, diffuse light that evokes the effect of light shining through Japanese rice-paper screens, *shoji*. In traditional Japanese architecture the *shoji*, a room divider consisting of translucent rice paper over a frame of wood, plays a very important role in the lighting in the house. The rice paper softens the strong natural sunlight and gently illuminates the interior of the house. It is very comfortable to stay in a place with light conditions created by *engawa* and *shoji*. In all my architectural projects I'd like to apply diffused lighting in combination with other qualities of light. When you arrange the lighting, you also change the quality of the shadow. Diffuse light can make shadow ambiguous. Ultimately, I like a situation where the light quality means that you can't experience shadow.'

What other light solutions have you come up with so far?

JI: 'Rectangle of Light, a house in Sapporo, lacks any windows to look out of. Instead it features a tapered light cavity affixed to the side of the house. The light cavity is a vacant strip 30 to 90 cm wide, with glass at either end, that provides the entire interior with soft, indirect light. From the living room one experiences this reflected light as if it came in through a huge, glass-less window. Instead of a house with curtains, I proposed a house without windows, gasping for light from the side only. House of Trough, a house in Shikao designed for a couple in their twenties, is composed of a "valley" sandwiched between two "mountains" made up of service zones. The strength of the interior lies in its stratification. The double-height area in the middle features a neutral palette and functions as a living room. The daylight-filled buffer zones accommodate areas for sleeping,

The 8.95-m-tall hallway exposes a sacred feeling and is lined with 'mysterious' rooms on both sides

Each room has a strong sense of being closed off, but is made comfortable using soft, indirect light that enters through skylights

bathing, storage and hobbies. Light flows through large openings in the walls separating the living room from the buffer zones – windows without glass, as it were – and is filtered by white curtains before reaching the living room. The solution of the buffer zone is also a variation on the concept of the Japanese veranda, which marks the transition from outside to inside. House O, a house in Kitami, is composed of 15 differently positioned black boxes, each containing one room. Light gives expression to a space. By a complex concatenation of boxes, each with a different height, the light intensity and light quality changes in an intriguing manner. With the expression of light, I search for a new universality. Each box has a complete different variation on light, orientation and height. By connecting all the boxes together into one entity, they are all ultimately of equal value.'

Why did you divide the geometric plan of House M into many different kinds of boxes?

JI: 'The clients, a middle-aged doctor and his wife, requested individual rooms in which it is easy to control the condition of the air and the light. The plan grew out of the state of the surrounding area, an urban condition where tall buildings loom right next to the lot. First I created a big plane and distributed the required rooms vertically across the site according to a standard zoning approach. Next I altered the height of each room to a variety of conditions. Each of the rectangular volumes has a strong sense of being closed-off. I opted for light coming in through a skylight, which produces a very comfortable atmosphere. The height of each room – the highest box reaching 9 m – is determined by the light conditions and fits its size and its function. It is a house made up of separate, closed but comfortable spaces.'

What is the spatial experience when walking through this agglomeration of boxes?

JI: 'Moving from one room to the other you will always find a level difference and a door. It means walking through involves stepping up and down, and opening a door before moving to another room, which heavily influences people's behaviour. I like to compare this action to the movement of walking in the forest or the bodily sensation of walking through a city with a dense urban infrastructure. With every step you discover something new. In spite of the limited space inside the house, the residents can feel a sense of infinity.'

What would this house look like if it were located in central Tokyo?

JI: 'House M is located in Asahikawa City in Hokkaido, the northernmost of Japan's four main islands, and stands in an urban condition. In my eyes, it has the same diversity as if it had been built in the centre of Tokyo. The residents enjoy the space as if it was a small city, at times a resort hotel, or a very intimate place.'

How did you control the air flow and lines of sight?

JI: 'The air supply inlet is located close to floor level. It is the height difference that accelerates the airflow to the top of each box where the air is let out. Sightlines through the house are based on the relationships among those living in the house. I didn't really control the direct visual communication between the boxes. It was more about making "a state of invisibility" and controlling the gaze that exists in our consciousness.'

What unique spatial experience do the residents of House M have because of the control on air flow, amount of sunlight and lines of sight?

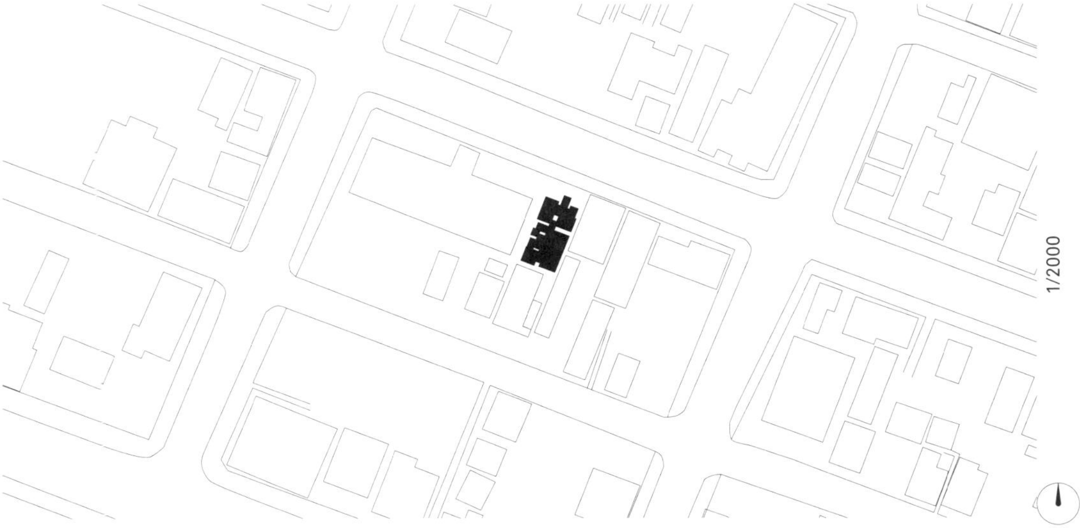
1/2000

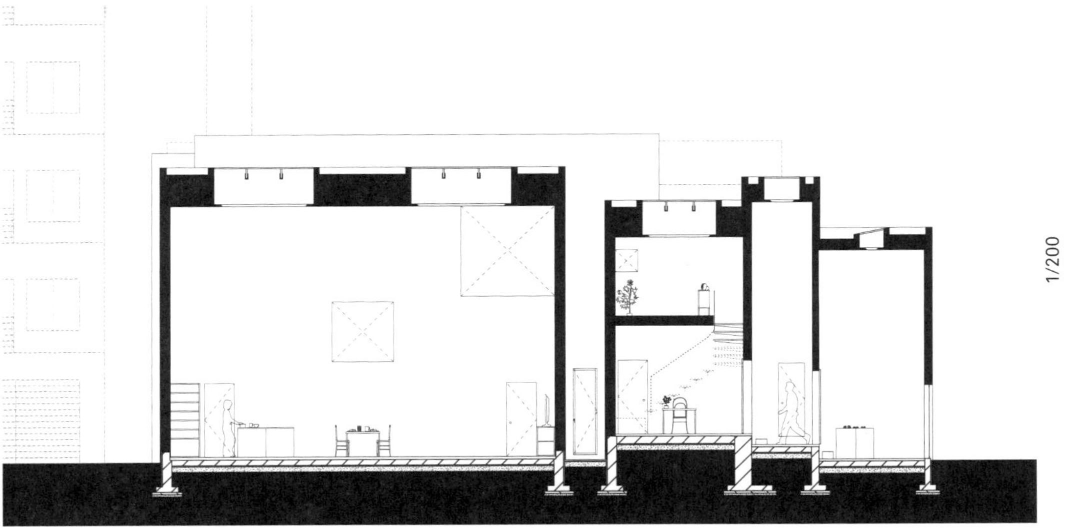
1/200

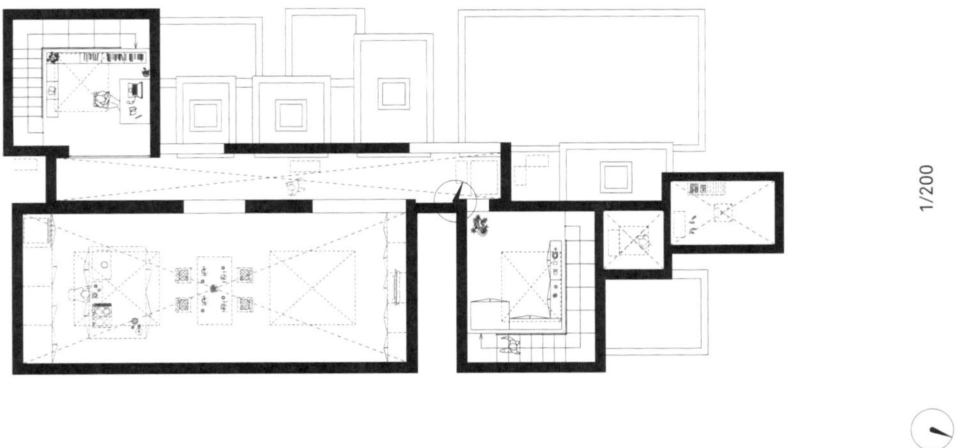
1/200

Doors and subtle level differences in the floor temporary intensify the movement from one room to another

An entresol above the entrance hall is designed as the guest room

The 7.95-m-high living room with kitchen island is the largest of all the volumes

JI: ‘At first glance, the house looks very introvert. However, soon you realize you can feel a very cosy and soft experience inside. That is because of the distance to the exterior as well as the distance to the light source in the ceiling. A high ceiling makes the existence of the ceiling seem to disappear from people’s minds. High ceilings are designed to create a sense of physical distance from the light. This distance diffuses light. Call it a “heavenly state”.’

‘INSTEAD OF DIRECT LIGHT, I OPT FOR A SOFTER VARIANT: REFLECTED DIFFUSE LIGHT THAT EVOKES THE EFFECT OF LIGHT SHINING THROUGH *SHOJI*’

JUN IGARASHI

FRIENDLY NOD
TNA

En elegantly curved façade camouflages Tokyo's strict building regulations and makes it look like the building is greeting passers-by with an impish nod

Project Name: Mosaic House
Location: Meguro-ku, Tokyo
Year of Completion: 2007
Client: married couple + one child
Clients' Profession: university professor/design critic + house wife
Site Area: 58.45 m^2
Built Area: 33.26 m^2
Total Floor Area: 84.50 m^2
Building Height: 9.30 m
Storeys: three
Structure: steel frame
Structural Engineer: Akira Suzuki/ASA

FRIENDLY NOD

ARCHITECT: MAKOTO TAKEI
Year of Birth: 1974
Education: Tokai University, Tokyo
Work Experience: Tezuka Architects
Masters: Kensuke Yoshida (b. 1938), Yoshiharu Tsukamoto (b. 1965), Takaharu + Yui Tezuka (b. 1964, b. 1969)

CHIE NABESHIMA
Year of Birth: 1975
Education: Nihon University, Tokyo
Work Experience: Tezuka Architects
Masters: Mayumi Miyawaki (1936-1998), Yoshihumi Nakamura (b. 1948), Takaharu + Yui Tezuka (b. 1964, b. 1969)

What kind of genuine characteristics have you picked up while researching sites prior to making designs?
Chie Nabeshima: 'At various sites both inside Tokyo and outside the city we discovered that although city and nature are almost opposites, both urban and rural sites contain the potential to create a very attractive relationship between the architecture and its ambient surroundings. Every detached house we designed so far also considers the area outside the site. Even if the size of the plot is very small, we think that the neighbourhood can benefit when one considers an area larger than the plot limits.'
Mosaic House is located in the midst of a typical Tokyo residential area. Why did the clients buy this site?
CN: 'The site is a corner lot facing two roads, one of which leads to an old shrine. During a *matsuri*, a traditional Japanese festival, the road becomes vibrant with people carrying portable shrines. This liveliness of a street filled with numerous enthusiastic pedestrians on their way to the temple is what the clients, a young couple and a little boy, had fallen in love with. Yet, when we first visited the site during winter, the place struck us as rather gloomy. The surrounding buildings cast a great deal of shadow.'
What was your response to the site?
Makoto Takei: 'We wanted to design a house that would receive enough light. Tokyo's strict regulations on maximum height, building volume and light penetration produce "truncated" geometric contours, seeking out the most extreme possibilities within the limits allowed. We tried to create a more elegant solution and designed a house that doesn't feel all those restrictions. By rounding off the sloping wall, instead of using the usual rectangular geometry, we made the restrictions virtually invisible.'
The result is a powerful, though very simple, shape.
MT: 'Simplicity is the result of a concentration of ideas, and not about leaving out ideas. We like to consider an idea from both the interior as well as from the exterior. For us, that's the very start of producing rich architecture. A tight

relationship between the building and its surroundings, composed into a very simple and compact form. Though it is of a completely different scale, we like to compare our architecture with *osechi*, the traditional Japanese New Year food. Dishes that make up *osechi* each have a special meaning and are displayed in a beautiful lunch box. Such a lunch box consists of seemingly very simple forms, though it has an abundant amount of functions and a beautiful shape. That is exactly what we are looking for in architecture.'
CN: 'When asked to think about the shape of a tree, people almost always think of the same iconic kind of shape. This shape is very natural and beautiful but at the same time there is a reason for the shape, namely the functional effect of photosynthesis. We are interested in such natural, powerful shapes that look the way they do for a reason.'
You mean that Mosaic House is more than an elegant landmark?
MT: 'We are not interested in simply designing a maximum volume on a limited-sized Tokyo plot. This way of building is too passive and negative. The shape of a building should be based on a way of thinking. We continually think of more fascinating forms, ones not defined by standard laws. The outcome should be something that looks heteronymous, but is in fact autonomous architecture.'
CN: 'There are so many invisible borders around us in Tokyo. It is fascinating to erase the borders for a moment and find the suitable architectural form in that way. We believe that by first solving the many relationships around a site and a house, a fascinating shape will eventually result.'
What kind of relationships are you talking about?
CN: 'One of our general interests is the contact point between architecture and the earth, or building and ground. The base of an architectural project is related to whether architecture moves or doesn't move, and this is the very essence of architecture. The base of Mosaic House is minimal, rising straight out of the ground. Even when you enter the house, the flooring seems to continue from the car park. We made it difficult to tell where the road starts and where the border of the neighbour's plots starts.'
MT: 'The site of Mosaic House used to be a parking space, so small that the parked cars were sticking out. With only 50 m^2, the design process of the house simply had to begin with figuring out how to accommodate the off-street parking. In reality, there were only two options: parking lengthwise, or along the broader end of the trapezoid site. We selected the second option. We left the concrete and the dividing lines of the existing parking space as it was and only excavated the footprint. You can still see the original car park.'
The house seems to make a friendly gesture by greeting passers-by with a bow.
CN: 'In an overcrowded environment like Tokyo, the question "how to touch?" is very relevant. Mosaic House touches the road and the parking lot directly. We removed the roof, so the house can directly connect and touch the open sky. It might look like the shape of the building was only influenced by exterior regulations, but the shape is also produced according to what is happening inside the building. The bowing figure is a coexistence of a consequential shape and a voluntary shape. This is exactly what gives people a complete new impression of housing.'
So we cannot speak of an icon for the sake of being a landmark?
MT: 'Whether this building uses a straight or curved line is not determined by

From the living/dining room on the top floor the residents can gaze out at the sky, and enjoy a changing scenery of clouds, rain and moon as if it were a living painting

Because of the gloomy site the house is orientated towards the sky, taking in light from a 23-m2-skylight rather than from the sides

A loft space above the kitchen unit is used as an extension of the living room

whether the form fits in the context of the street. It is a condensation of countless factors and consequently this shape came out. The curves are a coincidence.'

What is the story behind the façade texture?

MT: 'Mosaic House has an ordinary white façade. But when you look closer, it is made up of 1-cm mosaic tiles. The upper portion of the curved wall needed extra attention in regard to waterproofing. We clad the entire façade with mats, composed of 300 mm x 300 mm mosaic tiles, each 10 x 10 mm. Glued on the façade, the small mosaics easily follow the curvature. In fact, the whole façade of the house is finished with tiles for that reason. The mosaic tiles give the house a familiar texture that is reminiscent of a *sentō*, a Japanese public bathhouse, which once was a characteristic element of a neighbourhood like this in Meguro.'

What is the effect of the curved walls inside the house in terms of light quality?

MT: 'Inside we gained the maximum floor space, as the curved wall follows the track of a spiral staircase. The curves reflect the light that comes from the rooftop and bring it down into the house, from the second to the first floor. Seen from the outside, the curve on the northern side is an exterior façade as well as a roof, which brings the rainwater smoothly to the ground.'

The curves seem to provide a concentration of other advantages as well.

MT: 'Walking through this house makes you forget everything is the reverse of a normal house! The backward-bending wall creates a space-expanding effect, allowing the shelves in the kitchen to increase in depth as they go up. They also provide the residents with lumbar support while they read in the children's room. The curved wall becomes a pillow when one is lying in the bath, provides storage space for the shelves in an efficient way and serves as a carport roof. The other curved wall carries the light from the top all the way to the bedroom downstairs, providing sufficient daylight for the entire house. All of the family's activities take place in contact with the light from above, with the living room on the second floor being the centre of the house.'

Could the clients immediately recognize the value of your unusual proposal?

CN: 'The residents were quickly convinced that light from the top, in combination with an inverted layout of the house, would be very effective. Japanese people like the south side of a plot. But by taking in light from the top, even the lower levels on the north side receive enough natural light. The living room and bedrooms are normally situated on the preferred south side of a house, but in Mosaic House inferior functions such as storage, toilet and kitchen could be given this prime location.'

Did you include the usual hobby space?

CN: 'The husband loves outdoor sports. There is no roof on this house, as the ceiling is "finished off with the sky". When the sun is shining strong the husband, who loves to camp, "sets up a tent" in the centre of the house by closing off the skylight with horizontal blinds made of white fabric. The wife is a photographer and loves admiring the sky and the light in the shaft-shaped house through the enormous skylight. When the sky becomes beautiful, the wife takes pictures. Both clients can enjoy the change of seasons from inside the house. Besides a clear sky, it is actually very enjoyable to see the rain pouring down on the skylight, to watch planes go by or to just stare at the moon. The ceiling is not just a top light, but also an experience that makes you feel as if you are living outside. The residents forget that they are in the centre of the city.'

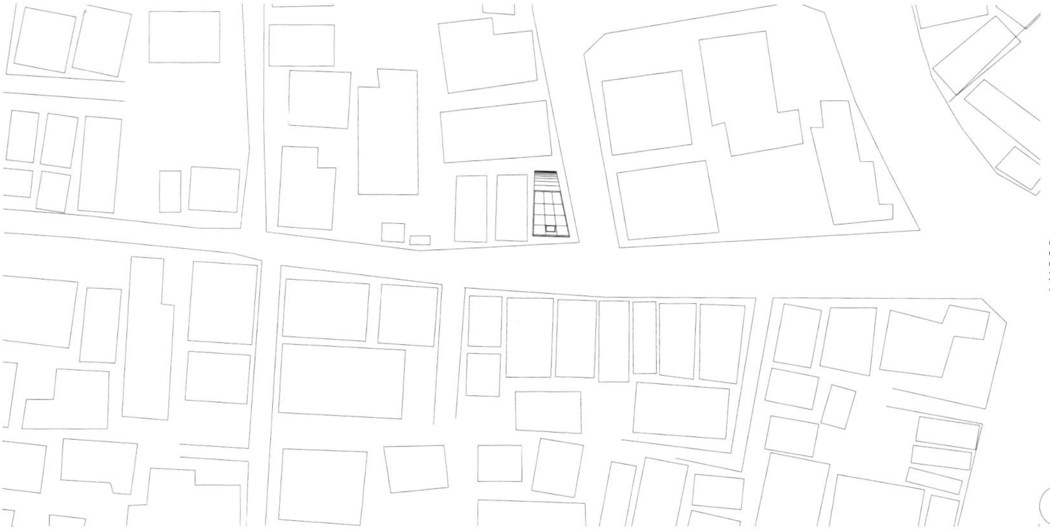

1/1000

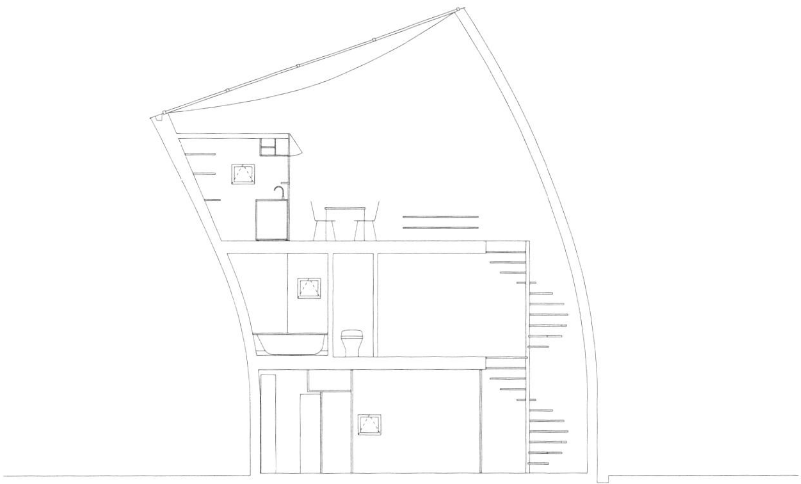

1/150

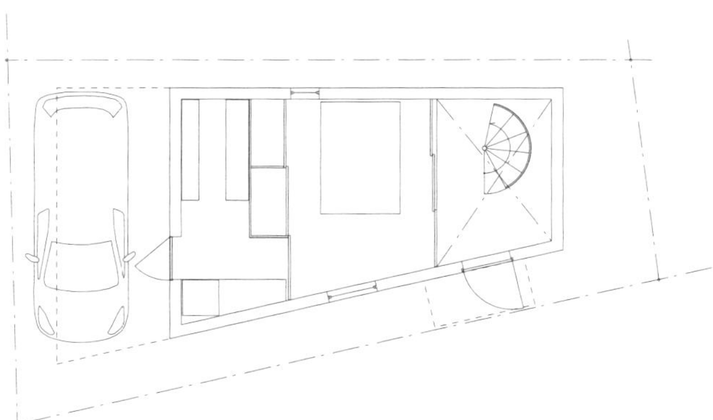

1/150

The sloping northern wall transports natural light all the way to the ground floor through the stair well, making the normally dark side the sunny part of the interior

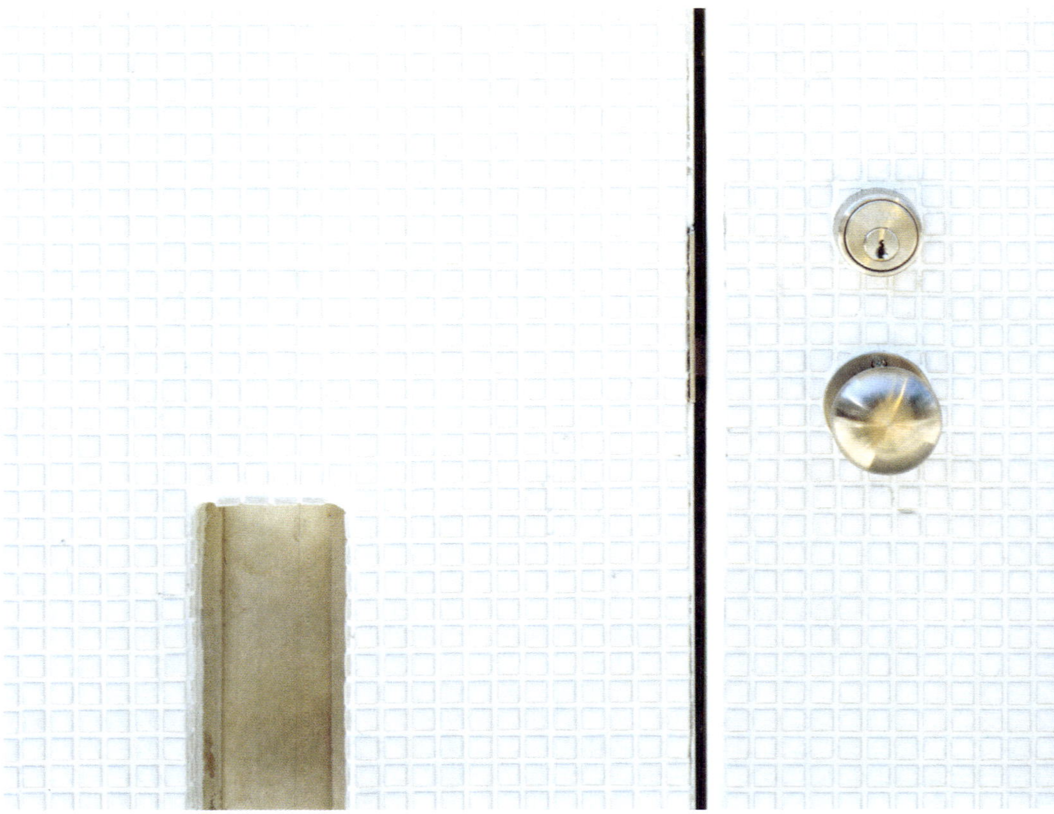

The entire exterior façade is clad with 0.30 m x 0.30 m white mosaic tile mats, a material that easily follows the curvature of the building volume and makes it waterproof at the same time

The entire skylight above the living room can be closed with a white canvas, turning the top floor into a camping-in-a-tent experience

Did the residents hear nice comments from passers-by?
MT: 'People seem somewhat startled as they walk past this unusual house. Because it is setback 1 m from the building line, it is not obtrusively present in the narrow streets of Tokyo. The bending form seems instead to be extending a friendly greeting to passers-by on their way to the nearby temple. Even without explanations, people understand that this house is rather simple; a small space in a crowded environment, so that is why the light is taken from the top. If Mosaic House were located in the countryside, it would actually be a very uninteresting structure.'
What would TNA like to add to the existing housing stock in Tokyo?
MT: 'By building a house we do not add anything to the programme of the house, but we are immensely interested in providing a blank space: a margin or a white space. For instance, when a tree grows it naturally keeps an appropriate distance from other trees and instinctively forms a blank space between the trunk and its ambient surroundings. At the same time, a large group of individual trees still feels like an abundant forest. We hope that the Tokyo house will mature like a tree in the forest, developing respect for other houses.'
Did you implement this idea in Mosaic House?
CN: 'Mosaic House turned the existing parking lot into a kind of blank space. The newly made garden is directly facing the street, without the use of a fence. It extends the borders of the site, like a ripple. Those kinds of chain reactions mean the city scenery is all around, having neither a rear nor a front side. That is exactly what makes Tokyo so attractive.'
And what is the role of a small single-family house in these chain reactions?
Takei: 'A group of small houses form a neighbourhood, and a group of neighbourhoods make up a big city. In the end, even though it is a small house, changing the typology of the house will change the city. We like to compare the impact of a single-family house on the city to that of an attractive-looking vineyard. A grape plant is independent from the vineyard, like a house stands independently in the city. But grapes need to be supported by a vine in order to make a bunch. Exactly this kind of relationship between the whole and a subordinate-superior part is what we can also find between a city and a small single-family house.'

‘SIMPLICITY IS THE RESULT OF A CONCENTRATION OF IDEAS, AND NOT ABOUT LEAVING OUT IDEAS’

MAKOTO TAKEI + CHIE NABESHIMA

A VIOLIN INSIDE A ROCK
Masahiro Harada (Mount Fuji Architects)

Thanks to the diagonal plan, the occupants have two outdoor spaces varying in character: a semi-public area facing the street and private garden to the south

Project Name: Rainy Sunny
Location: Suginami-ku, Tokyo
Year of Completion: 2008
Client: couple
Principle Use: private residence + office
Special Requests: A quiet, but open life
Site Area: 108.27 m²
Built Area: 53.08 m²
Total Floor Area: 79.51 m²
Storeys: two
Building Height: 7.00 m
Structure: reinforced concrete
Structural Engineer: Jun Sato Structural Engineers

A VIOLIN INSIDE A ROCK

MASAHIRO HARADA
Year of Birth: 1973
Education: Shibaura Institute of Technology, Tokyo
Masters: Kengo Kuma (b. 1954), Elias Torres , Arata Isozaki (b. 1931)

What do you find most curious about the urban context of Tokyo?
Masahiro Harada: 'I was born in Shizuoka, a city far smaller than Tokyo. It has relatively few houses situated on large plots. In Tokyo, on the other hand, there are many small houses lined up closely along a street. In every direction you look in Tokyo, you see man-made exterior walls. It means the exterior space feels like interior space. You could describe this as a negative aspect, but naturally architects should come up with an answer to an overcrowded man-made urban situation and the lack of nature. Making a good environment using a new kind of architecture is one answer.'
What new kind of architecture do you have in mind?
MH: 'Mount Fuji Architects does not support the assertion that the city is a problem and architecture is the answer. Architects who do that definitely make buildings that cause big problems for the city. That was exactly the mistake of the modernists. Architecture on paper, devoid of any substance, remains at a level of abstract purity that allows it to theoretically resolve the problem posed by the city. But with real architecture, an object made up of materials, it is another matter. Even when a building is designed as a pure answer, realized architecture, from the moment it imposes "mass" and becomes a built object, never manages to get beyond the "city = problem" equation. We are doubtless the first generation to become aware of the reality of the limits of modernism. We avoid dealing with architecture through concepts as much as possible. For us, the city is from the outset imbued with "substance", and the architectural process is the creation of "substance". The relationship between the pre-existing city and future architecture is never envisaged in a unilateral way, as one would do when providing an answer to a question, but rather a continuous and balanced "dialogue" between the old and the new "substance". This is especially important in Tokyo, as there are already so many different kinds of buildings next to each other.'
How do you picture this dialogue?
MH: 'The house should strike a balance between the interior space and its immediate surroundings. The site of Rainy/Sunny in Takaido is a popular residential area. It used to be a big plot with only one house. But in the 1980s the land was sold and subdivided into six smaller plots. Instead of one large house, a developer designed six small identical houses. Rainy/Sunny replaced one of the six houses and had to deal with a lot of harsh building regulations. So harsh that it was difficult to turn this plot into a happy space.'
What did you do to make Rainy/Sunny a comfortable living environment?
MH: 'In order to catch the sunlight from the south, an urban house in Japan is usually placed on the north part of the plot. In that way, there is just enough space to park their car in front of the house. With this type of plot layout and house

form, any stranger is able to look through the garden and parking directly into the interior. It is not good for having a comfortable life inside the house. As a result of this layout, people will not open their windows, as that would completely disturb their privacy. Therefore, we decided to place the volume of the house diagonally on the square plot. By cutting the site diagonally we realized two different types of outdoor spaces. One is a semi-public area facing the street on the north, and the other a private garden on the south. The north garden is used as the entrance for the house and as on-site car parking. The south garden is separated from the urban situation and allows the house to open up towards the south sunlight and the sky, in privacy.'

What are the consequences of this design solution for its residents?

MH: 'Everyone in the world has experienced rectangular volumes and their accompanying limitations. Such a floor layout is too clear to feel any depth, which makes the space feel limited. By introducing a unique geometry, using a diagonal plan and an opposite diagonal roofline, the house lacks spatial references. People have to discover its physical perimeters by themselves. This action blurs the borders of space. And most important, this kind of living space doesn't force the people to live in a particular way. If architecture can fix its form according to the climate, instead of social rules of what we call "house" or "family", people will be much better off. In the end, all we want is the effect of enlarging the very limited space of a small plot in central Tokyo.'

But you also kindly considered the neighbours.

MH: 'As I said, a house in a Japanese city is normally placed on the north side of a site, so that the garden on the south side is as big as possible. That means that the neighbours on the north side always directly face an exterior wall. By using a diagonal planning, we not only favour the clients, but also make it possible to present more space and natural sunlight to the neighbours on the north side. And because of the setback it also brings natural light and a breeze to the neighbour's window on the west side. You could also say that the volume of Rainy/Sunny acts like a barrier to protect the residents from the urban setting.'

What is happening inside the concrete shell?

MH: 'The client is a novelist who was in need of a quiet workspace with enough sunlight. He requested an interior space where he can feel nature in the middle of the city. As he and his wife already finished bringing up their child, they didn't need the house to be based on the family. Their life is kind of free now. We designed in two steps. First, we thought about how to realize a good liveable environment, a small cave or mountain. Secondly, we tried to change the cave into a liveable place. Rainy/Sunny looks like a rocky mountain from the outside, and a violin from the inside. It is a house that does not force the clients to live a certain way by naming the functions of the space. Instead, it is a space where clients can figure out their living space by themselves. First we prepared them a rocky mountain: a jacket that is tough enough to protect what is happening inside and with a suitable urban scale. But because it is too severe to present a rock as the final house, we needed another step. To bring this rock close to the sensitive scale of human beings we covered the entire interior – floors, walls and ceiling – with handcrafted woodwork. By using a herringbone pattern the interior doesn't have one single axis, and this also effectively softens the geometry.'

What did you have to do between step 1 and step 2?

Thanks to the diagonal plan, the occupants have two outdoor spaces varying in character: a semi-public area facing the street and private garden to the south

Because of the diagonal plan and an opposite diagonal roofline, the house lacks spatial references of any kind

MH: ‘In this case, there is no direct relation between the first and second steps. It is like two different architects in me. In Rainy/Sunny this division is very clear, perhaps more than in other projects. We wanted to realize a timeless building, as if it were a landscape. That was the hope of the client. The exterior will probably stay the same for a long time, but the interior will change over time.’

What is the violin aspect within?

MH: ‘The exterior is designed to fit the urban setting, but the interior had to be much gentler, according to us. Inside we work, sometimes without wearing any clothes, so the materials used for the walls should be very close to the human skin. The scale of the herringbone pattern is like a grain, because people can’t live and work inside a hard rock. In an earlier housing project we did, M3.KG (2006), the walls and floor have a very big texture. Because the 80-m^2 Rainy/Sunny is much smaller than the 260 m^2 M3.KG, the distance between human and material is smaller. We felt we should choose a softer kind of material for the interior.’

What is this sensitivity towards materials the Japanese talk about?

MH: ‘We Japanese like the art of *ukiyo-e* (pictures of the floating world). Unlike the real world, the idea of the floating world is born out of limitations. In order to live, we simply need to imagine extra space. The Japanese imagination is brought up like this. Moreover, our recognition of the world contains two phases: the real world and our imagination. We can discover a big space by just watching a television, looking at a small Kyoto Zen garden or looking into a white abstract space. All things unique to Japanese culture get a big space as an imaginary phase. The Japanese always think about how to connect to a bigger space, even nowadays. We included this idea in the Rainy/Sunny house and created darkness in the sharp corner of the living room. The space is not useful at all, but with the darkness we want to give the clients a connection to a bigger space. With this darkness they can imagine a connection to the floating world. Darkness is just one way to connect to another space. A white square volume could also connect us to an abstract space. In Tokyo especially, we need those two phases, because a real space is always too small.’

I am curious about the name Rainy/Sunny? What has the weather to do with the concept?

MH: ‘Although the climate is gradually changing, Japan still has a humid, monsoon climate. So the main issue when designing a house is how to keep it sound in a wet climate. The concrete exterior wall of Rainy/Sunny is a modern interpretation of *yoroi*, a traditional Japanese method for protecting an earthen wall from precipitation on Shikoku Island. To keep concrete over a long period, we need to keep alkali-ion inside the concrete. By making a zigzag in the exterior wall we can rapidly separate the raindrops. By manipulating the mould in which the wall was cast, we created the illusion of layers of samurai armour. Consequently, rainwater does not run down the wall in rivulets, but falls in drops from the “armour”.’

How do you expect Tokyo will develop in the future?

MH: ‘Architecture in Japan used to be temporary, made of soft wood. However, nowadays we have a lot of concrete and steel buildings, which have a much longer lifespan. We should change the architectural rhythm, and for reasons of ecology, the lifespan of a Tokyo building should be longer in the future. This short-lifespan architecture is starting to get boring, and the young generation of architects is starting to feel guilty about it. Architecture should not be like a temporary gadget,

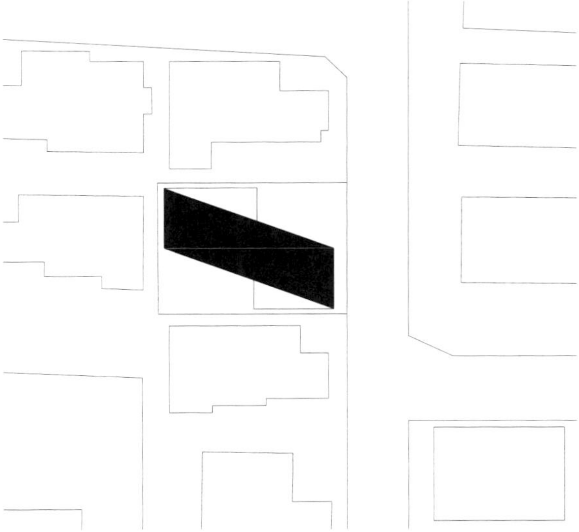

1/500

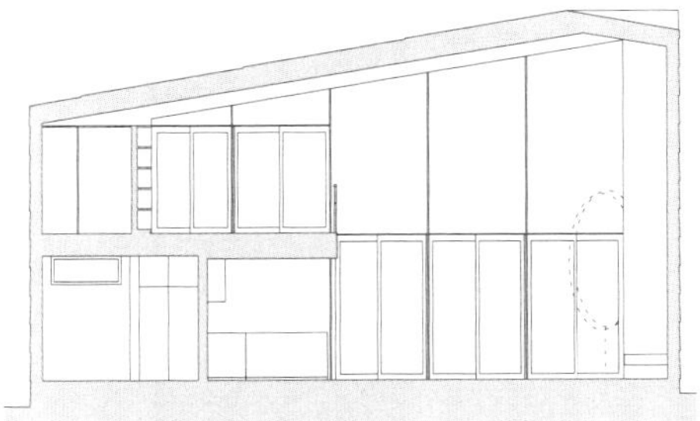

1/200

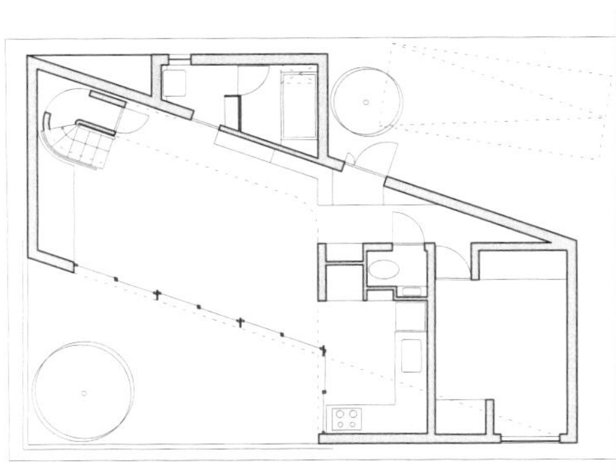

1/200

To give the reinforced concrete 'rock' a human scale inside, walls, floor and ceiling are covered with a random herringbone pattern made of wood that softens the geometry of the interior

but rather a part of the housing stock. If architecture could be stocked in the city, we could use big money for one project. We'd better start designing buildings that can last longer than the current average building lifespan in Tokyo of 30 years.'

Are you afraid that Tokyo will end up in a non-communicative concrete jungle?

MH: 'Natural science discovered that a separate way of living, with an equal density, is better in terms of exergy than living close together. I foresee that we should have a better balance between interior and exterior. We should gather together for concerts and performances, but in our everyday lives we should have more space and fresh air around us. I feel positive about a low-density, balanced city. It will make us more open-minded towards the community. If architects can realize architecture with a unique personality, buildings will start to have a conversation with the things around them, which is important for an intimate and communicative city.'

‘THE RELATIONSHIP BETWEEN THE PRE-EXISTING CITY AND FUTURE ARCHITECTURE IS A CONTINUOUS AND BALANCED DIALOGUE BETWEEN OLD AND NEW “SUBSTANCE”’

MASAHIRO HARADA

ALLEYWAY LIVING
Makoto Tanijiri (Suppose Design Office)

Behind the entrance hides an interior with the quality of an outdoor space

Project Name: House in Buzen
Location: Fukuoka, Fukuoka Prefecture
Year of Completion: 2009
Client: couple + two children
Clients' Profession: employees of a company that makes sanitary ware
Special Request: A bright residence with a courtyard
Site Area: 266 m^2
Built Area: 130.18 m^2
Total Floor Area: 130.18 m^2
Building Height: 5.40 m
Storeys: one
Structure: wood
Structural Engineer: Hidefumi Ohno [Ohno Japan]

ALLEYWAY LIVING

ARCHITECT: MAKOTO TANIJIRI
Year of Birth: 1974
Education: Anabuki Design College, Hiroshima
Work Experience: Motokane Achitects, HAL Architects
Masters: Foremen of construction firm Daiei Kogyo

Normally, architects design the main spaces of a house: the living room, bedrooms, the dining room. But you seem to be more interested in the spaces in between.
Makoto Tanijiri (Suppose Design Office): 'I believe what is important is the relationship between things. When you are interested in light, you also have to consider darkness. When you want a space to look bigger, you will have to incorporate narrow spaces. Making a certain atmosphere or environment doesn't mean you can just focus on making only that type of space. It is important to include the environment right next to your design as well. Even when you are designing a cup, for example, you should not just think about the cup itself. To make it a nice cup, you will have to consider the atmosphere in and around the cup. The first thing I do when starting to design a new building is to consider the surroundings.'
Similar to the way architects like Atelier Bow-Wow, Manabu Chiba and Katsuhiro Miyamoto are approaching architecture?
MT: 'Not really. I assume researching the surrounding site like they do is important, but it is not my starting point in design. I start instead from the characters of the people who are going to live there, their lifestyle, or the way they think. It is very important to look at the human scale and think of a city as a collection of personal belongings.'
What about your interest in the relationship between inside and outside?
MT: 'The planning of a house is usually conceived from the inside. This way of designing rigidly divides the outside from the inside. If you are lucky, rooms in a house in an urban situation have two sides facing the outside, but usually just one. I solved this problem in House in Buzen by breaking the house into several smaller units, so that each room has four sides facing the outside. In this way, each room has much more quality and comfort. It looks like the house consists of six different buildings designed by six different architects.'
If the exterior environment is so important for you, can you mention events or memories that show the fun of being outdoors?
MT: 'I was born in Hiroshima, a place with many alleyways. It was those narrow alleys that taught me how to play. *Roji* are a perfect place to play hide and seek, something you can't play in an open park. Japanese children actually don't really play in parks, but rather in the narrow streets of the city. As a child, you don't want to play in a place that is purpose-made. It is much nicer when you can discover a place to play on your own. I implemented this idea in House in Buzen. Children can discover for themselves where and how to play. The space between the boxes feels like a room to children, while parents and adults may experience it as a

street. The width of an authentic *roji* varies from 1 to 2 m. In this house, the in-between space is about 2 m, a little bit wider.'

Is that what the clients wanted, a house with the excitement of a roji?

MT: 'Usually, architects designing an interior space don't think at all about the outdoors. I start with thinking about what the quality of the outdoors is and hope to give the residents a sense of that inside. Clients always request privacy, a feeling of protection, but at the same time openness. That's what I call a real Japanese sense of *aimai*, ambiguous and doubtful! What clients actually mean is that they like a situation where they can feel the openness of the outdoors, yet still have the privacy of an indoor space.'

How do you design with such ambiguous requests?

MT: 'I don't interpret the urban structure only with my brain, but with my entire body. It is similar to appreciating art. First you feel if something is good. Then your mind will start questioning if it agrees with your feelings. Judging is not done by the eye alone. Smell, sound and taste are as important to get a feel for a space. Why do people feel this is comfortable? Why does a place feel bright? Why does this place feel like outside? What I mean with the garden is that even if it isn't outside, we can produce the feeling that it is exterior space. To give you an example, I have seen people using stairs in the park as a meeting point. A narrow stair can only be used as a passage but if the scale of the stair changes then stairs acquire another function. A lot of these intricate changes can be hidden in our daily life. To find these changes and reassess them can make us realize new values.'

So we should appreciate things more with our feelings?

MT: 'Adults take everything for granted, but children still have a fabulous curiosity about things. Who sees an adult jumping up and down from excitement like a child? What I like about children is that they ask questions before thinking for themselves first (*atarimae*), like "Why is this a cup?", "Why can we fill a cup with something?" Adults will just answer that a cup is a cup, as that is what they have learned. When I design architecture, I think with the curiosity of a child in order to make something that surprises adults. I hope adults can find creativity in a space, like children do. Places that stimulate your inspiration are very important, also for adults.'

How is this interior garden being used?

MT: 'They regularly put up a tent for the children inside the indoor garden; the adults make a terrace-like setting, while the children play badminton with their father between the rooms. They have shown me that it can be used in many ways, as if they were living in a small village using the in-between spaces of different houses. Inside the boxes, we find the master bedroom, the children's room, the bathroom and the dining/kitchen area. All the spaces in between are part of their extraordinary living room. The rooms contain glazed sliding doors. In winter, they can close the rooms individually, and heat the space individually. In spring, autumn and summer the weather is warm enough in Japan to leave the rooms open all day, and the house changes into one room. The rooms are mainly used at night and during the winter. They constantly use the garden space. For example, all family members use the dining table. While the children do their homework, the father reads the newspaper at the same table while the mother cooks at the other end of the table.'

Children recognize the space between the rooms as a playground

The different volumes configurate like a small village of six individual houses

To conserve energy, each volume can be closed off with sliding doors and heated individually

Is this how Japanese people typically use their garden?
MT: 'In fact, Japanese people don't use their gardens. For them, it is just something to look at. In most cases the garden doesn't even contain flowers or trees, as people fill the limited space with their car. Japanese people now around the age of 50 or 60 probably still prefer having a garden to look at. Young people, on the other hand, are fond of the idea of using the garden for relaxation, however small it is. The client of House in Buzen specifically asked to be able to spend time outside. The garden I gave them is like a small village of six houses with lots of narrow outdoor space between the rooms. Although the garden inside the house is not really in the open air, it does feel like being outdoors.'
Does the family have a different daily life since they live here?
MT: 'The family used to live in a standard rental apartment. They are really glad that, since they moved in here, they discovered that living can be so much fun. Here they receive many friends at home, something that wouldn't happen in the tiny apartment they had previously. They cook here together with their friends and hold dinner parties. People enjoy coming to the house so much they tell others about the fun. The house is a real place for gathering. Children also like the space. Obviously, they don't need any explanation on how to use it.'
How would you describe the atmosphere inside this house?
MT: 'It's like being outside, but because the garden is in between the rooms of your house it is an outdoor-garden-close-to-your-interior. See the house as a collection of small rooms – a small village – within a larger space. If the doors are all open, you experience it as a one-room space. When you are inside one of the small individual rooms you can still experience the entire space of the house. It's like a small miracle.'
How do family members find privacy?
MT: 'If Japanese people are completely separate from each other, they start to feel lonely. In this house you can always sense the other family members, even if they are inside one of the rooms. In fact, the space that is not occupied by people is used mentally. I did make sliding doors in each room. When the residents want to feel the openness of the building, they open the sliding doors. If they want their privacy, they can close the sliding doors to create smaller-scaled spaces. The character of the interior changes dramatically by opening and closing the sliding doors.'
Is the house as flexible as a traditional Japanese house?
MT: 'An important part of implementing successful new ideas on housing is to think about the past. I used to live in a very old Japanese-style row house, a *nagaya*, when I was a child. It was a narrow, two-storey house, 3.5 m wide and 25 m in depth. A garden in the middle of the house provided daylight in the rooms located on both sides of the garden. As a child, I didn't like to live in this house at all! The bath, just a tub heated by fire, was outside. It was very dark inside, and scary to walk around at night. It was very cold, so our breath would be white in wintertime. And because the house was big, we always had to scream for each other. All my friends at that time used to live in modern houses equipped with modern luxury amenities. It was only when I started to study architecture that I realized a *nagaya* was a high-quality house. In a *nagaya* you live very close to nature. And because of the inner-courtyard garden, you can feel the change of

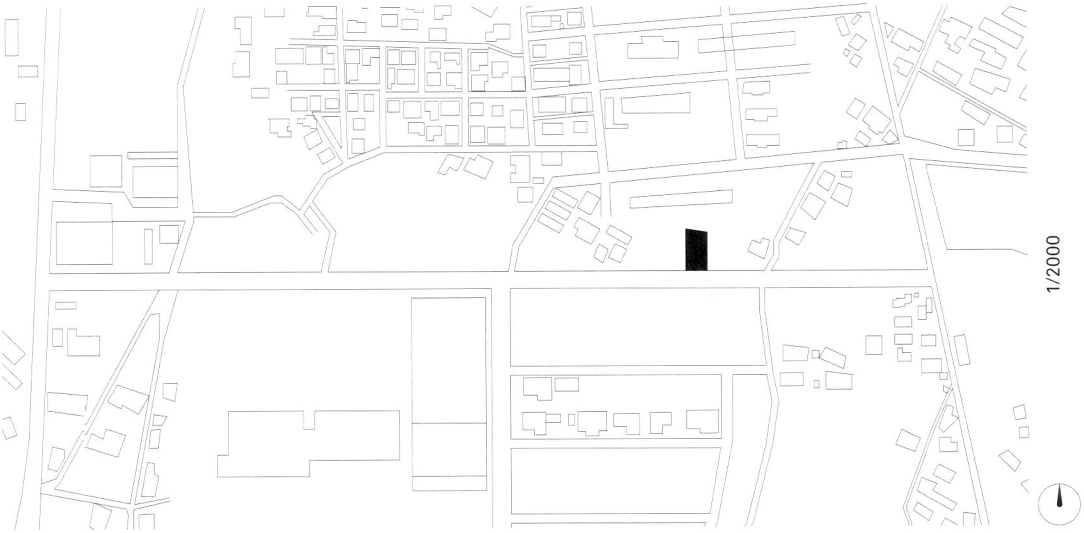

1/2000

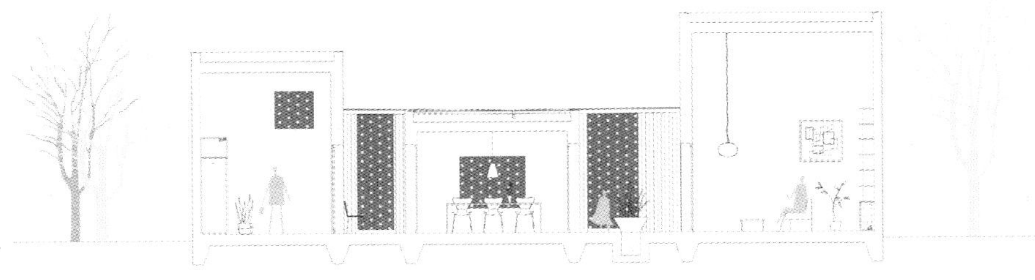

1/200

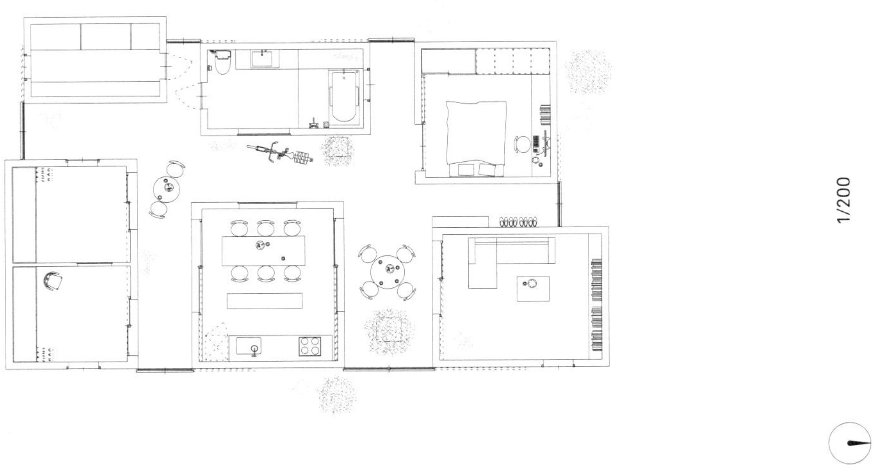

1/200

The path between the individual rooms acts like an narrow street

Each room faces the exterior on four sides, which produces a layering effect of interior/exterior/interior

The residents enjoy the openness of the outdoors within the privacy of an interior space

the four seasons inside the house. I thought it was important to translate this idea into a more comfortable one: a permanently roofed garden.'

New ideas are hidden in the old?

MT: 'It is not that I only look at the past. My aim is to design something that makes people aware of new possibilities. It is very possible to find something new by changing the scale and reconsidering things found in everyday life. At first glance an everyday object or experience might not be something that relates to architecture, but when looked at carefully there might be a point where it interacts with architecture. It is not wise to design by just looking at the essence of things. We should look at what surrounds the essence and the relationship between them and also think about the impossible relationships.'

Designing a blurry line between inside and outside has been done for a long time in Japanese architecture. In what sense do you think differently about this?

MT: 'When not thinking about architecture, we almost naturally blur the transition from indoor to outdoor. But as soon as we start creating architecture the interior is almost automatically divided from the exterior. Up to now, a building creates an inside, while the rest of the site becomes forgotten exterior space. Architects make the inside, but I want to make the outside and inside at the same time. I think from the very start of the design process about a new way of making inside space and exterior space, not only inside the building, but throughout the entire site and beyond. Bringing a variety of exterior spaces into a building so that you have no idea if you are really inside or outside, for example. Designing the exterior is considered the task of a landscape designer. For me, the design of the exterior can start with architecture.'

‘I THINK WITH THE CURIOSITY OF A CHILD IN ORDER TO MAKE SOMETHING THAT SURPRISES ADULTS’

MAKOTO TANIJIRI

LIVELY BALCONIES
Go Hasegawa

Contrary to the closed modern residential high-rise towers in Tokyo that completely depend on air conditioning, Apartment in Nerima contains semi-outdoor spaces that allow for a more open lifestyle based on natural ventilation

Project Name: Apartment in Nerima
Location: Nerima-ku, Tokyo
Year of Completion: 2009
Client: private individual
Special Request: A variety of rooms for different types of young people, both students and workers
Site Area: 352.22 m^2
Built Area: 223.58 m^2
Total Floor Area: 1054.27 m^2
Building Height: 19.98 m
Storeys: seven
Units: 22
Structure: reinforced concrete
Structural Engineer: Kanebako Structural Engineers

ARCHITECT: GO HASEGAWA
Year of Birth: 1977
Education: Tokyo Institute of Technology, Tokyo
Master: Yoshiharu Tsukamoto (b. 1965), Taira Nishizawa (b. 1964)

You were a student of Yoshiharu Tsukamoto's at the Tokyo Institute of Technology (TIT). Did his contextual approach leave any impressions on you?
Go Hasegawa: 'Tsukamoto studied the spatial composition of contemporary Japanese houses when he was a student himself at the TIT, so I learned his point of view on housing design. In his laboratory, I joined several of his research projects, including *Made in Tokyo* and *Pet Architecture Guidebook*, and became familiar with his way of analysing urban spaces. It's mainly these ideas on the relationships between buildings that influenced me, perhaps more than his architectural designs.'
After your graduation you worked for three years in the office of Taira Nishizawa, the brother of architect Ryue Nishizawa. What did you learn from him?
GH: 'While Tsukamoto always looks at architecture from the outside, Nishizawa thinks about architecture from an interior point of view. I learned from him that it's not important what you're striving towards; it's the striving itself that is valuable. He taught me how to strive for what I want to reach. Or, to put it in other words: the object of a discovery isn't important; it's the act of discovering that counts. His ideas still influence the way I approach issues I am confronted with in everyday life.'
What do you strive for when you're designing a house?
H: 'Generally, I'm interested in the transitional spaces between inside and outside, half private and half public. In Gotanda House (2006), for example, I have taken the narrow space that any Tokyo house shares with the house next door as a concept for a house that incorporates such a space in its own volume. In Saitama House, a project now underway, I am investigating the character of the *engawa* (veranda), *koya-ura* (attic), and *doma* (earthen floor), aspects of the traditional Japanese house. All those spaces subtly determine the relationship between a house and its surroundings. The roof, attic, yard and terrace accommodate the space between inside and outside. They are the commonplaces of architectural vocabulary, but precisely because of that they lend themselves to investigation.'
Why this interest in everyday architectonic elements like roofs, attics, gardens and terraces?
GH: 'Transitional spaces are very often leftover spaces, without a specific purpose. These ambiguous spaces are very important to make a good house. According to the Japanese dictionary, the word room means "a space with a certain purpose". I believe every private house should have spaces without any particular purpose. I am interested in creating a new experience that could expand our sense of body and that has no name yet. I also think that a new experience must be very old at the same time, because our sense of body is

strongly connected with history, culture or lifestyle. So, we should observe an old experience when we try to produce a new experience.'

Is there an everyday example of your 'view on old things' that clarifies this idea?

GH: 'Of course, oldness is not always good. But basically things that are old carry the fact that they survived up to today. For example, the languages we speak must have started out as cries or shouts. Gradually, people increased the number of words to communicate with other people. Because human beings live only a tiny part of the entire human history, it's hard to imagine how language developed. Through architecture I would like to confirm that we have lived, are living now, and will live in the future. That's why I like to keep respect for old things.'

How did the concept of Nerima Apartments come about?

GH: 'At first we looked at many apartments in Tokyo and noticed that the façades are very introvert. Almost all windows in Tokyo contain a closed curtain and are in fact not a window anymore. One of our conclusions was that Tokyo windows forget to make a relationship with the city. The balconies of the apartments also didn't work well. Generally, the balcony of a Japanese apartment is a very functional thing: a space for machinery, the evacuation route, the clothes-drying space, and so on. It is a part of the building, rather than a space for human beings. This generates a very ugly façade. I thought about assigning another activity to each balcony. In Nerima Apartments we proposed large terraces that are used as an extra room, and almost the same size as an interior room. The result is a very difficult puzzle, as each terrace had to function as a space for machinery and as an evacuation route as well.'

The balconies form the 'transitional spaces' in Nerima Apartments?

GH: 'Yes, you could say that. In Nerima Apartments I imagined a lifestyle where people easily cross the boundary between inside and outside. We can live in a city with so many people because we allow a variety of people to live there. But it is important to have a sense of living with other people so that we feel the relationship with the city from both inside and outside. But on the other hand, there is a contradiction between this relationship and privacy, because people need their privacy. A solution to this duality is to control the relationship between inside and outside and privacy with 'transitional spaces' and make the experience in the city richer and more attractive. I have a dog that goes outside every morning and comes back in when he feels hot or cold. He really shows us the way of using the outdoors instinctively!'

How did you make Nerima Apartments part of its surroundings?

GH: 'I always take care of the relationship between a house and its surroundings. I neither deny nor affirm the context. I like my proposals to go beyond denial or affirmation. A house or apartment building should look independent and at the same time it should involve its surroundings. Nerima Apartments is built along a street that is connected to a new train station, which was built ten years ago. I expect that this new main street in town will be uniformly lined with apartment buildings in the near future. It's kind of a strange phenomenon, as we are talking about a very local road. It sounds very natural when I talk about buildings aligned along a road, a common phenomenon in European cities with a strict urban structure. However, in Tokyo this is not usually the case at all. That is why we'd better imagine Tokyo developing into a more open, flexible and tolerant city than those in Europe. With Nerima Apartments, I tried to create a new look for an

Each apartment is equipped with a distinctive kind of terrace (atrium type, long and vertical type or corner type), inviting its residents to spend more time outside

The terrace-like balconies trigger a new way of looking out onto the neighbourhood, looking down on the street or looking up at the sky

apartment building that is freely open to all directions. We thought it might define a new landscape for the city of Tokyo.'

What did you want to accomplish with this project?

GH: 'As I explained, balconies in Tokyo are usually just a space for drying clothes and storing garbage. They function purely as a by-product of the living room. In Nerima Apartments the terraces are almost the same size as the apartments. Each terrace has a specific shape: a tall terrace, a long terrace, an L-shaped terrace. Each room is characterized by the type of terrace, rather than by the interior plan. People living in this apartment block can arrange furniture and plants on their terrace, and use it as if it were their living room. It is something very common in Europe, but not in crowded Japanese cities.'

Making use of balconies and actually enjoying the outdoor space is very European. Where did you discover the quality of balconies?

GH: 'The word balcony might be a European invention, but in Japan we also have a balcony-like space, which is called an *engawa*. An *engawa* refers to a veranda-like space just outside the main room of a traditional Japanese house. People use this space to drink and eat outside while looking at the cherry blossoms in spring or at the full moon at night. Because there is a beautiful changing of the seasons in Japan, we historically know the delightfulness of outside space, In fact, we love to stay and drink with friends in the outdoors.'

How do you hope the residents will use the outdoor spaces?

GH: 'Basically, I want them to use the outdoor spaces as they like, but I would be glad if these balconies could naturally help residents to be rougher towards the outside and not be so nervous about people passing by . . . like a kind of device. There are just a few spaces like this in Japan. One of the residents told me he likes to read a newspaper on his terrace every morning, with a coffee and a cigarette. As his room has a 7-m-tall terrace, it's a perfect place to smoke. The owner of the L-shaped terrace, which is directly connected to the corridor, uses his outdoor terrace as a privileged parking space for his nice bicycle.'

Taira Nishizawa indirectly taught you that 'the object of discovery isn't important; it's the act of discovering that counts'. When reflecting on the design process of Nerima Apartments, how would you explain this method?

GH: 'We made various terrace shapes. For example, from the L-shaped terrace the resident can look around at the surroundings; from the double-height terrace the resident can look up to the sky or look down to the city. It's is up to the residents to select a room, and thus the type of experience. In this apartment building people select a room as if they were selecting a plot, including its surroundings. Rather than just thinking about the variation in space inside the apartment, there is also the possibility of choosing between various types of relationships between the apartment and the connection with the city.'

Can you compare the flexibility of a traditional Japanese house with that of Nerima Apartments?

GH: 'The flexibility in a traditional Japanese house comes from the *fusuma*, light walls which can slide from side to side to define spaces within a neutral, homogeneous room. I gave each terrace in Nerima Apartments a clear character so residents can face its spatial quality and begin to imagine how they can enjoy this outside space based on that quality. The differences in flexibility between a traditional Japanese house and Nerima Apartments are the system of

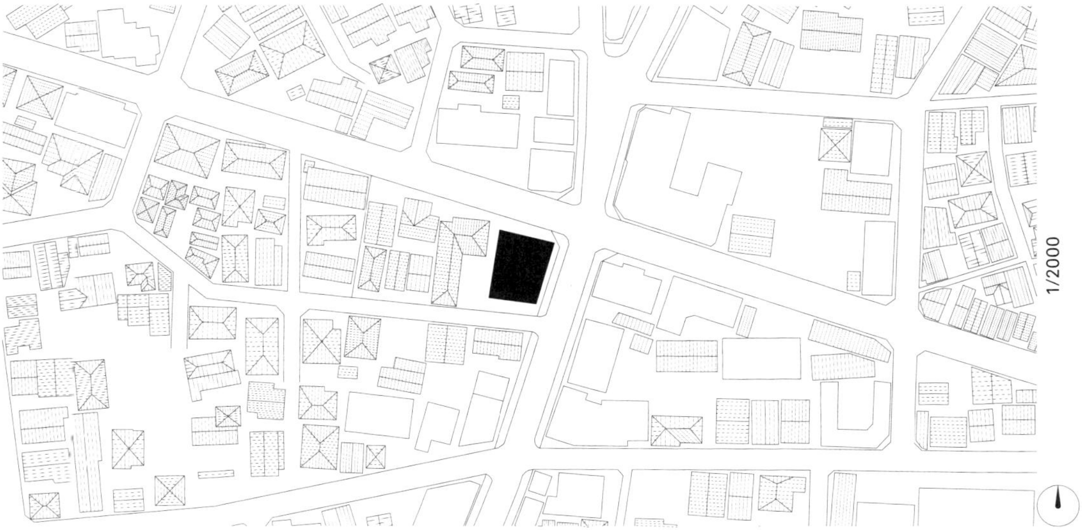

1/2000

1/300

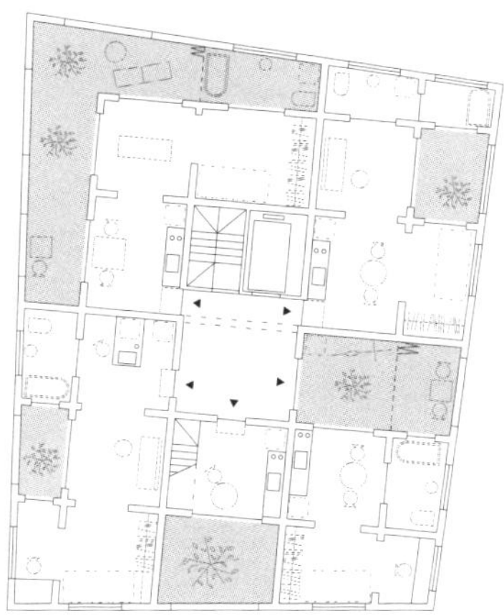

1/300

The semi-outdoor space can be as large as the apartment itself and is intended to function as a extension of the living room

adjusting a neutral space and the imagination of a resident that stems from the characteristics of a space.'

Could your designs be built in Europe, or are they very much tied to their sites?

GH: 'What is important to me is the relationship between inside and outside, architecture and city, individual and society, imagination and space. In each project, I like to make an alternative relationship, rather than a new architectural concept or form. This way of solving problems is useful in any country. The outcome just depends on the ties with the site.'

‘THE OBJECT OF A DISCOVERY IS NOT IMPORTANT; IT’S THE ACT OF DISCOVERING THAT COUNTS’

GO HASEGAWA

EMPTY HOUSE
Hideyuki Nakayama

The earth-coloured, pitch-roof house neatly follows the building code, but its unusual layout triggers a form of communication between neighbours that was apparent in historical Kyoto but has been lost in many places today

Project Name: O House
Location: Kyoto, Kyoto Prefecture
Year of Completion: 2009
Client: couple (professor/design critic and wife) + three children
Site Area: 83.33 m^2
Built Area: 42.9 m^2
Total Floor Area: 59.71 m^2
Building Height: 7.39 m
Storeys: two
Structure: steel frame
Structural Engineer: Mitsuda Structural Consultants

EMPTY HOUSE

ARCHITECT: HIDEYUKI NAKAYAMA
Year of Birth: 1972
Education: Tokyo University of the Arts, Tokyo
Master: Toyo Ito (b. 1941)

How do you start designing a house?
Hideyuki Nakayama: 'I am more interested in stories than in shapes. The stories are not narratives, just small relationships. But an architect cannot just make stories, so I think from the scene and situation in order to make a shape.'
That sounds very paradoxical.
HN: 'I draw a line on a white sheet of paper. With the line the paper is divided into two spaces. When you look at the paper now, you can discover a perspective. But what is the meaning of this line? If I draw a chair next to the line, the line starts to look like a floor mat. If I draw the shadow lines of the chair, the line starts to look like the divider between a floor and a curved vertical wall. And when I erase some lines of the chair, the line starts to look like a table with a chair underneath. This is the interesting thing about drawings. It is not reality – it can only happen in drawings.'
How do you take the step from sketches to an actual design?
HN: 'In our office, an imperfect way of communication is very important. For example, my sketches and perspectives of my architectural ideas are deliberately ambiguous. I pass them on to my staff and they have to detect a shape. The drawings can be read in different ways, because of the distorted perspective. Every time you look at the drawing from another viewpoint, you will receive new information. Because at that stage I haven't made any actual 3-D designs yet, I am usually very surprised by my staff's interpretation of my drawings. Just by the placement of furniture, there are many ways of reading my drawings. After my staff has made different 3-D models, I start drawing more imperfect sketches to add new information. The staff can now modify their models. This is our way of making a shape out of stories and lines.'
A project is always a scene in your mind?
HN: 'I am not interested in the story itself. If I don't draw the chair next to the curved line on the white sheet of paper, the line stays a carpet. Only when I draw a chair does the line start marking different areas and the chair become important information: now we can distinguish a floor and a table or a floor mat and the ground. It is not my intention to produce a very concrete image. Misunderstanding is the key of our work. Imagine that E.T. were to visit your house. He wouldn't understand how to use the objects. Everything would be strange to him. But he would try to find a way to use them, regardless of whether it is the appropriate way we, humans, would. I want to create such kinds of uses.'
What kinds of sketches formed the start of O House?
HN: 'It started from the city landscape regulation requiring a gabled house form on this site. We read the form as the existing "geography". The house as a "geography" created many different conditions. We tried to characterize those

conditions and appropriately position furniture, such as table, kitchen and bathtub by surrounding the "geography". In the process of sketching them, we found that some spaces could be narrower or wider for each quality. Through this study of distortion, the "geography" located in the middle of the site was consequently formed into a slightly curved, narrow long space.'

O House is like a walking trail?

HN: 'The main housing functions are arranged around the house. We put a simple sloping roof on top. As a result, the "geography" located in the middle of the site was left as a void forming a typical gabled house. We opened this void towards the street to create a different meaning for the inside of the house. Now this idea raises a question: "Where is the life of this house?" The answer lies in the gap between this house and the house next-door. If the street grows by building houses next to each other, I can say living in O House gives you the feeling of living outside of the house and in the street.'

What was your intention with this design?

HN: 'The traditional Kyoto style of living is an urban block made up of long, narrow houses. Within this urban block there used to be a very intimate kind of communication among residents. Nowadays, however, plots in Kyoto are marked by the walls of freestanding houses. In between two neighbouring walls is the inevitable 50-cm gap. It gives the neighbourhood a lack of flow in terms of communication. The spaces between houses feel very uncomfortable. I'd like to restore the possibility of communication by inviting residents to use the borders of their plots and be able to see each other.'

Does designing for the former imperial capital of Japan, a traditional city full of UNESCO World Heritage shrines and gardens, present any restrictions?

HN: 'Kyoto has a local building code. It is necessary to make a slanting roof and use mid-tone grey or earth colours for the façade. A flat roof and the use of black, white or any vivid colours are out of the question. Even making a rooftop garden was not an option.'

How did you get round the regulations?

HN: 'O House, as the project is called, neatly follows the building code. However, due to the specific design, the family doesn't really live inside the house-that-follows-the-building-code, but rather lives around it! The house is a long, slender and slightly curved two-storey building, placed in the centre of the site. Around it, I arranged spaces such as the bathroom, the kitchen and three small gardens.'

Why these regulations? Does Kyoto, as opposed to Tokyo, want to keep a homogeneous urban landscape?

HN: 'Kyoto authorities think that by prescribing a shape you can retain authenticity in the city. In my opinion the building code is old-fashioned. With such regulations we can never expect communication between neighbours to return. The rules ensure privacy, but completely ruin the neighbourhood atmosphere. I made an empty house as a statement.'

But what is the use of making an empty house?

HN: 'If every house in the neighbourhood would adopt this kind of organization, the communication between residents would revive, like in the old days of Kyoto. Maybe my concept sounds cynical, but in the end it will ensure a very interesting lifestyle.'

How do the clients use the house?

All functions except sleeping are planned on the periphery of the site, leaving the house in the middle as a curved void

Four consecutive doors in the living room either open to an interior or an exterior space, softening the hard distinction between indoors and outdoors

A 7-m-high curtain behind the street façade (seen from the first floor) gives the house a theatrical character

HN: 'We divided the plot into three zones: the kitchen, the empty main house and the bathroom. As the plot is very narrow we had to curve the main house so that we would manage to fit a dining table in the kitchen zone. The main house has two floors that can be used for the children to play in or to receive guests. The bedroom for the couple and their three young children is a slab hanging from the roof, like a bed in a night express train. When the children have grown up we might add an extra hanging bedroom. Because the facilities are accessible through the gardens, daily life can unfold independently from the central building. On the ground floor, the empty house has four doors, like the corridor of a hotel. The first door connects to the outside, the second and third door to the bathroom and the fourth door to the outside again. Because the living areas around the empty house can either be seen as part of the street or as part of the interior, inside and outside in this house feel the same. The curve in the house and the rounded end produce a special effect: seen from the street, the house seems endless. The curved white shape makes it look like a photographer's studio.'

What is the large curtain doing there?

HN: 'The 7-m-high curtain is similar to the ones used in theatres. A recent graduate of Kyoto Institute of Technology and a former student of the client designed it. The large window that slices open the front of the house makes it look like a dollhouse. With the curtain it becomes a theatre. The idea behind the curtain is to switch the house "on" and "'off". By closing the curtain, the family can change their dollhouse into an ordinary home.'

What if the clients are tired of intrusive eyes and opt for permanently closed curtains?

HN: 'If the family chooses to turn their back on the city, it is OK with me, as long as the house has the possibility to open up. A house with a wide range of options is important in order to be able to choose one's own living style, and not one decided by building codes. And of course I thought about privacy, as sleeping takes place on the second floor. People can't see the bedroom from the street, even if the curtain is open. The stairs to the second floor start outside the empty core. It would be possible to live in this house without ever stepping inside the central area.'

Can the neighbourhood learn a lesson from O House?

HN: 'Enjoy living! Nowadays, people walking on the street can't get any information about how people are living inside. Houses are closed off for privacy and security reasons. People passing by O House walking their dog around the same time every day are amused, wondering if the curtain will be open today or not. Sometimes passers-by will catch a glimpse of life inside, other days not. This makes the house become a part of the scenery of the city again.'

What impact can we expect the house to make on Kyoto's residential neighbourhoods?

HN: 'O House represents a tiny step towards a changing vision on how to think about the boundaries of a plot and the meaning of a house on its plot. The shape of O House follows the building code, yet the house demonstrates that we can break down conventional barriers.'

Does the neighbourhood welcome the newcomers?

HN: 'I don't believe the people think that a strange family has moved into their neighbourhood. Most neighbours have visited the house and liked the intimate

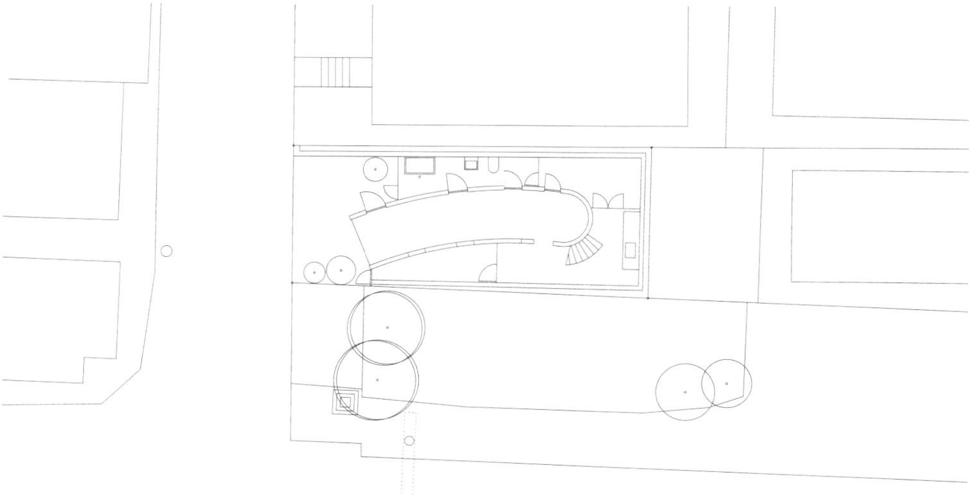

1/300

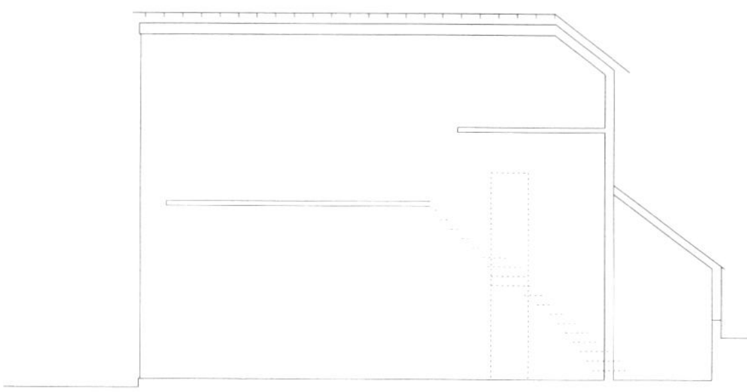

1/200

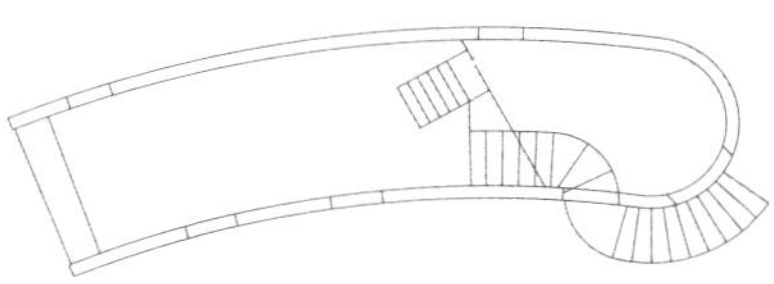

1/200

The kitchen and dining area (left) contradict the empty central void and can be considered part of the street, or part of the interior

The bathroom is set on the periphery of the site and connects with the living room, the back garden and the public street

communication. Those who have only seen the house from the street accept its openness, I think, because the house looks so enjoyable to live in.'

Is your design method of sketching stories different from the commonly applied planning studies in architecture?

HN: 'I question some common manners in life. What do you think of the life of the broken glass cup that you usually throw away? Throwing something away doesn't mean that you environmentally dispose of it. The broken glass cup is processed and cleaned somewhere else. It used to belong to where you are, but it becomes a part of another life outside once it is thrown away. Now you realize the method of thinking of boundaries in the lives of things in terms of places where they exist. Before we just talk about ecology and sustainability, it is more important to think about the boundaries where we define these and make them tangible. Therefore thinking about a house also makes me think about boundaries in living. I want to observe a glass cup and city at the same scale, but it is difficult to study this with small models. This is why I started sketching, to capture differently scaled elements and events in the same scale. My sketches are never a way of creating a particular story generated by different details of positioned furniture.'

In what sense is O House still an 'unfinished' design?

HN: 'We think short legs are for a bed and a long structure is for a slab, but there are more different aspects and variations with structure and plane in architecture. Unfortunately we haven't seen much different potential yet. This doesn't mean that I want to describe everything that we can think of. I simply imagine one day we could have a totally different world with a new way of acting and use in architecture. Even if the purpose is switched between table and slab, so that you put a glass at the edge of the slab and you stand on a table to look around the room, it could give you a state of mind to question and think more about boundaries in different spaces. My approach for O House was to redefine and configure space to generate unexpected relationships by placing furniture between houses, and bringing the street into the house.'

‘IT IS NOT MY INTENTION TO PRODUCE A VERY CONCRETE IMAGE. MISUNDERSTANDING IS THE KEY OF OUR WORK’

HIDEYUKI NAKAYAMA

UNREACHABLE SPACE
Yuko Nagayama (Yuko Nagayama & Associates)

How can openness, enough daylight and privacy be achieved on a 50-m²-site that sits uncomfortably on a hill, in between buildings and opposite a school yard?

Project Name: Zenpukuji House
Location: Suginami Ward, Tokyo
Year of Completion: to be completed (2013)
Client: Couple (architect and designer) + one child
Special Request: Flexibility to change into an office
Site Area: 50.83 m^2
Built Area: 25.27 m^2
Total Floor Area: 76.24 m^2
Storeys: four (1BF-3F)
Structure: reinforced concrete
Structural Engineer: Yasushi Moribe

ARCHITECT: YUKO NAGAYAMA
Year of Birth: 1975
Education: Showa Women's University, Tokyo
Masters: Hisako Sugiura (b. 1958), Jun Aoki (b. 1956)

In what way is Tokyo an inspiration for your design projects?
Yuko Nagayama: 'Compared to European cities, Tokyo is an immense, extensive city. Within this sprawl there exist many scales, such as high-rise buildings along major boulevards next to small wooden structures in narrow back alleys. The existence of such complicated multilayered scales in the city naturally influences your design process. To me, it is about how to utilize a sense of distance and different scales.'
What exactly does distance mean to you?
YN: 'How to take a distance to one's environment and surrounding objects depends on the culture. I believe such notions of distances originate in the climate of a country. Looking at traditional Japanese gardens, we can get an idea about the Japanese notion of distance. Unlike European garden design that uses a physical, perspective manipulation to overlook an entire garden, Japanese gardens provide only a hint of depth. Providing only an indication of an invisible depth is what stirs the imagination of the onlooker.'
How do you translate these scale experiences into a design concept?
YN: 'My design for the commercial building of Urbanprem Minami Aoyama clearly represents the character of Tokyo. It is an 11-m-high mini-tower located in a small-scale housing area, just one block away from Aoyama Boulevard, which is crowded with high-rise buildings. The site represents a drastic scale gap typical of Tokyo. My intention was to realize a building that doesn't belong to either of the two extreme sizes. By removing the sense of scale, I represented the ambiguity of Tokyo. People standing on the opposite side of the narrow lane are not able to see the roofline or even figure out the real height of the building, as it has a bulging façade that seems to rise continuously. Lots of small windows in unexpected places confuse the sense of scale even more and cheerfully send misleading messages about the total number of floors to outside onlookers.'
In all your projects it seems you leave something to the imagination.
YN: 'I try to find a certain rule in primitive and universal components, such as light, gravity, connecting distance and time, which I then turn it into a design. By doing so, I achieve a universal design that is flexible to trends but also tolerant of the ever-changing diversity within an urban landscape like Tokyo.'
What kind of atmosphere did you feel when you first visited the site of Zenpukuji House?
YN: 'The site, only 50 m^2, is small, but it also felt very small. It is situated on top of a hill, open only on one side towards a road. The other three sides of the house are enclosed by neighbouring houses. The orientation of the house was thus determined by the conditions of the site. The very first challenge was how to open the house towards the roadside, which at the same time sits, uncomfortably,

opposite a schoolyard. I first thought about how to ensure a maximum amount of natural lighting. Next, I thought about how to achieve a spacious openness from this small plot while following the strict buildings regulations. The solution was incorporating a tilted floor. The tilted floor angles natural light downward. And because gravity will not allow you to leave objects on the floor, the tilted floor becomes an abstract void space between the indoor space and the outdoor landscape. It is like a buffer zone connecting the interior and exterior space.'

The house is a permanent residence for you and your husband. What kind of lifestyle is it supposed to accommodate?

YN: 'What I had in mind is a comfortable and attractive space, adaptable to changes. I don't think it's necessary to have a big space when living in the city centre. If you need a larger space, you'd better move to somewhere in the countryside. I love to gaze out at the city from a big open window. My solution for this lifestyle is to connect each room with the outdoor stairs. In other words, the individual rooms are piled up. Although I now think of it as a residence, I would like to use the building as an office or a gallery in the future, depending on what may happen. Rather than owning a house, I prefer to think about owning a place where I can do things freely in the midst of a metropolis.'

You 'cheated' on the legal amount of square metres for the floor space, didn't you?

YN: 'The site is only 50 m^2. According to the building regulations we could build a total floor area of 75 m^2, including the basement. But the tilted floor is not calculated as legal floor area. It enabled us to make a more spacious kind of architecture. The tilted floor can never be untidy because nothing can be left on it. In other words, there will always be an empty space. It reflects my positive view on the contrast between the untidiness of everyday activities and the neatness of an extraordinary space.'

What do you mean by 'extraordinary' space?

YN: 'A space that has no functional use, such as a *tokonoma*, an alcove in a traditional Japanese home where people display art or flowers. Such spaces add and extraordinary or abstract space to our everyday life.'

Are the Japanese so fond of collecting things that they need a tidy space?

YN: 'A consequence of the tight urban situation is that people have very little storage space. The Japanese therefore tend to devise their storage space very well. One way to store your belongings is by simply hiding the mess. Another way is to design a scene with a lot of things stocked in place. My ideal solution is to design an architectural space that will not be influenced by objects scattered around.'

Like all your other projects, Zenpukuji House displays a discrepancy between what is visible and what is physically within reach.

YN: 'I've made unreachable situations in other projects as well, but this house is different because the actual unreachable part is connected to the living space. By connecting the two different domains, this small space has achieved an ambiguous boundary. For example, in an earlier housing project, Hill on a House (2006), I literally made an unreachable space, as it is situated behind fixed glass. In Zenpukuji House, the unreachable tilted floor is a space that people cannot step into yet is incorporated as one space and right in front of their eyes. I would rather call it an ambiguous boundary. The *engawa*, a veranda-like porch found

Three tilted floors bring natural light into the house without worrying about the peeking eyes of passers-by

Because gravity doesn't allow objects on the tilted floor, it is an unreachable abstract void that phsychologically increases the small interior

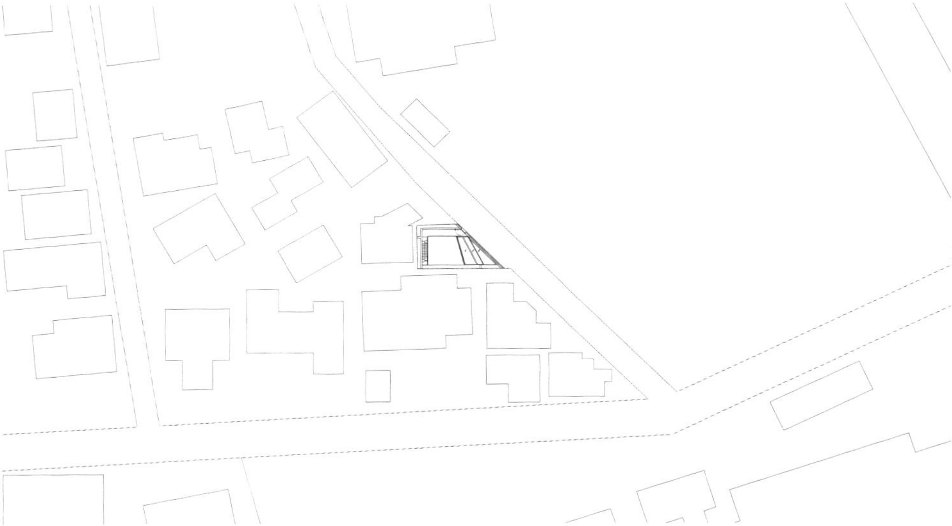

1/1000

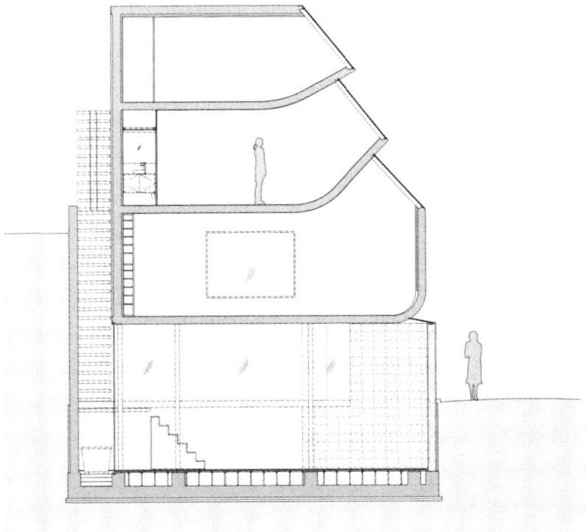

1/200

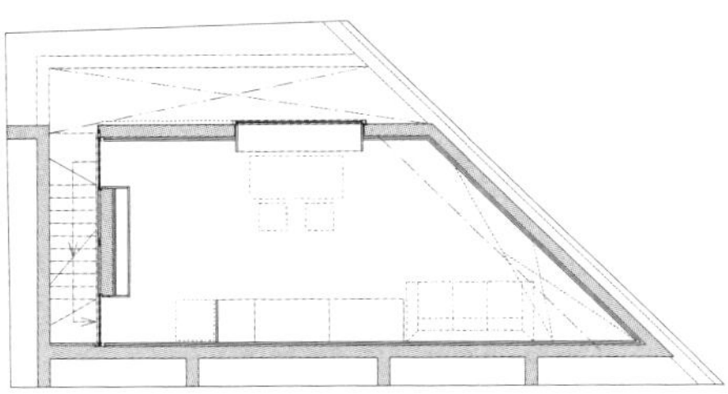

1/200

in traditional Japanese architecture, reflects a similar ambiguous boundary. In that case it carries the intermediate function of connecting the interior with the garden. The biggest characteristic of Zenpukuji House is its smallness. By using the concept of depth and making a special untouchable section, I realized psychological spaciousness. It feels like an unlimited extension within a limited small space.'

It sounds like a place to treasure.

YN: 'I'm very interested in traditional Japanese gardens, as these are places you don't enter: they are designed to be looked at from an adjacent room. The physical restriction of not being able to enter frees the imagination and leads people to focus more on the space they cannot reach. It is this awareness of looking into the garden that impacts the onlooker. In Zenpukuji House, I put a neutral space between the surrounding urban landscapes. This symbolic space gives the impression that natural light is sliding down. It is my interpretation of the traditional Japanese architectural feature of an *engawa*, a space between the interior and exterior.'

What caused the shape of the house?

YN: 'The form, and thus the floor plan, is mainly determined by the Japanese diagonal offsetting regulation and the irregular shape of the plot. In accordance with building regulations, I designed full zigzag openings and considered how light penetrates the interior and how this results in different atmospheres in each room. I found out that the zigzag shape makes light come in multifarious ways, which diversifies the relationship with the urban landscape outside. The rooms are identical, but the angles of inclination and the volume of the skylights give a different character to each room. Light is an important component for the character of walls, floors and ceilings. Unlike materials or textures, light is a variable element; it changes over time and influences the atmosphere inside the rooms.'

How does this house communicate through its zigzag openings?

YN: 'Whenever I design a house in Tokyo, I always keep in mind the idea of living without curtains. In densely built-up Tokyo lots of people draw their curtains and window shades. One solution is to think about how to avoid other people's eyes. Zenpukuji House naturally avoids the eyes of pedestrians. The tilted floor area works as a buffer zone. The angled openings make it hard to look into the interior from outside. But for the residents, the house is open to its surroundings.'

What kind of living spaces do Tokyo residents require nowadays?

YN: 'The lifestyles of Tokyo residents are shifting from a family-based to an individual-oriented lifestyle. Various individual-oriented lifestyles are supported by new urban infrastructures such as networking environments and convenience stores. My approach towards housing is to create a metabolized space. The space does not necessary have to be determined by functions. The function can change over time. More importantly, I think a house needs a boxy shape to keep an adequate distance to the city. A box can turn an urban site into a place to reside, into an office or into a shop. Those multiple functions allow an unrestricted floor plan, similar to the adaptability that makes Japanese traditional architecture so unique. Because of the changes in lifestyle from family-based to individual-oriented, the previously required instantaneous physical shift of space is no longer valued. I expect that from now on the changeability of the meaning given to a space will have more emphasis. Zenpukuji House might end up being an office or a gallery, or perhaps other people will end up living there. I must say it is not an elderly-friendly house, but this is okay with me. As long as it is an attractive place, people can make the most out of the space. The possibility and the capacity of space to be edited and re-edited is the method for the future of cities.'

'BY USING THE CONCEPT OF DEPTH AND MAKING A SPECIAL UNTOUCHABLE SECTION, I REALIZE PSYCHOLOGICAL SPACIOUSNESS'

TRANSPARENT SCENERIES
Junya Ishigami (junya.ishigami + associates)

House H is a proposal for a lifestyle that mixes an outdoor and indoor experience within a slender steel structured box

Project Name: House H
Location: Saitama Prefecture
Year of Completion: to be completed (April 2012)
Client: Family
Site Area: 115.40 m^2
Built Area: 69.22 m^2
Total Floor Area: 69.22 m^2
Building Height: 6.70 m
Storeys: 1
Structural Principle: Steel
Structural Engineer: Jun Sato Structural Engineers

ARCHITECT: JUNYA ISHIGAMI
Year of Birth: 1974
Education: Tokyo University of the Arts, Tokyo
Work Experience: Kazuyo Sejima & Associates
Master: no statement

Let's talk about the scale of your work – you make things three, four, even five times longer or narrower than we're used to seeing. What's this obsession with scale?
Junya Ishigami: 'Rather than the plan itself, scale and proportion can make a space. Changing the scale changes the atmosphere as well. A solid wall adds strength to a space, whereas something extremely tenuous has a completely different effect. Living rooms or streets are spaces in which we can immediately feel the organization, because they have edges or borders. But what if a space and its organization are one and the same thing? That's what I'm trying to achieve with my thin, elongated structures that seem to defy gravity.'
Does your architecture merge with art? Or perhaps product design?
JI: 'I'm an architect, not an interior designer or a product designer. I consider all my projects from an architectural point of view. It might be that some people think my designs look like products, but it's architecture I want to make, even inside a building. In 2004, for example, a client in Yamaguchi Prefecture asked me to design a restaurant interior, complete with furnishings. At the time I had no experience in furniture design, but I knew how to make architecture, so I approached the design of the required tables and chairs as though they were small pieces of architecture. My image of the space to be designed was not that of a room but of a building site with small architectural volumes on it. I put those tables into the space as I would have erected buildings on a site outdoors.'
When you set up your own practice after working for six years with Kazuyo Sejima, did you have a specific goal you wanted to achieve?
JI: 'Architects make models that help them understand the spatial content of just about anything, even the smallest of objects. Most people look at a coffee cup and see nothing special, but I see it as a container with a small space inside. A cup viewed as a drinking vessel is a small-scale product and nothing more. But an architect looks at it and sees the object on any number of scales.'
You are talking about another scale of architecture?
JI: 'Yes, I want to bring scales into architecture that could never be realized before. Think of the vastness of the sky, the liberating feeling of a landscape extending forever, or the lightness of a cloud. Architecture that floats in the air like a cloud, vast and enormous but without substance, or to conceive a building in such a manner that it produces a horizon – that is the kind of architecture I pursue!'
Why this urge to renew? What is wrong with the magnificent buildings produced by modernist architects?
JI: 'The modernists were all aiming for the same primary goal. Theirs was an

age-old architectural approach that demanded a strong concept. The situations and objects that characterize today's architecture, however, do not always require a strong concept. In my opinion, it's all about balance and about the right distance between one thing and another. Although my initial plan always has a strong concept, I make it weaker as the design process continues. A design based on a strong concept forces people to look at it from only one perspective, whereas a less assertive concept leaves room for interpretation.'

If you say you can even discover a valuable space inside a small cup, does it mean that a model is just a smaller version of a single-family house?

JI: 'Architecture and product design are very different. Product designers can design on a 1:1 scale because the project is very small. But architecture is so big. Even a model of a small house can't be made on a 1:1 scale. Every time the architect makes small drawings and small models, the scale is expanding and made smaller at the same time. Architecture is much more abstract than a product and architects have to work on an imaginary scale. It means that space is always abstract. Architects always have to imagine a space from a drawing or model. It means the model is not a product. But an architect can feel the space and recognize a space. Architecture thus includes a lot of space and scale. Compare it with travelling around the world. If you don't know the earth is round, you won't recognize the total distance you travelled. This is because the earth is big and you can't recognize the entire space at once. Only when you look at a world map can you sense the real distance you travelled. This is similar to how architects deal with scale models.'

When we look at the current housing situation in Tokyo, a landscape filled with prefabricated detached houses and small free-standing buildings, is there anything you dislike?

JI: 'Actually, I like the typical prefab house or Tokyo apartment. They all have exactly the same repetitive style and floor plan. What is different is the location. That's interesting! The exterior environment of those houses significantly influences the interior life. A house in the Asakusa neighbourhood is very different from one in the neighbourhood of Shibuya, just because of its location, not because of the floor plan. That's why I like moving from house to house in Tokyo. When I'm lucky I might have an extra window if the plot next door happens to be vacant, but there's a big chance that the layout is exactly the same.'

Do you feel a similar affection for the urban landscape of Tokyo?

JI: 'Tokyo doesn't have a master plan like a European city – it's a kind of landscape in itself. Within this landscape, tall buildings are suddenly constructed, while other buildings are suddenly demolished. In my eyes, this is the difficulty of Tokyo. The buildings are not architecture but look more like events. Look at the series of tall, commercial buildings recently developed in Tokyo by real estate developer Minoru Mori.'

What is the role of one single-family house in such a landscape of events?

JI: 'A private house in a city like Tokyo is not just a shelter for living, but an environment in itself. From the time the clients return home late after work every day until they leave early the next morning it should be a place to relax, similar to a weekend house. They return to the house to refresh their minds. Le Corbusier and other architects in the twentieth century wanted to make architecture as a kind of prototype. That is difficult today in Tokyo. Everybody has a different

In Ishigami's housing proposals the distinction between interior and exterior is made uncertain, accomplishing a miscellaneous interior landscape (for example the Row House)

situation, so each building is another situation. Although their houses are situated in a very dense urban setting, residents should have a very comfortable environment inside their single-family house.'

What is the idea behind House H?

JI: 'This house is about making a garden inside the house and about making a landscape by means of furniture. The clients are a couple in their 30s, like me, with one child. They didn't have any image in their mind for their new house. The wife's father owns a furniture company, so it was decided from the beginning that they would bring in a lot of furniture themselves and didn't want to have a closet designed by the architect. The house became a very simple one. In fact it is just a raised floor.'

What other kind of subtle differences do you have in mind to blur the line between the interior and exterior on the scale of a house?

JI: 'When I make architecture, I in fact make the surroundings. And it is the surroundings that make the interior space. When implementing this idea in architecture I imagine, for example, a house that is very transparent and has a ground floor that appears to continue into the landscape. Its core includes trees, so that the house itself is like a little forest in the middle of the city. My purpose is to create a new kind of architecture, one that seeks out a new environment. New architecture, in my eyes, makes a space and at the same time scenery. In Japanese, we have a very nice word for this: *fuukei*. *Fuukei* can be translated as atmosphere, but also carries the meaning of space, scenery or landscape. I want to make a new kind of *fuukei*. Compare it to the scene at Roanji Temple, a Zen garden in Kyoto that radiates an atmosphere strongly influenced by its surroundings. This ambiance is vital to the space itself. How can the feel of the surroundings be distinguished from the residential space in the same way the distinction is made at Roanji Temple?'

What is the new kind of *fuukei* in House H you designed?

JI: 'I wanted to make a space as empty as possible. The client already prepared the furniture and they wanted to have a big void space. For the city, people walking on the street can peek inside. The privacy is preserved but they can see the plants. Inside and outside is mixed, outside as well as inside the house.'

It is a very flexible space. What kind of possibilities do the clients have to develop their own lifestyle within the ambiguous space you designed for them?

JI: 'Basically, the clients can plan the position of the furniture themselves. I designed two spaces: the floor and the soil. Within this garden, I arranged the trees. The plants and furniture are of equal importance. In this house, furniture and plants make the atmosphere, not the structure or the composition of the space.'

In what way does this new atmosphere you made influence the clients' way of living?

JI: 'Even when inside the house, the clients are changing shoes all the time! Typically, the Japanese take off their shoes before entering the living room. But in this house, the people wear shoes because the living space is just an earth floor. In the bedroom and terrace, which is paved, they take off their shoes. Nowadays, the function of architecture has become so boring. Architects just make thick walls with insulation and precise climate control. I don't want architecture to become a shelter. The clients should be able to choose their own way of living.

1/140

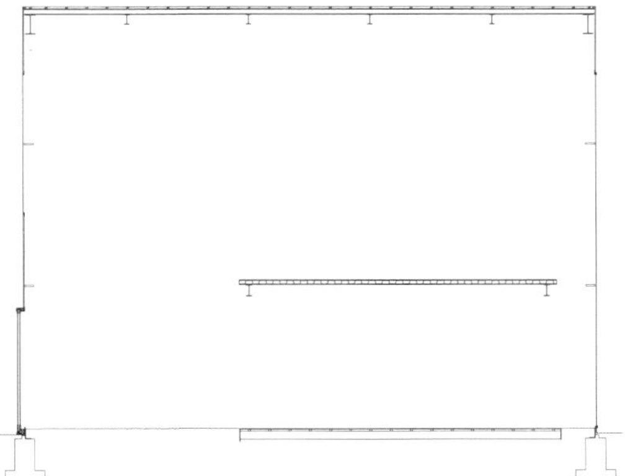

1/140

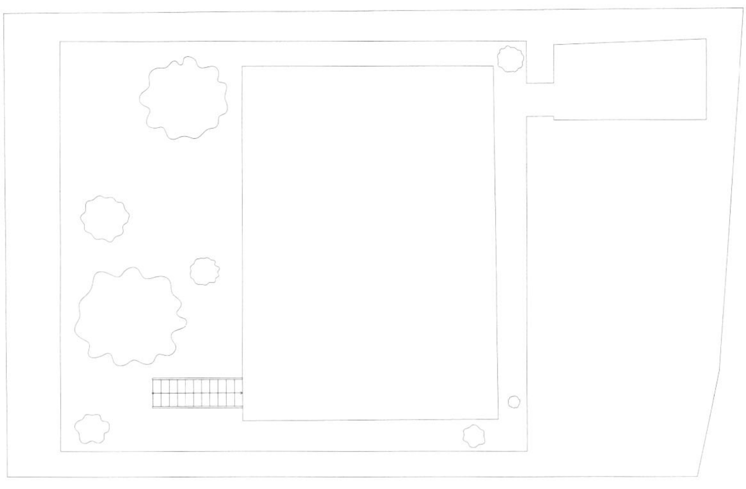

1/140

This house has almost no appliances. When it is closed, it could be a winter garden.'

You are of the opinion that an architect can just provide the basic structure? That is enough?

JI: 'No, the structure alone is not enough. That's why I designed a landscape. Although the structure is simple, the space itself is complicated. The position, height and varieties of the plants are all decided, as well as the position of the furniture. Although I decided a lot within this landscape, the clients have the flexibility. All the same, I did advise the clients about the position of the furniture.'

What is the level of transparency you wanted to achieve in this project?

JI: 'I didn't just want to make transparency, but rather a new boundary in architecture. Sometimes this is transparent, but sometimes I use a very thick wall. Even a big open space between two points could carry the meaning of a boundary. It means that scale can at the same time be the borderline. Transparency is not just talking about materials but something that equals the architectural elements. When you have transparent architecture, the interior and exterior look the same. In House H, the interior of the house is exterior and interior at the same time. But like the furniture, walls and trees, I consider them all equal. That is transparency for me.'

How do you envision a new environment on a slightly larger scale than one house or building?

JI: 'A plot is something we cannot design. As the site is usually very small in Tokyo, the shape or environment of the plot is very important for the planning of the house or the building. If architects could design the site itself, I imagine we could make a more flexible environment. Imagine a big plot that is freely divided! Developers always make those boring linear divisions, so architects tend to make boring buildings on those boring plots. But what if we divided a plot in a very inspiring way, with curves and all?'

What does your future Tokyo look like?

JI: 'In a European city a road name usually takes the name of a person, but in Tokyo the name of the place refers to scenery. For example, *kuramitaka* means 'dark slope', *fujimidori* stands for 'view of Mount Fuji Street' while *ondendori* refers to a hidden rice field. So each place in Tokyo reflects a certain image. It would be nice to connect all the different sceneries of Tokyo.'

Your living proposals go beyond the single-family house. What kind of radical examples do you have in mind for high-rise living?

JI: 'The world takes on an entirely different scale when we move vertically instead of horizontally. At a height of 30 m, the scenery is already completely unlike that of the ground level. Contemporary high-rise buildings fail to exploit the possibilities of vertical changes in scenery. I would like to conceive new proportions for buildings and build on the sky. I foresee that the sky's environment itself can become the environment of architecture. For example, high-rise buildings with very tall ceiling heights produce an airiness akin to being high in the heavens. The huge distance between floors results in an entirely different vista just one level up. If buildings were to reach higher and higher, further from the ground, eventually the concept of height would merge with that of distance. In this future city with very tall, slender high-rises, the feeling of super-density would be non-existent. The natural environment residents would experience in such high-rises is not one of land and trees, but of sky and clouds.'

Living is going to be different from now on? Will the single-family house as a typology still exist?

JI: 'Lifestyles will change drastically.'

'WHEN I MAKE ARCHITECTURE I IN FACT MAKE THE SURROUNDINGS. AND IT IS THE SURROUNDINGS THAT MAKE THE INTERIOR SPACE'

RULER OF THE SITE
Ryuji Nakamura

How can the incomprehensible urban scenery of Tokyo be appreciated through a window?

Project Name: HOUSE GH
Location: Minato-ku, Tokyo
Year of Completion: To be completed (2013)
Client: couple
Special Request: Soft, white square house with a room for the husband's cars + a room with a terrace for the wife's cats
Site Area: 112.61 m^2
Built Area: 78.39 m^2
Total Floor Area: 140.81 m^2
Building Height: 6.35 m
Storeys: two
Structure: wood
Structural Engineer: Konishi Structural Engineers

ARCHITECT: RYUJI NAKAMURA
Year of Birth: 1972
Education: Tokyo National University of Fine Arts and Music , Tokyo
Masters: Jun Aoki (b. 1956)

Your interiors and products border on art. Is that because you studied at Tokyo University of the Arts, the alma mater of many well-known Japanese artists?
Ryuji Nakamura: 'I was a student of the Japanese architect Koji Rokakku (b. 1942). He taught me that art is something on the border between two things. Rather than saying that the field of art exists prior to anything else, he explained to us that art exists in any field, including architecture. During my studies I was also inspired by the creations of students from the other departments in my university. Every day, students made strange large objects, almost the size of architecture, that suddenly appeared in the courtyard of the university. Their work taught me that art is something on the border of two things.'
What lessons did you learn while working for Jun Aoki?
RN: 'Aoki has a certain "sensitivity" to the experience of a space. Of course, he works with a theory, but the feeling or emotion the space conjures is more important to him. In his eyes, a project is not finished with the completion of the building. We always discussed the atmosphere within the project once it had been realized. Aoki's architecture is like an art installation in its ability to imbue a space with atmosphere. The longer you look, the more beautiful it becomes, just like art. During the three years that I worked in his office, I learned not to have a final image in mind during the design phase. All the projects I worked on shared the philosophy of not having a clear, holistic overview and so were the sum of the differing parts. But it was obvious nonetheless that a part was equivalent to the whole.'
Why this interest in designing the part instead of the whole?
RN: 'Rather than just thinking about parts, I'm making a point of the relationships that tie those different parts together. Objects look different because of the shapes and size of the parts and the joints between the parts. Two projects that clearly show this idea of "parts rather than the whole" are *Atmosphere* (2009) and *Cornfield* (2010). For both projects, I first set a volume and only then did I think about how the volume should be filled and what kind of material to fill it with. Atmosphere is a stage design for the opera *Le Grand Macabre* that was held at the New National Theatre in Tokyo. The director of the opera, Yasuki Fujita, tried not to direct the singers himself but wanted to use the scenery to do so. I designed a stage design that functions not as a mere background but as scenery that brings a certain kind of inconvenience to the singers. *Atmosphere* consists of 242 catenaries, ribbons hung between two points from a height of 11 m. The air of the stage is filled with dynamic curves arranged in a distorted grid to emphasize the perspective. By slowly moving ten batons at the same time the entire "volume" of the ribbons moves up and down, transforming all the time. Glossy white fibres are woven into the

ribbons. Although the parts are very thin, lit by stage light they give a very strong impression.

'*Cornfield* (2010) is a 100-m^3 structure made entirely of 1-mm-thin vulcanized fibre paper. The planar shape is a triangle of 30, 60 and 90 degrees. The height is about that of a person, the length of the longest side around 16 m. The structure is uniformly filled with paper frames. When you walk along the exterior, your view will change due to the many lines that are drawn one on top of the other. The structure itself is subtle, almost becoming a part of the scenery. Instead of viewing the structure itself, *Cornfield* is the space from which the view of the other installations will constantly alter as you walk by.

The difference between the two projects is that *Atmosphere* is a hanging structure without an exterior that fills the entire stage. *Cornfield*, on the other hand, is an independent structure placed in the middle of a large exhibition room. In this case, it does have an exterior. Because I mainly design interior projects, I never thought about the exterior up to then. Making *Cornfield* made me realize the importance of designing an exterior in architecture.'

How did this idea of the parts instead of the whole develop after you opened your own office in 2004?

RN: 'My concepts are simple, but I wouldn't call them minimalistic. I want to make a harmonious yet complex composition, like we find in nature. My interior designs are comparable to a homogeneous space in which countless elements, each slightly different from the rest, are repeated: think A, A', A'', A''' rather than simply A and B. What I strive for is a small wave of water, as in a river, from which beauty gradually emerges. Usually, this involves a palette of white with pale wood and indirect light. White light is composed of a rainbow of colours, so when it shines on a white surface it creates the kinds of gradations that interest me. When I design I always use a rule or some kind of order. In my eyes, there are many kinds of simplicity. One kind of simplicity cannot be made by rules, while another one can. I follow the latter approach.'

What do your interior designs reveal about your way of thinking about architecture?

RN: 'Architecture is very big compared to interior design, furniture or installations. For instance, a glass cup can be made from just glass because its size is small enough. Architecture, however, is too large to make from one single material, so it has to be made as an integration of parts of a certain size. It means we need joints between the pieces, and joints may cause a defect in the design from a functional point of view. You may consider this the weak point of architecture, but to think about the joint and how to connect the pieces is the essence of architecture to me. I look forward to anything that only architecture can create. For instance, there are huge numbers of tiles covering the façades, and the same for a roof covered in roof tiles and for a glass curtain wall. I like to look at the unusual nature of the quantity even though it has become a common daily backdrop for most people. Finding new possibilities in architecture within such anomalies is my interest.'

What kind of concept did you come up for your first housing design?

RN: 'I wanted to draw out the property like a ruler. To do so, I used exactly the same windows and doors to compose an entirety. The same rounding of the windows and doors draws out the property like it is a mathematical ruler of the architecture. By placing the same windows and doors evenly, people can

All of the windows are the same size and are homogeneously spread accross the façade, acting like a ruler that draws out the property

Looking out the exact same windows from differently sized rooms, the inhabitants are able to feel subtle differences between their views of the same surroundings

The geometrically equal windows make the residents more conscious of the differences in room size

feel the differences of each room and the outdoor environment. Because each window acts like a ruler, the clients can feel the outside environment much more accurately.'

In what sense does GH House conjure up an emotion or feeling?

RN: 'I would like to know what kind of sensation the relationship between the windows, doors and rooms can give us. In order to find out I gave each of the 17 "rooms" in this house – including the corridor, the toilet, the bath, and terrace – a different size. The design and size of all the windows, however, is the same and the windows are placed evenly, without considering the differences of the rooms inside the house. By giving equality to the windows and doors, people can feel the differences in room size and the outside environment they look at through the windows. In general, a large room has a large window and a small room has a small window. That is situation A. My starting point was the difference between situation A and situation B: if all of the rooms have the same windows, I believe you will feel more conscious of the difference in room sizes in the latter (B) than in the former (A). Accordingly, I think that in a room you sense the relationships with all rooms, and then you can measure the relationship to the outside by the house. Any house is like this to a certain extent, but I think if you can make this stronger, it also makes a house more attractive. I can't explain why this is attractive, but there is no doubt it is about the relationship with the outside. It is therefore very good to be strongly aware of it. For instance, a "one-room-like house" is so attractive because it is easy to understand the entire house. This, in turn, makes the relationship with the outside clearer. Drawing out the property like a ruler is one of the methods to maintain a sense of the attractive even when the house is subdivided into rooms.'

Can you link this concept of a ruler back to your interior work?

RN: 'I have designed interior spaces that evoke a kind of scale because their walls, ribbons or steel frames are arranged at equal intervals. It is like drawing a grid in the entire room.'

Do you have a similar mathematical view of the Tokyo urban landscape?

RN: 'Tokyo has an urban landscape to appreciate and to enjoy. Buildings are made freely, though the forms are defined by many social, physical and structural rules. All of the buildings are different, but at the same time they are in a sense alike. It is the unexpected scenes that those buildings conjure up that make Tokyo an interesting city.'

How is your stance reflected in the design of GH House?

RN: 'Probably the Tokyo landscape is not considered "beautiful" in a Western sense, but I believe that any view becomes beautiful when picturing it with a frame. Maybe it is the contrast that makes the ugliness beautiful. I want the clients of GH House to appreciate the Tokyo urban landscape from the windows. They will notice the differences because the window frames and door are of equal size. Consequently, the rooms in GH House acquire different characters because of their different proportions. The proportions make the difference even if the size of two rooms is the same. I want the people to feel what the planning of this house on this site does. For example, the scene that people see from the small room is different than the scene people see from the big room. Why did I not simply paint the rooms in different colours? That effect would be far too strong!'

What is the interaction between GH House and its neighbourhood?

1/1000

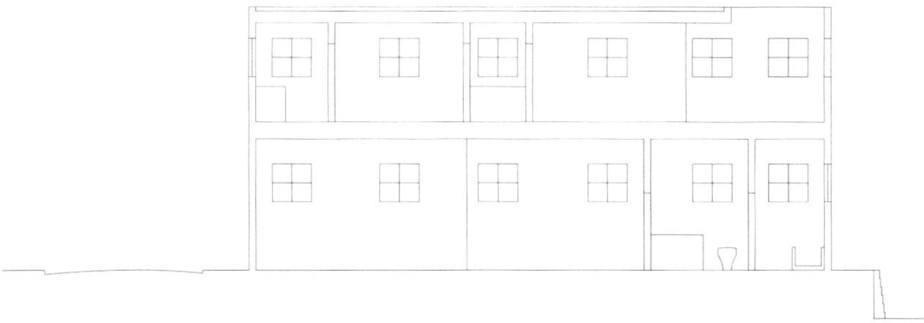

1/200

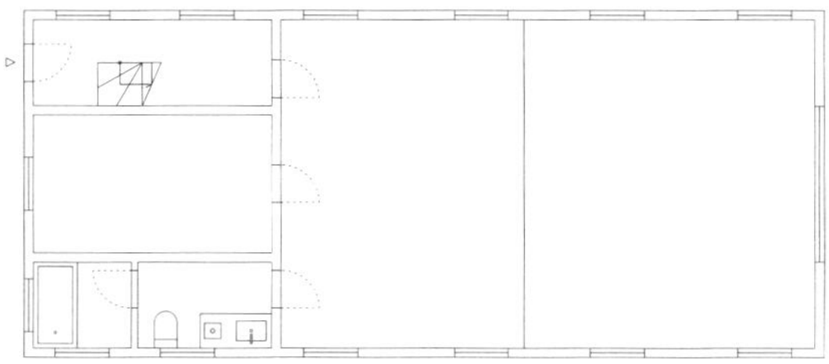

1/200

RN: 'The 112-m^2 site is located in a residential area in Aoyama, from where you can see the Tokyo landmarks of the Roppongi Hills and Tokyo Tower. The house faces a crossing, so that we can always see at least two of the house's façades from the street. Because GH House looks so simple, its occupants, a couple in their 40s working at an advertising agency, will probably think that the neighbourhood looks very complicated. The incomprehensible urban scenery starts to feel fresh when framed by the same kinds of windows.'

In what sense did aspects of traditional Japanese culture inspire the design of GH House?

RN: 'Traditional Japanese architecture includes devices to take in the environment from the outside. One of them is "borrowed scenery". It is the way to take in the nearby trees and distant mountains, not only things in our site. Windows, fences and walls play an important role in this technique. By appropriate trimming, obscure scenes are united and emerge into our mind.'

I feel you have narrowed the themes to an even more select range than before. What is the secret of your original design methodology?

JI: 'I guess I am the only one thinking one trivial thing over and over again.'

‘THINK A, A’, A’’, A’’’ RATHER THAN SIMPLY A AND B’

NEW DIRECTIONS
Monologue by Jun Aoki

1940s versus 1950s

'The Japanese architects of my generation, like Kengo Kuma, Kazuyo Sejima and Kazuhiro Kojima, were born in the 1950s. We respect the generation of architects before us, such as Toyo Ito, Riken Yamamoto and Tadao Ando, but at the same time we feel we are constantly competing with them. The 1940s generation was very active during the student revolutions in 1968, the year of the barricades. That year served as a symbol of everything an entire generation of young people detested about their parents' generation. Architects shared a lot of ideology about socialism and anti-imperialism and talked about the city of Tokyo as if it was a huge issue. But when this movement failed, they changed their minds. As a consequence, our generation didn't believe in big ideas anymore. First, we felt inferior to the older generation because they were aware of the big problems at hand. But after having seen that their awareness did not solve anything, we consciously backed off from this 'awareness of big problems'. They were very conscious about the relation with the city. To be precise, for them it was either about opening the doors to the city or closing them. The very first houses designed by Toyo Ito and Tadao Ando were houses that literary turned their backs on the city. When they take the relationship to the city as the main topic of architecture, architects look down at things from above. They don't take the viewpoint of people walking at street level. For our generation, this ideology comes close to the idea of an architect excluding himself from society and the city, observing the world only as an outsider. We felt we had to follow a more fundamental approach and not strive for a social change, but rather for a change in attitude. The architects of my generation started their career by making very authentic modernist architecture. That is the sense of beauty and architectural thinking we share. But our aim is to go beyond modernism. This zigzagging in and out of modernist ideas is typical of our generation. Because we have grown up with it, we can never get completely rid of it; we always come back to it.

1960s

While my generation has a strong reluctance to the top-down view of the 1940s generation, the 1960s generation has a lot in common with the 1940s generation. They try to adopt the same stance toward the city and society, without any reluctance towards the 1940s generation. The architects born in the 1960s, like Yoshiharu Tsukamoto, Manabu Chiba, Ryue Nishizawa and Katsuhiro Miyamoto, seem to be the last generation of architects who started their careers designing houses and gradually obtained bigger projects like museums, schools and concert halls. They talk easily about comprehensive issues. Yoshiharu Tsukamoto and Momoyo Kajima (Atelier Bow-Wow), for example, have a clear focus on Tokyo. They research how the city is formed, and by analysing it, they attempt to build a Tokyo-like architecture. Ryue Nishizawa started experimenting with collective housing. Instead of considering collective housing as one building type, he re-examined the typology. His Moriyama Apartments is like a densely built housing district in itself. The architects of the 1960s generation are very powerful because they not only think about social issues but also propose solutions.

1970s

There is no generation as free as the 1970s generation. This is not only because of their age, but also because of the situation in Japan. They have quite a hard time being independent architects, as they can obtain only small-scale projects, like installations, interior projects, renovations, shop designs and tiny single-family houses. Ryuji Nakamura's very first work, for example, is an interesting series of chairs that he made all by hand, by himself. I would say the 1970s generation is not as conceptual as those born in the 1960s, but work with a natural attitude towards specific issues. Although they have fewer possibilities because of the economic situation, this doesn't stop them from having completely different ideas about architecture. I believe they can turn Japanese architecture in an entirely new direction.

Hideyuki Nakayama, for example, makes a very compositional kind of architecture. To him, architecture is like a story or a scene. Basing architecture on sketching stories is an idea that never occurred before in modernism. Ryuji Nakamura is very interested in the repetition of natural elements. In modern architecture, repetition is something very artificial. For Nakamura, the leaves of a tree may look the same from afar, but when you take a closer look you can discover subtle differences among the leaves. This difference between natural repetition and artificial repetition is a new starting point for design. By using slight differentiations, Nakamura can reinterpret the usual composition into another meaning. Takei Makoto and Chie Nabeshima (TNA), on the other hand, are like natural modernists. Their work is softer, clearer and more natural than modernists. They sort out the complex, entangled requirements thoroughly before tackling them. Then they create clear and beautiful architectural solutions. Makoto and Nabeshima are very good at formulating the problem and presenting their answers. The process of realizing their solutions comes from modernist aesthetics in which a balance is cherished. It results in a very soft expression. Instead of making one complete work, Junya Ishigami's design ideas are open to changes. Although Ishigami cannot control the people and objects within his projects, he is able to create a very strong feeling by creating a good balance among concrete things, like rough furniture, and abstract things, like openness or distance. Kumiko Inui's architecture exceeds the existing building typology. She finds a need to reconsider the prerequisites. Her Small House H can be formally referred to as a vacation house. However, it produces a new form that nobody had thought of and can be described as 'a mechanism that projects a cut-out scenery'. Yuko Nagayama's work is characterized by mixing form with a sensation, without any ideology. Go Hasegawa responds with extreme sensitivity to the surrounding environment of his sites. His concepts go much further than just showing concern for the surroundings. He strives for an architectural method to proactively enjoy the surroundings more. The ideas of this generation of architects are not just simply innovative; they reinterpret the existing style.

Compared to older generations, young Japanese architects don't seem to feel any stress and take a more natural attitude towards things. They are at ease with complicated requirements from the clients, the site and the building code and come up with very innocent propositions or a new diagram. The basic attitude of this generation is to find a good viewpoint or main issue within all those requirements. The building itself is the answer. It means they build up their own questions and at the same time provide the answers. This kind of design method can be very effective, because in a complicated situation clarification is a very important issue. And the clients seem to be very satisfied with their solutions; the architects often receive new commissions through the very same clients. But if we are critical, their way of designing is also a bit of a game. If you were to look at their work from another viewpoint than the one the architects selected, or if you were to add another viewpoint, I am not sure the designs would still work well. I wouldn't call this a bad thing, though. It is just a very unique attitude towards architecture.

If I could give the young architects a piece of advice, I would tell them to think more about the construction. The sets of questions and answers they propose are very smart, but to realize the concepts with such high precision, as is required now, is difficult. The composition might fit the requirements of the clients and the site perfectly, but it doesn't always work from the construction point of view. Such high-level precision construction is possible in Japan with incredible effort, but it will not work smoothly when building overseas. If the workers fail to build precisely, they will have to redo the entire building. While in modern architecture the structure of the building was a very economic one, the young generation of Japanese architects doesn't care about this issue. They are eager to maintain their own attitude towards architecture and find the right client – one that matches their design approach. The young architects should either integrate the structure better, or think about simplifying the joints between different materials. With such high-end construction techniques, their architecture is craftwork in itself. Though if they can continue their tough work for another ten years, I am sure they will become well-established architects.

ESSAYS

In Building K, Ryuji Fujimura put the shared outdoor space of the mega-structure facility – a residential/ commercial typology that is typically covered with air conditioning units and plumbing equipment – to use as a place to enjoy.

ARCHITECTURE AND THE CITY

ON URBAN PLANNING, TRUNCATED BUILDING FORMS AND BOTTOM-UP INTERVENTIONS

BASED ON INTERVIEWS WITH THE FOLLOWING EXPERTS:
Riken Yamamoto × Manabu Chiba × Ryuji Fujimura

The longer you stroll through Tokyo, the harder it is to describe this city. Its immense complex visual appearance makes you wonder whether Tokyo actually has a master plan. Of course it has, though it is not as clearly discernible as in European cities. Those who have the historical maps of Tokyo imprinted in their minds can discover the two-layered logic behind the planning. The most obvious layer, the one we see immediately, is the modern layer of high-rises and large thoroughfares. The other, hidden layer dates from the Edo period (1615-1868), with a planning system adapted to the city's microtopography and its wooden architecture. It incorporated natural elements like hills and waterways, resulting in a maze-like network of small streets and neighbourhoods. Over time, the streets remained, but buildings were replaced at a rapid pace, providing Tokyo with its unique dual character: both village and metropolis.

ARCHITECTS AS TOWN BUILDERS

As in most developing countries, urban planning in Japan is initiated top down. Therefore the basic driving force for current planning comes from the central government's modern initiatives on an overall scale, or *toshikeikaku*. However, these mass-scale urban initiatives coexist with *machizukuri*, the involvement of citizens in planning and implementing new ideas in their community on a small scale. The two seemingly contradicting planning methods make the Japanese city difficult to comprehend from a Western point of view. One needs to concentrate on the smaller scale of the architectural activities in order to get a sense of how the individual parts of the neighbourhoods become part of the larger city. Rather than built urban forms, strong social networks have tended to determine the character of neighbourhoods.[1]
These social networks are also the reason architects and local residents are able to participate in town building in a 'soft', bottom-up way. 'Instead of looking down from the sky and deciding where to put roads and other infrastructure,' explains Manabu Chiba (b. 1960), an architect and assistant professor at the University of Tokyo, 'this smaller, bottom-up approach is more efficient, influential and also very practical.' According to Chiba if you look closely at the relationship between two buildings you can discover a nice harmony, a dialogue, between them. 'I am not talking about a similar colour, building material, volume or texture, but about an interactive relationship.' 'Tokyo's master plan determines building codes, such as floor layout and maximum height,' adds architect Ryuji Fujimura (b. 1976), a student of Yoshihara Tsukamoto (b. 1965). His contemporary Yoshimura Yasutaka (b. 1972) researched this phenomenon extensively in his book *Super Legal Buildings* (Shokokusha, 2006).[2] Using 77 photos of Tokyo buildings with a wired look, Yasutaka visualized what defines the townscape of the city. Red lines

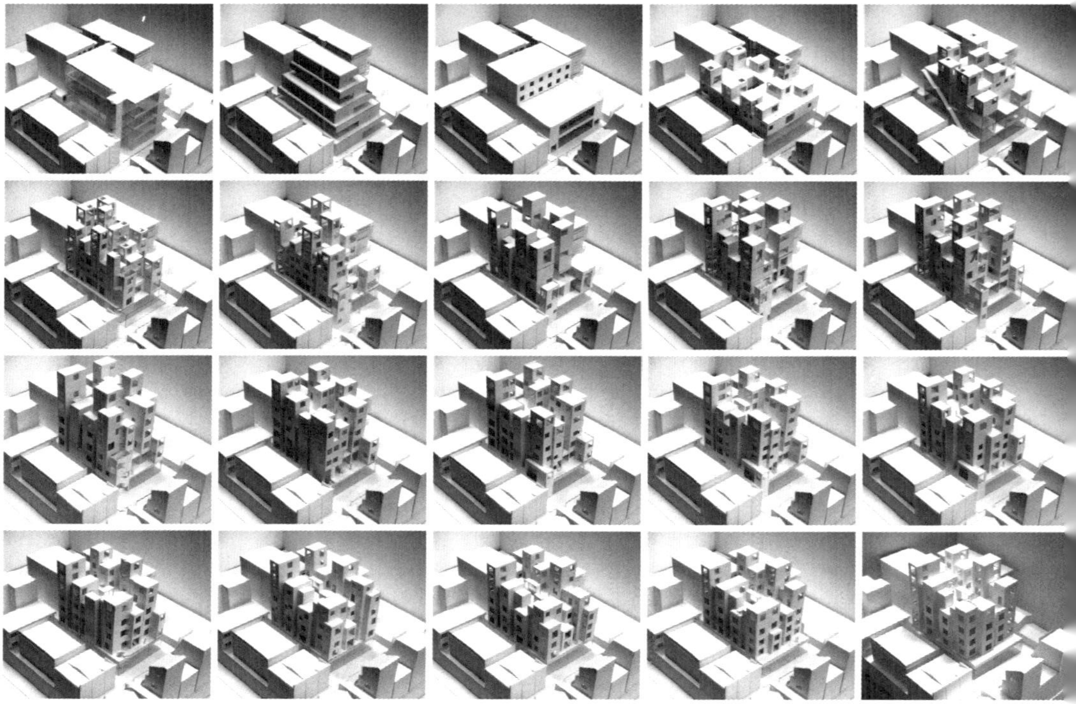

Ryuji Fujimura designs and documents the entire building process in clear steps (example Building K)

drawn on top of the buildings reveal invisible auxiliary lines, explaining in the process how building codes affect the appearance of construction in Tokyo. 'The urban design of Tokyo is often said to be elusive because it was originally a rough and squalid city that expanded into the suburbs without any thought,' Yasutaka comments. 'I show that it is the building codes that determine the outline of buildings and city.'

THE INFLUENCE OF THE METABOLIST MOVEMENT

In the late 1950s, architects like Kenzo Tange (1913-2005), Takashi Asada (1928-1987), Kisho Kurokawa (1934-2007) and Kiyonori Kikutake (b. 1928) proposed grand utopian visions for large-scale, flexible and expandable structures that evoked the process of organic growth. The most famous built contribution of the Metabolist Movement in Japan, and a typical example of an adaptable plug-in structure, is the Nakagin Capsule Tower (1972) in Tokyo designed by Kisho Kurokawa. The movement's members came together in 1959 but soon went their own way after the World Expo in Osaka in 1970.

The Metabolist Movement was the only major architecture movement in Japan that addressed the scale of the city, and their ideas have enjoyed a continued latent currency among architects. According to Chiba, the most surprising aspect of a project like Tange's *Plan for Tokyo Bay* (1960) was not the creation of a large-scale development but the idea of expanding the city into the water of Tokyo Bay. 'Tange showed architects how to discover the frontier of Tokyo,' Chiba says. Japanese architects have recently started to pay attention to the ideas of the Metabolism Movement again.

Instead of large infrastructural works

for Tokyo, their interest in Metabolism focuses on growth and effect. 'In times of rapid economic growth the expansion ideas of the Metabolist Movement worked really well,' Chiba explains, 'but especially during the current period of economic recession, making mega-structures like Tange's as a way of organizing the whole would not work well, as it basically means denying the city.' Instead of overlaying the existing structure as the Metabolists were doing, architects in Japan now use a similar concept but on a smaller scale, which is more powerful and realistic for current times. Chiba explains the most fundamental aspect of Metabolist thinking: 'Think of *shiatsu*, a traditional hands-on therapy originating in Japan. When you push on certain point of your body, you can become really strong or active. If you push on points in an urban plan, you can influence the entire urban structure.'

REINVENTING METABOLISM

In 2010, architects Koh Kitayama (b. 1950), Ryue Nishizawa (b. 1966) and Yoshiharu Tsukamoto (b. 1965) presented their urban research project *Tokyo Metabolizing* at the 2010 Venice Biennale, a study obviously inspired by the Metabolist Movement. In their manifesto they claim that Tokyo, a city 'covered almost infinitely with small two and three-story houses with tiny gardens or greenery inserted in gaps between them' has a very sustainable urban morphology. Because of the short average lifespan (26 years) of the independent structures, the Tokyo landscape is constantly changing and automatically regenerates itself in a very healthy way.
Their study acknowledges the reference to the Metabolists of the 1960s but emphasizes an essential difference. The regeneration of the city, unlike the architecture designed by the members of the Metabolist Movement, does not take place around a core but around a void space: namely the obligatory interstices between two buildings. Rather than just an ugly urban concrete jungle, *Tokyo Metabolizing* sees the urban morphology of Tokyo as an incubator for new forms of architecture and even new urban theories.
Fujimura, a student of Yoshiharu Tsukamoto who learned a lot about process making during his studies in Europe, is somewhat sceptical, however, about the *Tokyo Metabolizing* theory. 'It is a very clear strategy for explaining the situation of Tokyo to Western people, but for the Japanese it is nothing new,' Fujimura says. 'They did a great job finding a method of showing what Tokyo is like, but their theory is not a powerful idea for showing future visions.' He also criticizes the claim that Tokyo is built up democratically. 'In reality we have many codes,' Fujimura says. 'If you want to talk about the city you also have to look at the political and economic systems active in the city.'

SOCIETY DESIGNERS

Beyond merely designing a shelter for their specific clients, Japanese architects feel a general responsibility for society when they tackle the design of a single-family home. Architects often use the term 'city' to refer to spatial ideas that go beyond the physical boundaries of the site, but in fact they are addressing issues on the scale of the neighbourhood. The interventions apply to the level of surrounding buildings and passers-by, rather than trying to improve the entire metropolis. With a commission for a single-family house the architects try to redesign the 'city' in miniature: how the house sits on its plot and

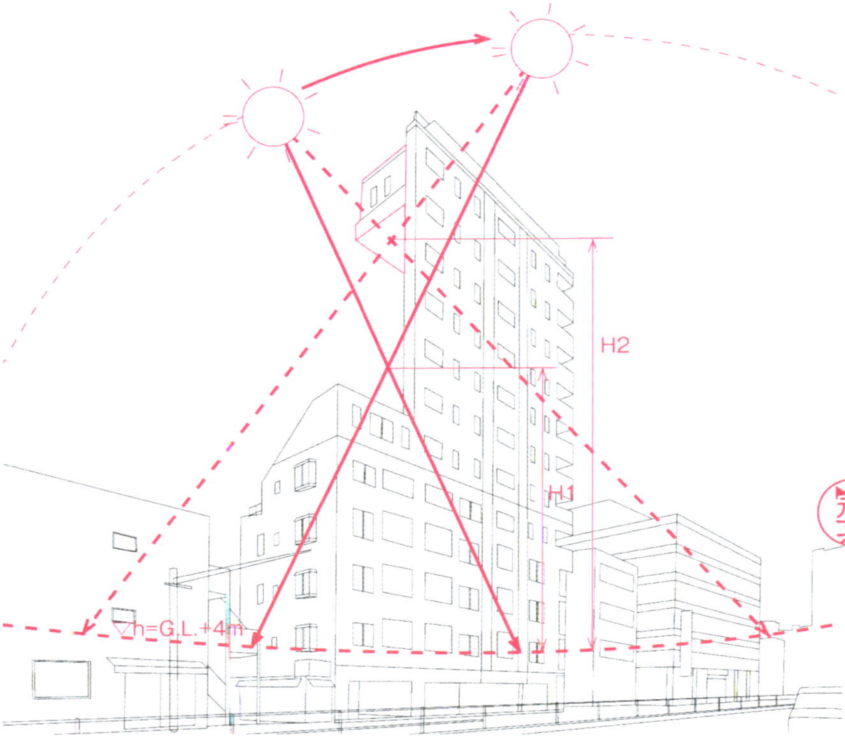

‘Giraffe Building’ is an example from Yasutaka’s book Super Legal Buildings showing a building curved by the Shadow Code. Because shadows formed on the upper floors move faster than those on the lower ones, this building has a bigger volume on the upper floor

communicates with the rest of the neighbourhood. ‘Through our sensitivity, we can discover the charm of the neighbourhood we are designing for,’ Chiba says in explaining his design approach, which starts with the ‘rule of the site’. Once he has found the rule, or common factor, he designs the house accordingly.

To architect Riken Yamamoto (b. 1945) the twentieth-century city was centred on the promotion of economic activities, rather than on creating a habitable city. Yamamoto’s vision is to restructure the city into a habitable place using a new form of collectiveness, which he calls the *Local Community Sphere*. Fujimura would like to move beyond a city filled with box-like dwellings. He has developed a growth model that should produce buildings that can be constructed rapidly but will be more contextual and complex ‘Europeans always talk about political aspects, while Japanese architects like to focus on sensory aspects, things like the physical perception, thin walls, and a light volume,’ Fujimura explains. ‘My aim is to bridge those two aspects.’

SHRINKAGE

The overall population of Japan has been declining since the 1980s. According to the Statistics Bureau of the Ministry of International Affairs and Communications, the proportion of citizens 65 years of age and over was the highest in the world in 2010, constituting 23.1 per cent of the total population. Along with a declining birth rate, Japan’s population is aging much faster than in advanced Western European countries or the USA. The question for architects in Japan is what the city is going to look like in the future and how large the urban population will be. ‘It is a natural movement that when

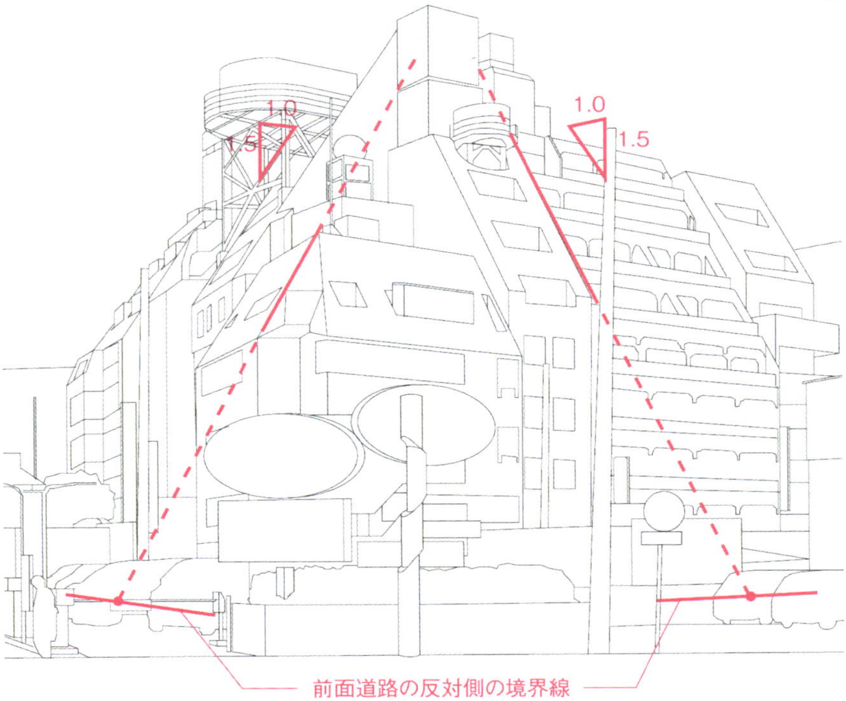

The Building Height Code prescribes that all buildings must be lower than tilted lines at certain degrees, resulting in a gothic-shaped tower called 'Setback Cathedral' by Yoshimura Yasutaka

a city grows, administrative initiatives try to make suburbs,' Chiba comments. 'Even when a city starts to shrink, as in the case of Tokyo, suburbs keep on growing.'

Growth and shrinkage are happening at the same time in Tokyo, but not two-dimensionally. The numerous vacant storeys in office towers in central Tokyo produce a situation of three-dimensional vacancy, which is reinforced by developers who continue to build new high-rise towers. Chiba attributes the paradoxical situation to developers who keep on building new towers because of their power rather than in response to demand. Like many of his colleagues, Chiba is positive about the success of Tokyo's small scale, and says that Japanese companies, generally very small, do not require offices in big high-rise towers but can work fine in the existing smaller buildings. 'Those towers will be empty soon,' warns Chiba. 'In the worst scenario Tokyo will become a ghost town with empty high-rise buildings.'

TOKYO FOREST

Yamamoto, Chiba and Fujimura are nevertheless positive about Tokyo's future, provided architects address certain issues. Yamamoto is especially concerned about living conditions for elderly people in Japan. 'We have an aging society, and it is up to the architects to come up with good ideas of ways of living together in the city as well as in the suburbs,' Yamamoto says, referring to his ideas on the Local Community Sphere. 'I suggest to students a way of creating a new system for different people living together, rather than inventing a way of living for a single family.' Chiba sees the potential of a rapidly changing Tokyo by focusing on the parts that are not changing, for example the amount of void spaces within the city. He admits he finds the way Tokyo is organized more interesting than the rigid way of planning streets and city centres in Europe. Rather than the Western preference of preserving buildings and keeping their ensemble, 'we should look at a city as a forest that is always growing and receiving new energy so it can survive in many ways.' It is up to the architect to react to the topography and create architecture that can start a dialogue with this rule of the site.

'Nowadays we just build bigger and bigger, and the relations between architecture and topography become weaker,' Chiba says. 'This is not about simply going back to the Edo period but about reconsidering how we can create a good relationship between the underlying topography and architecture once more.' Fujimura's solution is a step-by-step design method in which he neither skips steps nor goes back. Each step is visualized in models to facilitate collaboration between specialists and users, which helps to create consensus and make the design proceed in a more complex though speedy way.

'During Prime Minister Junichiro Koizumi's urban renewal campaign between 2001 and 2006, over 200 super-skyscrapers (higher than 100 m) were built,' Fujimura points out. 'Like New York in the 1920s, modern Tokyo is driven by a huge system on a scale that goes beyond the imagination of the architect.' The reason Japanese architects do not talk about the entire city anymore is not a matter of personal attitude, but a matter of social organization, according to Fujimura. Since 1970, due to the complexity of the projects, design firms have been divided into small individual studios and large design firms. Gradually the architects in design studios began to focus on private residences, while the larger firms designed major commercial projects, without any shared discourse between the two. 'But to compete with the speed of global economic activities of the city, we need to restore the uniqueness of a project, and involve experts.'

1 C. Hein, '*Toshikeikaku* and *Machizukuri* in Japanese Urban Planning – The Reconstruction of Inner-City Neighborhoods in Kobe', *Jahrbuch des DIJ* (Deutsches Institut für Japanstudien) no. 13 (2001), 221-252.

2 Y. Yoshimura, *Super Legal Buildings* (Tokyo: Shokokusha, 2006).

Riken Yamamoto's proposal for a Community Area argues that a house should not be an envelop that encloses a singel family, but a gathering place for people whose ties go beyond that of a family

About the experts:
Riken Yamamoto
Year of Birth: 1945
Profession: Architect at Riken Yamamoto & Fieldshop
Education: Nihon University/Tokyo University of the Arts, Tokyo
Academic Career: Professor at Kogakuin University (2002-2007) and Yokohama Graduate School of Architecture (2007-2011)
Vision: Societies should be based on community living

Manabu Chiba
Year of Birth: 1960
Education: The University of Tokyo, Tokyo
Profession: Architect at Chiba Manabu Architects
Academic Career: Assistant Professor at The University of Tokyo
Vision: Making architecture is about discovering formats that are unique to particular places

Ryuji Fujimura
Year of Birth: 1976
Education: Tokyo Institute of Technology, Tokyo
Berlage Institute, Rotterdam
Profession: Architect at Ryuji Fujimura Architects
Additional: Editor, Curator
Vision: The process of building design is approaching media design

Window House is Kengo Kuma's contribution to MUJI's infill houses and allows clients to choose the position of their windows, strategically framing the views outside like pictures frames

Home builder company Daiwa House sells around 300 of its best-selling prefabricated home 'xevoE' per month (~ from 167,000 yen/m2). It is made of standard prefabricated items that can be arranged in many different ways

ALTERNATIVES TO AN ARCHITECT
ON HOME-BUILDING COMPANIES, HOUSE PRODUCERS AND PREFABRICATED DESIGN HOMES

BASED ON INTERVIEWS WITH THE FOLLOWING EXPERTS:
Kazuhiko Namba × Shigeru Oshima × Tadashi Fukuoka

Tokyo consists of a sea of single-family detached houses, free-standing multiple-unit blocks and towers. The housing stock is an eclectic mix of traditional homes, modern homes and one-room 'mansions'. In this vast tapestry, the single-family house designed by an architect is an exception. Just to provide an idea: in 2011 the Tokyo Metropolitan Area totalled 5,940,000 dwellings, of which 1,687,000 were detached houses, 94,000 tenant houses, and 4,135,000 apartments. The gross of the 'boxes' you see in the urban landscape are prefabricated houses. Of all single-family houses, 15 per cent are purchased through a home-building company, while local contractors make up the other 85 per cent. In only 2 per cent of these single-family houses was an architect involved in the design. But if you can get a custom-made house designed by an independent architect for the same price as an ordinary one or less, why do the Japanese still opt for a repetitive prefabricated catalogue dwelling?

PREFABRICATED HOUSES

In the heyday of post-war construction, home-building companies entered the housing market with the idea of industrializing the construction process. They invented ready-made houses that were easy to supply, as there was such a great need for housing. Daiwa House started in 1955, while Sekisui House, currently the largest, and others soon followed. Their contribution to the current building stock is indispensable and obviously present. 'What people expect from a home-building company is safety, security, a sound company and a reliable maintenance programme,' explains Shigeru Oshima, who works for the home-building company Misawa Homes.

Daiwa House, currently the second-largest home-building company after Sekisui House, sells about 10,000 prefabricated houses a year; key words are welfare, speed and comfort. 'Performance certificates and full-size structural tests mean most Japanese prefer a house built by a home-building company rather than by an independent architect,' explains Tadashi Fukuoka, chief of the housing development department at Daiwa House. 'Moreover, home builders guarantee the maintenance of the house.' The first 20 years of the warranty are included in the sales price. After that, homeowners can buy 10-year extensions up to the maximum building lifespan of 50 years.

Corporate identities like Sekisui Homes, Daiwa House and Misawa Homes are big in Japan. Aside from designing and building detached homes, they are also involved in the construction of medium- and high-rise buildings, as well as in more comprehensive urban development projects. Because of their corporate identity, home-building companies find it easier than independent architects to develop new materials, products or systems in-house, such as

Daiwa House commissioned architect Akihisa Hirata to develop the concept model le no le, which could show the company's in-house designers about the meaning of a roof in comtemporary housing

special ceramics, new window sashes or photovoltaic power generation systems.

At a certain point housing was standardized in Japan, and people were not so much aware of other options. It was not until independent architects started to design completely different kinds of houses about 20 years ago that a number of Japanese started to question this copy-paste mentality in housing. Home-building companies have to keep up with new requirements and frequently launch a new home type, with colourful names such as 'Future Home', 'Beverly Hills', 'Smart House', 'Zero-Energy Home', or '100 Per Cent Recycled Home'. When a potential client approaches a home builder, they can take an orientation tour of a model park in the suburbs with all the different housing types on show. A client either picks one of the standard designs or asks the in-house design team to propose a free layout within the template the company can offer. 'Exceptional requests from clients, such as a window larger than 2300 mm by 3500 mm, are practically impossible,' Fukuoka notes. 'They require special permission, which can take up to two years.'

Although wooden structures allow for more variation in layout, prefab houses with steel structures are more popular among the Japanese. Because the structures are prefabricated, the system is approved in advance, so the construction process can be as fast as three months. More and more house-building companies are trying to make their selection more exclusive by involving independent architects. Daiwa House, for example, developed a luxury prefab home in collaboration with architect Edward Suzuki (b. 1947), a new type currently selling around ten units a month. 'It is difficult for

Akihisa Hirata used mountains as a metaphor for an innovative housing concept featuring an oversized roof with three distinct summits that allow many people to share a single living space without entirely sacrificing privacy

an architect to work with a home-building company,' Fukuoka admits, as a house-building company cannot give an architect very much freedom. 'They have to work within the template of the company and stay close to the corporate style.'

Independent architects who collaborate with house-building companies only in idea workshops enjoy greater freedom. Daiwa House, for example, asked Sou Fujimoto (b. 1971), Akihisa Hirata (b. 1971) and Yoshimura Yasutaka (1972) for radical new ideas on housing. 'It is not that we intend to feature the results in our catalogue, but they inspire our design team and we have developed themes from them.'

CREATORS OF ARCHITECTURE

A recent phenomenon in the design of single-family houses in Japan is the involvement of a so-called 'producer'. Due to the cooling economy and housing market since the late 1990s, opportunities to work on actual projects have become scarce for young architects. This new system benefits both architect and client. A producer introduces the clients to an architect. As the producer coordinates the entire process (including budgetary planning and requests) until the building is completed, the architect can fully concentrate on the design. On the other hand, clients can express their desires and questions without hesitation through the 'mediation' of the producer. One such producer is Shigeru Oshima. Although he officially works for the large home-building company Misawa Homes, he manages his own subdivision, 'A-Project' (A for architecture) within the company. A-Project supports the design process leading to the completion of independent single-family houses

Coordinator Shigeru Oshima (A-Project) collaborated with architect Hiroshi Kikuchi on House 222 oiz because the site was small and irregularly shaped, and it was therefore not posible to use a prefab system

and housing complexes designed by independent architects. As a producer, Oshima intercepts clients who initially opted for a prefabricated house from Misawa Homes. But because they have purchased a plot with an awkward shape – triangular, for instance – a prefab is not flexible enough to adapt to it. Oshima then offers these clients a safe solution and guides the clients through the normally uncertain process of the independent architect. Misawa Homes allows him to collaborate with a 'competitor' – an independent architect – because this is seen as part of the company's high-level of service of the company. 'Misawa Homes does not want to disappoint its clients,' Oshima explains. By paying an extra 10 per cent on top of the architect's fee, clients receive the guarantee that their architect-designed house will actually be completed and obtain a maintenance warranty, just as they would if they bought a prefab house. A-Project tends to select young architects with a lot of talent who are still working for somebody else. 'Many talented young architects cannot start their own career because of the difficult economic situation,' Oshima explains. 'With a real first assignment, they can finally make the move to do so.' Oshima has helped a lot of young architects, such as Hiroshi Kikuchi (b. 1972) and Go Hasegawa (b. 1977), start their career, as well as now-renowned architecture firms like Atelier Bow-Wow and Mikan.

PREFAB DESIGNER-STYLE

Another development that foresees more variety in the current housing stock market is Muji's initiative to ask renowned designers to develop a prefabricated house with a touch of design. The Muji Company was founded in Japan in 1980 during the economic boom as an antithesis to the habits of consumer society at that time.[1] As a critique of expensive foreign-made brands and cheap, poor-quality projects, Muji restored the vision of products, combining the idea of the non-brand (*mujirushi*) with quality projects (*ryohin*). Through rationalization and meticulous elimination of excess, it re-emphasizes the natural appeal of an object.

In its 30 years of existence, the company has developed over 7,500 household articles, consumer electronics, home appliances, furniture, clothing and food, all demonstrating a desire for moderation – the plain and unadorned. By carefully selecting materials, omitting wasteful production processes and simplifying packaging, Muji wants to make users feel the beauty and pride in living a simple and modest life again.

As a logical extension of their projects, Muji started to produce houses. At first, Muji collaborated with designer Tokujin Yoshioka (b. 1967) and architects Koh Kitayama (b. 1950) and Kazuhiko Namba (b. 1947). Namba designed one of the three houses that were eventually brought onto the market. His Wood House is a wooden structure with a characteristic galbanum exterior. Misawa Homes's chief designer, Motochika Kawamoto, designed Morning House, and Kengo Kuma (b. 1954) designed Window House, with distinctive wooden window frames. Namba's Wood House is Muji's best-selling house, with around 400 homes sold and built in Japan. A 105-m^2 configuration of the three types ranges from 180,000 to 200,000 euros. The package deal includes the shelter, the frame and equipment such as lighting and floor heating. The clients can then fill their house with their own choice of kitchen supplies, bedding and electric appliances from – obviously – the Muji store. Namba explains the sales strategy of the house: 'Muji only proposes the system. Small construction companies around the world buy the system and Muji teaches them how to design and construct it.'

FAMILY-STYLE LIVING

'The Muji house lifestyle is about communication, Namba says in explaining how the concept of the Muji House is reflected in his Wood House. 'Partition walls are almost absent, and it has a big window facing the street.' Muji targets couples around 35 years of age with one small child who feel home-building companies define the lifestyle of a client too much in advance. The clients are usually not aware of what an architect could mean for them or do not know how to approach an architect. Namba expresses his concern about his changing society: 'Japanese children and parents now lead very separate lives. A young couple nowadays does not even know how to manage a family,' he explains. The Muji solution to the problem – which should prevent *hikikomori,* the withdrawal from social life or the seeking of extreme isolation – is a one-room space. The idea is that parents can always add partitions later. Namba's Wood House, with the simplicity of its one-room space, is akin to a traditional Japanese house from the Edo period. Husband, wife and child sleep in one room, just like the old times. The current version of Wood House is designed for a suburban plot, is easily expandable and is available in up to 200 different combinations of floor plans. A special version is being developed that can also fit within tight inner city plots, with a footprint as small as 50 m^2.

Kazuhiko Namba's Wood House for MUJI is designed to stimulate communication among its residents as well as interaction with the neighbourhood

GOURMET FOOD, FASHION AND ARCHITECTURE

In the 1980s, many Japanese lifestyle magazines started to cover architecture in their magazines, along with fashion and gourmet food. Widely available in all convenience stores and bookshops, these magazines have had a major impact on the requirements of clients looking to create their own homes. The unique lifestyles exposed through such magazines have led a broader public to commission independent architects. 'Within today's chaotic mixture of Japanese culture and post-war influences, it's equally important to seek and construct a new Japanese housing standard,' says Oshima, outlining the response of Misawa Homes to the changing requirements of its clients. For his part, the producer says he is interested in the custom-designed house because architects can realize a lifestyle that specifically suits a particular family and a particular house. 'In times when things are rapidly changing, the same can be said about people's way of living. With the help of young architects I believe we can invent new and better housing for the near future, which people would prefer to what they are used to live in.'

1 J. Morrison, N. Fukasawa and K. Hara, *Muji* (New York: Rizzoli, 2010).

Wood House is designed as a one-room space to help young couples with small children manage a household and to strengthen the family ties

About the experts:
Kazuhiko Namba
Company: KAI WORKSHOP
Alternative: Architect who designed flexible open plan house for MUJI

Shigeru Oshima
Company: A-Project (division of Misawa Homes)
Alternative: Mediator between clients of Misawa Homes and (young) independent architects.

Tadashi Fukuoka
Company: Daiwa House
Alternative: One of Japan`s largest homebuilders inspired by independent architects

Mount Fuji Architects realized the feeling of being 'under a tree' in their Tree House by using laminated veneer lumber (51 x 286 mm) and wooden joists crafted to perfection

TRADITIONAL AESTHETICS OR MODERN ETHICS?

ON HARMONY WITH NATURE, MODERN BUILDING MATERIALS AND WORKERS' COMMITMENT ON THE BUILDING SITE

BASED ON INTERVIEWS WITH THE FOLLOWING EXPERTS:
Kengo Kuma × Yasuhiro Yamashita × Masahiro Harada

Traditional Japanese architecture is known for its extremely delicate use of natural materials. Since as far back as the sixth century, the Japanese have been building elegant wooden structures with gigantic, straw roofs. The abundance of forests and a natural preference for wood produced some of the most advanced wooden architecture in the world. Unlike Western architecture, which tries to keep the elements strictly outside, the Japanese have always opted for an architecture in harmony with nature. With their choice of materials they maintain or even enhance the natural state. Floors covered with rice-straw *tatami* mats, paper *shōji* windows, sliding paper-thin partitions, bamboo fences, bamboo furniture and hand-laid stone paths are key features of traditional Japanese architecture, which can still be found in the thousands of well-preserved temples and shrines throughout the country and in traditional-style houses in the countryside. Although those aesthetics are still an important aspect of present-day Japanese culture, such sensitivity is no longer evident when one walks the streets of contemporary Tokyo. The city simply looks like a jungle of buildings built of concrete, steel and plastic. What happened to the sensitivity with which the Japanese used to handle natural materials?

THE WEAKNESS OF WOOD

Practical reasons such as fire, maintenance and costs partly explain why natural materials are almost absent in the contemporary Japanese cityscape. The weak point of wood is that it is flammable, something extremely dangerous in a city that used to be densely packed with only wooden houses. The result was that Tokyo lay in ruins twice during the twentieth century: the 1923 Great Kantō earthquake and the bombings during the Second World War both razed the city to the ground. 'Tokyo has had so many problems with fires that about 100 years ago buildings made of mortar and concrete were introduced,' explains the ever-innovating architect Yasuhiro Yamashita (b. 1960).
There was even a short period of interest in the use of Western-style brick with the Ginza Brick Town, but this did not last long. It soon became clear that brick cannot resist strong earthquakes and is not suitable for the hot Japanese summers. Yamashita explains the mentality change: 'Traditional Japanese construction is sustainable and lasts at least 100 years, but modern techniques such as those seen in today's prefabricated homes are made to last about 30 years.' During the period of rapid economic growth starting in the 1960s, the Japanese government provided many houses in a very short time. This was when house-building companies entered the housing market, introducing safe prefabricated homes made of steel, a trend that continues to this day.
'Natural materials like wood require

Earth Brick House is Atelier Tekuto's first house built with the new brick and contains no less than 2600 hand-made earth blocks, weighing 20 kg each

a lot of maintenance,' architect Masahiro Harada (b. 1973) of Mount Fuji Architects explains. 'Clients prefer maintenance-free materials nowadays, as this is cheaper.' Master architect Kengo Kuma (b. 1954) has shown many Japanese architects a new way of using traditional techniques and materials, and explains the current situation with a sense of nostalgia. 'We used to have an interesting lifestyle that blended with nature, because traditional Japanese homes did not have glass. The interior was separated from the exterior by means of thin rice paper. It was after the Second World War that big, strong concrete buildings appeared and destroyed the original "soft" urban fabric of Tokyo.' When the Japanese government surrendered to the Americans and their allies in 1945, the US military occupied Japan for several years. The Japanese started to regard their American occupiers and all things American as new symbols of happiness. Western lifestyles and housing layouts rapidly took over and Japanese urban people consequently 'lost their happy relationship with natural materials', according to Kuma.

AUTHENTIC OR AVANT-GARDE?

To understand the rapid changes modern Japanese architecture underwent after the Second World War and the resulting attitude towards materials, we can distinguish two directions among Japanese architects. One group consists of those Kuma calls the 'authentic modernists', following avant-garde architects like Kenzo Tange (1913-2005), Fumihiko Maki (b. 1928), and Toyo Ito (b. 1941). The other direction features the traditional architects who follow Isoya Yoshida (1894-1974), an architect who became famous for a new *sukiya* style: a combination of traditional Japanese

Extensive research initiated by Atelier Tekuto resulted in an innovative earth brick (made primary of soil, water and magnesium oxide) that meets Western building codes

Six thousand pieces of cypress wood make up Kengo Kuma's GC Prostho Museum Research Centre; an elegant three-dimensional lattice 9 m high

architecture with modernist elements. His portfolio includes the recently demolished *Kabuki-za* theatre in Tokyo's Ginza district, several houses for Japanese prime ministers and major traditional Japanese restaurants. 'Yoshida established a truly modern Japanese style, different from authentic traditional Japanese and freed from international modernism,' Kuma explains. 'When architects opted for working with natural materials, it would automatically mean they were going in the direction of Yoshida. For many young architects this was "going backwards", a dichotomy that stayed in the minds of the Japanese architects long after the Second World War.' According to Kuma, many architects from Toyo Ito's generation (the 1940s generation) and his own generation (the 1950s) are afraid to use natural materials. Kuma himself is obviously an exception. He reinvents traditional architectural details using new materials, or improves existing methods of detailing using new features.

With his progressive attitude Kuma opened the road for many other Japanese architects. He enthusiastically teaches younger architects that this kind of separation between traditional and modern is not effective. His design methodology – using materials in their most honest way, as pure façade materials rather than as wallpaper covering a structure – resembles the basic idea of the prehistoric structure of Stonehenge in the UK, built of large standing stones. 'People can feel the strength of the material from the stone itself,' Kuma explains.

Architect Yasuhiro Yamashita, who has realized over 171 uniquely designed single-family houses in his career so far, has an exquisite interest in

By using strong cypress wood, the lumber could be sculpted into new shapes while keeping the wooden elements as thin as possible – without requiring the use of bolts, glue or nails for the joints

technical innovations and materials. After the Glass Block and Aluminium Ring Houses experiments, he recently developed a Soil Brick made of 100 per cent recycled materials. With the natural additive magnesium oxide, in combination with sand, loam, water and gravel, Atelier Tekuto developed a 40 x 20 x 19 cm unfired brick. The new brick more than satisfies Japanese construction standards, which are the strictest in the world. The first single-family house made of these soil bricks was hand-built in Chiba Prefecture, using 2,600 soil-brick blocks.
Harada, who has had his own practice since 2004, naturally acquired his affinity toward materials while working at Kengo Kuma Architects & Associates. With partner Mao Harada (b. 1976) he designs buildings that try to redress the lack of natural materials. The architect duo frequently travels the country to find new master craftsmen to collaborate with, as they believe in the qualities of the carpenter. 'Materials themselves are designers,' Harada explains poetically. 'Only when we keep our mind silent are we able to hear the small voices of materials. In "fake" materials like plastics, the voice is kept inside and we can't hear what it wants to say.'

ECLECTIC MIX

Recent housing designs in Japan show that Japanese architects are slowly recovering from the American 'deconstruction'. Housing concepts are now often related to aspects of traditional Japanese culture, although the architects themselves may not be immediately aware of this. 'Everybody my age grew up with plastics,' says 39-year old Harada, worrying about the commonness of such artificial materials. 'We are so surrounded by computers, iPhones and iPads that

Kengo Kuma's Yusuhara Bridge Museum is a outstanding example of modern Japanese timber construction of a large yet delicate cantilever made of small-sectioned materials assembled together

people start to feel sympathy towards plastic.' He does not want to imply that we should not use plastic at all, providing plastic is used as plastic and not as a fake alternative for wood, stone or paper and as long as it remains in balance with natural materials.
Unlike the post-war generation of architects, the younger generation has been growing up in a fairly global world, in an urban environment and with products based on American culture. Harada: 'American culture has been the substitution for "the order until then" which was destroyed during the Second World War. This new order has always been around us. Not as a new "subject of admiration" but as something extremely ordinary.' Harada elucidates his statement with the house in which he spent his childhood. Like many of his contemporaries he grew up in typical post-war housing with a 'Frank Lloyd Wright taste'. This kind of eclectic architecture mixes traditional Japanese elements with Western aspects. For him and many other young architects this eclectic style has become the standard, not only in house designs but also in food, fashion and music. Pure Japanese is something extraordinary nowadays; eclectic is the norm. Take classic Japanese garments like the *kimono*. The T-shaped, straight-lined robes with wide sleeves are now only worn during traditional events, and most Japanese walk around in Western-style outfits.

COMMITMENT ON THE CONSTRUCTION SITE

Although the application of traditional Japanese construction techniques is the exception rather than the rule today and building materials have radically modernized over the years, the commitment of the workers on site in Japan is still among the highest

The Yusuhara Bridge Museum shows Kengo Kuma's preference for architecture inspired by traditional techniques

in the world. Construction is carried out with the utmost care, turning single-family houses into incredible examples of craftsmanship. 'Japan is a small country and we therefore expect details on all levels,' says Yamashita to explain why things in Japan are generally made well and with great care. During the construction process, the building contractor is a friend rather than a rival of the architect. To uphold the pride of the construction company, contractors search – in discussion with the architect – for the best execution possible within the available budget. Japan also owes the high level of detailing and unique site-specific solutions to its editing culture. 'Japan is quite limited in resources, but we have learned how to use the available materials in many different ways,' Yamashita says. 'Take tofu, the dish made from soybeans. Japanese manage to create many different tastes out of the same source. We keep the original taste, smell and character of the material but we edit in many ways to create different products out of it. Although the beans are crushed, we can still taste the soybean.' A similar attitude towards editing can be found in Japanese architecture. Structure, furniture, decoration are made with respect for the material. Architects think about the taste and the texture of the original material, they never forget the original source.

INNOVATIONS IN MATERIALS

What Kuma, Yamashita and Harada have in common is the belief that 'earth' will be *the* keyword for future architectural constructions. Soil, as Yamashita explains, is everywhere in the world and has zero transportation costs. Ideally, the three interviewees prefer not to use materials transported from other places, but in a city like

Tokyo this is impossible because of the lack of natural materials and natural soil. 'Using earth, people can get a very warm feeling,' Kuma says. Harada picks up a second point of interest. 'The most important aspect of Japanese sensitivity towards materials that has been preserved is the sense of humidity,' Harada says, referring to the country's wet climate. 'Humidity wakes up the grain of a material. Without humidity, all grains are closed.'
Because of the humidity, people cannot see the outline of a building clearly, which automatically emphasizes the *feeling* of textures. This sensitivity stems from Japanese tradition, where the most important thing was to feel the materials at close range, rather than seeing the outline of architecture. Compare this with Greek architecture, where the outline plays such an important role. 'I feel very familiar with the paintings of *suiboku-ga*, Japanese monochrome ink paintings,' Harada says. 'Take the paintings by Tōhaku Hasegawa (1539-1610), for instance, an ancient Japanese artist whose aim was to draw the humidity using only black ink.' Modern Japanese author Jun'ichirō Tanizaki (1886-1965) described this phenomenon beautifully in his book *In Praise of Shadows*,[1] claiming that the Japanese prefer 'a pensive lustre to a shallow brilliance'.
Throughout their history, the Japanese have been skilfully enhancing beauty by using the conditions of humidity and darkness. Although darkness and humidity tend to be obliterated these days, Harada sees a great need for these conditions to survive. A recent example is the monster earthquake that hit northern Japan on 11 March 2011, when many cities were required to save electricity by switching off lights. 'We felt somewhat relieved by this inconvenience,' Harada admits, as people realized how unnatural bright and nervously lit up cities are. 'Switching off lights reawakened a natural feeling of comfort with darkness.' Although globalization is conquering the world, Harada believes that local cultures will be more respected and maintained in the future and a new Japanese style will take hold from here. When it comes to the use of building materials, Kuma's advice to young architects is clear and bold: 'Be free from any political and ethical standards.'

1 J. Tanizaki, *In Praise of Shadows* (Stony Creek: Leete's Islands Books, 1977), 11.

Atelier Tekuto's A-ring is based on a self-developed prefabricated system using aluminium for the structure and well as a thermal heating device (radiator)

About the experts:
Kengo Kuma
Principle at Kengu Kuma Architects & Associates (KKAA)
Year of Birth: 1954
Special Interests: Using materials not merely as cosmetics, but also to show its structural qualities

Yasuhiro Yamashita
Principle at Atelier Tekuto
Year of Birth: 1960
Special Interests: Innovating building materials and building performance

Masahiro Harada
Principle at Mount Fuji Architects
Year of Birth: 1973
Special Interests: Building materials contain a message of how to use them

Jun Sato translated Sou Fujimoto's concept of hovering floor slabs into a flexible welded steel frame of 55 x 55 mm solid steel columns, 32 x 65 mm solid beams and a minimum amount of braces

THE ROLE OF STRUCTURE
ON ARDUOUS SEISMIC CODES, DEDICATED CRAFTSMEN AND SMART ENGINEERS

BASED ON INTERVIEWS WITH THE FOLLOWING EXPERTS:
Jun Sato × Hidefumi Ohno × Ryota Kidokoro

In the old days, the professions of structural engineer and architect did not exist in Japan. Traditional craftsmen called *miya-daiku* designed and constructed wooden temples and shrines, the kind of architecture Japan became famous for around the world. 'Workmen didn't solve architectural issues thanks to structural calculations but rather thanks to experience,' explains the young independent structural engineer Hidefumi Ohno (b. 1974). 'Their extensive knowledge and skills concerning wood joinery were passed down through the apprenticeship system.'
Today, there are roughly 10,000 structural engineers in Japan working for large construction companies. A mere 500 engineers work independently. 'In Europe, structural engineers are educated in a university's department of civil engineering, but in Japan engineers and architects are both educated in a department of architecture,' structural engineer Jun Sato (b. 1970), who frequently collaborates with young Japanese architects, explains. Architects and engineers study the same subjects, such as architecture history, design and structure for the first two or three years. After that, engineering students go deeper into their own subjects. 'The advantage of such a system is that architects learn about the importance of a good structure, while engineers can imagine what the architects are thinking,' Sato says. 'We communicate with each other in a common language.' Without a doubt, this system of education contributes to the enthusiastic collaborations between young independent architects and independent engineers we see happening in Japan today.

THE GROWING ROLE OF THE ENGINEER
According to Sato it was structural engineer Toshihiko Kimura (1926-2009) who advanced the role of structural engineers in a design project about 40 years ago. Kimura started the trend of working closely with Japanese architects, like Fumihiko Maki (b. 1928), Arato Isozaki (b. 1931) and Yoshio Taniguchi (b. 1937). Stimulated by the Metabolist Movement, architects felt an urge to build tough and heavy structures, which they obviously could not design solely by themselves. 'Structural engineering used to consist of calculating and drawing figures, with the engineers faithfully fulfilling their duty towards the architects,' Sato asserts. 'Architects didn't have many problems, but neither did they ask the engineers to develop the idea of structures further.' Only a few specialists or professors at universities worked as advisors on a few exceptional architectural projects. In the last 20 years, the opportunities for independent structural engineers to be involved in the design process have significantly increased, because independent architects are designing more exceptional single-family houses. Instead of merely calculating the structure, structural engineers also take on the role of designers these days. Their structural concept is expected to

Ryota Kidokoro (ARUP) helped architct Akira Yoneda out with an acrobatic structure in his K-clinic: a 16-m-long cantilever covered with steel deck plates and a heavy slab as the counterweight

strengthen the architectural concept. Structural engineer Ryota Kidokoro (b. 1976), born in the USA but a Tokyo resident for 11 years as well as an engineer working for ARUP Japan, can assess this from a foreign perspective. 'Mutual respect between architects and structural engineers in Japan is on a much higher level than in other countries,' says Kidokoro, who often comes across foreign architects jokingly saying they are fighting with their structural engineers. 'If they understood each other's work, such friction between architects and engineers would not occur.'

THE POWER OF STRUCTURES

What can a structural engineer add to the architectural concept of a single-family detached house? On a tiny plot of land many things, including the structure of a house, have to fit, so a slim structure immediately pays off. On the other hand, beautiful slim structures obviously run counter to the strict building regulations related to earthquake readiness in Japan. The massive forces a building has to resist in Japan in the event of a major earthquake almost automatically assume a need for structures with large dimensions. 'No wonder structural design heavily influences the design of a small house in Japan,' says Kidokoro with the two constraints in mind. Ohno, who has been running his own firm, OHNO Japan, since 2005 adds, 'A structural engineer is the one who decides the dimensions and the position of the structure as well as the kind of material. During the process of the design, the architect and structural engineer share the architectural concept, clarify it, and refine it until a very pure product comes out.' What structural design also offers to the design of a single-family

The skin of Hiroshi Sambuichi's Rokko Mountain Observatory is designed by Kidokoro as an interweaving network of slender and branch-like elements that naturally shifts out-of-plane to turn into a three-dimensional frame

home, according to the three young engineers, is that it should seem almost non-existent. In small projects like detached single-family houses the structure is supposed to disappear and evoke the feeling of a single entity. 'The architectural houses may look dynamic, but that is not because of the presence of the structure,' adds Sato. Ohno agrees, saying that 'when a structure is minimized and arranged properly, the structure almost becomes part of the furniture of the house.'

BIG OPTS FOR SMALL

For Westerners it may seem unbelievable that a small architecture firm would knock on the door of a world-renowned mega-firm like ARUP. The prime reason ARUP Japan works with young architects is that, unlike their other branches spread over the world, the Japan branch is relatively new and thus less established. 'We started only 15 years ago and have to get to know the architects before they explode into fame,' Kidokoro says, explaining how the company starts building relations while practices are still very small. 'In Japan, architects always start their career with the basics of architecture, namely residential buildings,' Kidokoro continues. 'For us, it is a great way to get to know the architects.'

When ARUP's engineers are inspired by the exceptional ideas and thinking of a particular architect, they may accept projects as small as an 80-m^2 single-family house. 'If architects have enough confidence to knock on our door, it shows they have courage and perseverance,' Kidokoro says. He frequently works on challenging constructions for architectural projects by Japanese architects like Akira Yoneda (b. 1959) and Hiroshi Sambuichi (b. 1968), saying that the small projects are fun to do. How

Hidefumi Ohno collaborated with architect Nobuhiro Tsukada on the structure of Earth House; a hollow reinforced concrete structure that is packed with soil at the top to form an elevated garden

much time does a big company spend on such small projects? 'These small projects are a big pain in the butt, as we work on them 15 times longer than on big projects,' Kidokoro admits. 'But because of the scale the projects are completed relatively fast, an exciting contrast with our usual big-scale projects that take at least ten years to realize.'

THE CHALLENGES

Major earthquakes and the resulting strict building codes mean that structural engineers in Japan work at the limits of their profession. They are obliged to design structures that can withstand a wave velocity of 50 cm per second. Roughly speaking this is equivalent to an earthquake with a magnitude of 7 on the Richter scale. 'Technically speaking it's not exactly true, but it's close enough to get a feel for the design criteria,' Kidokoro explains. 'Remember, it's all guesswork, since no one can ever know the exact characteristics of an earthquake.' Sato emphasizes that the job of a structural engineer is a lot more complicated in Japan than in countries that do not experience earthquakes. 'Besides the static forces of gravity on a building, we also have to think about the dynamic forces of both earthquakes and strong typhoons,' Sato explains. 'The latter causes positive and negative types of loads in both the X and Y direction, which means that we have to deal with four different directions plus gravity on a single structure.' Because it is impossible for an architect to imagine such complex forces, collaboration with a good structural engineer becomes indispensable. Despite all the strict regulations and strenuous seismic codes, Japanese engineers are convinced that they can realize every possible shape, because

Earth House's structure embraces the entire house like an umbrella and defines the interior space with undeniable strength

there are excellent techniques for welding, moulding concrete, and traditional carpentry available in Japan. Moreover, Japanese craftsmen still possess the centuries-old sense of precise manufacture.

HEAVY VERSUS LIGHT

The monstrous earthquake that hit the coast of Northern Japan on 11 March 2011 with a magnitude of 9.0 proved that buildings in Japan are designed by highly skilled and trained structural engineers. No buildings collapsed as a consequence of the earthquake. The design code apparently incorporates sufficient safety factors to withstand such big earthquakes. 'Modern buildings designed under the most updated codes will most likely withstand up to a magnitude 7.0 or greater,' Kidokoro asserts. In spite of the earthquakes, small houses in Tokyo seem very light. Unlike taller buildings in which earthquake calculations are usually more clearly visible, small houses have those 'invisible' structures. 'Arduous seismic codes, excellent guidance references, strict checks and the education system all play a big role in the good quality of Japanese structural design, but most of all it is the *majime* nature of Japanese people,' Kidokoro says, referring to the serious earnestness that eschews cheating or cutting corners. 'That's why in Japan safe buildings with a high quality are constructed.'

As an everyday example of this cultural aspect he mentions how Japanese people, obsessed with safety, patiently wait for the light to turn green before crossing the street, even if there are no cars in sight. For the same reason it is not so surprising that lost wallets are returned to their owners with all the cash still inside. 'Even when an architect does not consider

Mount Fuji Architects collaborated with Jun Sato on a centrifugal structural solution for Tree House in Tokyo to bring in light on a dark site without sacrificing the residents' privacy

the dimensions, the importance of the structural elements cannot be disregarded,' Ohno concludes. 'A structural engineer is the specialist who decides the dimensions of the structure appropriate for the concept.' Kidokoro's advice to architects is not to think about structure at all when they start their design. 'We engineers want to see what you as an architect want to make – your ideal vision. Together we will find a way to realize it somehow.'

Jun Sato translated the architects' geometry of a polar coordinate system with laminated veneer lumbers that extend from a central column at a radial interval of 11.25° and a small vertical displacement

About the experts:
Jun Sato
Technical Adviser at Jun Sato Structural Engineers Co., Ltd
Year of Birth: 1970
Education: The University of Tokyo, Tokyo
Work Experience: Toshihiko Kimura Structural Engineers Co., Ltd
Specialism: Flexible structures (that have the ability to be deformed by load) composed of delicate elements
Collaborations: Sou Fujimoto, Mount Fuji Architects, CAt, Coelacanth K&H,
Riken Yamamoto, Kengo Kuma, Junya Ishigami, Makoto Yokomizo, Atelier Tekuto, Kumiko Inui

Hidefumi Ohno
Structural Engineer at OHNO Japan
Year of Birth: 1974
Education: Nihon University, Tokyo
Work Experience: Masahiro Ikeda Architecture Studio
Specialism: All objects in which form is decided by dynamics
Collaborations: Takaharu+Yui Tezuka Tezuka Architects), Go Hasegawa, Makoto Tanijiri (Suppose Design Office),
Yuji Nakae (Nakae Architects), Fuminori Nousaku

Ryota Kidokoro
Associate / Structural Engineer at ARUP (Tokyo office)
Year of Birth: 1976
Education: Cornell University, Ithaca
Work Experience: Thornton Tomasetti + ARUP
Specialism: Unconventional structures of all shapes and sizes
Collaborations: Maki and Associates (Fumihiko Maki), Riken Yamamoto & Field Shop, Kuma Kengo Architects and Associates, Shigeru Ban Architects, Hiroshi Sambuichi, Akira Yoneda

Yoko Ando designed curtains for Teppei Fujiwara's design of House in Kamiuma in Tokyo that are more than simple blinds

INSIDE THE HOUSE
ON LIFESTYLE, INTERIOR DESIGN AND DECORATION

BASED ON INTERVIEWS WITH THE FOLLOWING EXPERTS:
Yoko Ando × Naoki Terada × Kyoichi Tsuzuki

Where do Tokyo residents actually sleep? Any visitor walking the streets of Tokyo probably wonders where the vast streams of people crossing the streets, stations and subway tunnels in the daytime end up spending the night. Some people may end up sleeping in front of the subway station waiting for the first morning train, while business people might opt for one of the many convenient hotels or capsule hotels around any of the train stations. Couples in love who cannot return to their parents' home due to the lack of privacy might check into a love hotel for the night. The homeless end up in the public parks, while teenagers go for a cheap overnight party in a karaoke or game box. Naturally, besides these typically urban lifestyles, there are also ordinary family lives. These lives habitually unfold in a modern apartment building with a highly standardized floor plan. In such apartments, parents, children and perhaps grandparents share a 3LDK, which stands for a living/dining/kitchen space (LDK) with three individual bedrooms. The apartments are located in high-rise towers built in newly developed areas by big developers such as Sumitomi or Mitsui.
Besides residential towers and multi-unit buildings, the urban landscape of Tokyo is filled with an endless repetition of single-family detached houses. Such detached houses are prefabricated and constructed by home-building companies like Daiwa House, Sekusui House, Misawa Homes or by local contractors. After buying a plot, clients can order a ready-made house from a catalogue. Only the truly daring commission an architect to build them a custom-made home. After all, when you team up with an architect the final result is not at all clear from the beginning. The total budget, how long the construction will take and the structural performances are all uncertainties that are eliminated if you buy a prefabricated house.
'People who buy land and build their own house are often young couples in their 30s who work for a television company or an investment bank and plan on having children in the near future,' architect and designer Naoki Terada (b. 1967) goes so far as to stereotype. Location is a priority for those kinds of clients, although this means even fewer square metres of usable floor space. 'In a typical Japanese family, the father works outside the home until quite late while the mother spends a lot of time in the kitchen preparing all the meals. Children keep themselves busy in the room chatting with friends or playing computer games,' photographer Kyochi Tsuzuki (b. 1956) says in describing the average life of a family. He has photographed tiny Japanese apartments – the antithesis of designed ones – overstuffed with objects. His images demonstrate a respect for a Tokyo urban lifestyle about which people are usually ashamed.[1]

ULTRA-CONVENIENT
Living in the metropolis of Tokyo,

The curtain serves as a optical structure to temporary fill the intentionally made slits and margins in the walls

with its high level of facilities and exceptional level of services, has its consequences for the definition of a house. In Tokyo, you do not need to have your own bookshelves, because late-night bookstores around the corner from your house allow you to browse freely. You can do without a large kitchen, because there are plenty of good and cheap restaurants catering to all early-morning and late-night commuters. And why should you consider buying a fridge when you can purchase all your chilled foods in the 24-hour convenience stores down the street? What you need for a comfortable life in a metropolis like Tokyo is a 'base camp': a small place in a central location to stay the night. The city itself is an extension of your private living room, and that is exactly how individuals and couples in Tokyo spend their lives and enjoy the vibrancy of this city. Because Tokyo is made up of many neighbourhoods, each with its own character and atmosphere, location is of prime interest. Your favourite café can be the reason to move to a certain area. Subsequently, the kitchen of that particular café becomes the alternative to your own tiny kitchenette at home.

In busy family lives, with parents working late and children joining after-school and sports clubs, it is not surprising that the most important request from clients is a shared space where family members can enjoy time together. 'The reason people spend so much time outside instead of at home is because they don't like the home they live in,' Terada points out. 'The layout of these apartments is so standard that it doesn't fit anybody's lifestyle.' He has observed that the consequence of these uninspiring homes is that teenagers start to hang around in sport clubs or drink cheap cups of coffee at

Rather than merely blinding a window, Yoko Ando's curtain can cover the entire surface of the wall in the bedroom

McDonald's instead of returning to their own family home.

For Japanese architects the challenge is to design a better living environment that fits the particular lifestyle of a family. A good house design can break the vicious circle and make family members at ease again in their own abode. Numerous talks with new residents confirm this hypothesis. A custom-made design can improve the quality of the living environment in such a way that it makes its residents happier.

HOUSES LIKE PAPER SCALE MODELS

Aside from the entrance area or genkan and the kitchen, bathroom and toilet, rooms in traditional Japanese homes do not have a designated use. All necessary furniture is movable and stored in a built-in cupboard when not in use and thus flexible in organization and usage. With fusuma, sliding doors made from wood and paper, residents partition the main space and decide on the size of a room. All you need for a basic Japanese housing unit is a kitchen, a bathroom, a toilet, a genkan and one multipurpose living space. However, the reality is that modern Japanese homes are stuffed with colourful items and Western-style furniture, resulting in interiors that more often than not break with the efficiency and sobriety of the traditional Japanese house.

'Have you ever seen Zen simplicity in contemporary Tokyo?' Tsuzuki asks, referring to the architecture magazines that picture modern Japanese lives in white, sterile 1:1 mock-ups. 'That kind of minimalist look might be visible in a few houses owned by very rich people,' says Tsuzuki, who got bored photographing expensive villas. 'Japanese people are so happy to have many gadgets around them nowadays.

Walls, floor and ceiling of Naoki Terada's Stomach House in Tokorozawa are painted in a soft Kimono Green

Most of them don't care about design at all.' 'However uncomfortable it might look to Westerners, smallness is not a real constraint for Japanese to live a happy life,' Terada points out. 'The Japanese dream of having bigger houses, but as we cannot afford this we just stick to the concept of non-privacy,' he says, quickly adding, 'of course the Japanese want to Westernize, and mothers dream of American-style kitchens, big living rooms and barbeque spaces, but in Tokyo that is not reality.'

The Japanese notion of limited space is casually mixed with a Western way of living with furniture that requires space. The Japanese are used to the space-efficient foldable futon mattresses and flexible-use tatami mats for a lifestyle that takes place on floor level. Nowadays many Japanese cram Western-style chairs and beds into their apartments and disregard the efficiency of the traditional Japanese home. Japanese architects designing uniquely custom-made houses lend a helping hand in making an eclectic mixture of lifestyles. They handily incorporate the shift from a floor-sitting to a chair-sitting culture in Japan and mix the traditional notion of personal space with Western spatial ideas, resulting in surprisingly new lifestyles.

Terada, a good home chef himself, likes to compare the design of a modern house with preparing modern Japanese food, 'delicately mixing all kinds of styles in tiny bits together'. Yoko Ando (b. 1968), a textile designer who used to work for the renowned NUNO Corporation, confirms that the Japanese are used to living in small spaces. 'Europeans might think of 100 per cent privacy, but the Japanese think differently and try to manage with in-between feelings,' she argues. 'Instead

Natural light coming in through the large floor-to-ceiling glass façade blends with the green tint of the interior in a mixture of colour gradations, creating a soft, mellow mood

of making a 100 per cent closed room, we Japanese would rather opt for 50 per cent transparency so that we can feel a larger space around us.' As a result, she asserts, people can be in an enclosed space but still feel or imagine that the space continues on the other side (of a curtain) and are therefore able to stand a small space.

Ando designs curtains for architects. Her curtains function as an instrument to adjust lighting and to make a connection between the exterior and interior, rather than merely closing off the exterior. Her curtain designs have the quality of traditional fusuma in the sense that they absorb light but do not show the life inside directly. 'Especially in Japan where houses stand close to each other, people like to have sunshine in their house,' Ando says. 'At the same time, clients don't want to display their private life to the street.'

INTERIOR DESIGN OR DECORATION?

Buying and owning a space is quite a new idea in Japan. Until the 1960s, more than 90 per cent of city dwellers did not own property. Renting was the norm and many landlords rented out apartments in the city. Once a family got bigger, it would move to a larger apartment. 'The Japanese are accustomed to a temporary style of living and thus not very familiar with a total redesigning of a space according to their specific taste,' Terada explains. 'We just put something in our apartments to show that it is our space and personalize the city apartment with a curtain, some favourite furniture items or by pinning up souvenirs.'

Japan caters to all these do-it-yourself decorators. The 100-Yen shops, found in every residential neighbourhood, sell everything from paperclips to grass mats for just 100 Yen (1 euro) each. Muji (Mujirushirohin), as its

name ('non-brand') suggests, offers simple but beautiful products in a style that fits any apartment in Japan. People therefore say Muji sells an all-in lifestyle perfectly matched to the standardized Japanese apartment. And then there is IKEA. 'In contrast to Muji, IKEA sells a jumble of things, full of colours and different shapes,' Terada explains. 'You can combine any style and material. The variety offers much more freedom in arrangement, which might explain why IKEA is so popular among families in Japan nowadays.'
Tsuzuki points out that the unique aspect of Tokyo is that people do not have very strict rules as to which class of people should use which brand of furniture. Louis Vuitton fashion or Italian designer furniture made for high-end people? In Japan people do not care much about this. People with a tiny apartment can have an exceptionally expensive sofa, while everything else in the house is cheap. It is similar to fashion. Young Japanese kids may wear inexpensive Uniqlo clothing but at the same time carry a super-expensive Louis Vuitton handbag. 'There is a true democratization of products in Tokyo,' Tsuzuki states.
When Ando collaborates with architects, the architects design the actual space but they expect her to enhance the space with her curtains. 'Some people think a curtain is a kind of room decoration, but I disagree,' says Ando, who uses her textiles as a building material, as if it were glass, wood or concrete. Her textiles appear in the space as a tapestry or curtain but at the same time serve as the finishing. 'The interesting point of curtains,' she points out, 'is that when you are inside, you can see the exterior from the inside. But from the outside, the inside cannot be seen.' Different from a traditional fusuma, a curtain as Ando designs it opens up a space without losing privacy.

ERASING DISCIPLINES

Young Japanese architects may succeed in proposing a new lifestyle to their clients using spatial features, but they still have to learn about interior design, according to the three interviewees. Tsuzuki: 'Architects spend a lot of time in university and usually enter an architecture firm straight after graduation without having any kind of experience in life. They should first leave the island of Japan and make a long trip abroad, and experience what it is to be in a really good and really bad place and discover the big contrasts.' To Ando, the interior is part of the architecture, and so are lighting, fabrics and furniture. Young architects should try to collaborate with specialists in this field. Terada concludes that architects always want to make a clear division between architecture and interior. 'It is time they learn that architecture is not just the completion of a paper model, and cross the boundary line between the discipline of architecture and interior design.'

1 K. Tsuzuki, Tokyo: A Certain Style (San Francisco: Chronicle Books, 1999).

Yoko Ando designed a curtain for Toyo Ito's Tama Art University Library that provides a soft and light atmosphere, which is in sharp contrast to the hard and strong concrete architecture

About the experts:
Yoko Ando
Independent Textile Designer at Yoko Ando Design (previously at NUNO Corporation)
Year of Birth: 1968
Education: Musashino Art University, Tokyo
Special Interest: Treating curtains as if they were building materials

Naoki Terada
Architect and Designer at Teradadesign Architects
Principle Teradamokei
Year of Birth: 1967
Education: Meiji University, Tokyo
Special Interest: Don`t limit yourself to designing form when humans can sense 3D space and colour with their eyes. Form and colour should enhance each other.

Kyoichi Tsuzuki
Independent Photographer, journalist, editor, art curator, and book publisher
Year of Birth: 1956
Special Interest: Unsung places

BIBLIOGRAPHY
HOW TO MAKE A JAPANESE HOUSE

Ashihara, Y., *The Hidden Order: Tokyo Through the Twentieth Century* (Tokyo: Kodansha International, 1989)

Atelier Bow-Wow, *Pet Architecture Guide Book Vol. 2* (Tokyo: World Photo Press, 2002)

Atelier Bow-Wow, *Bow-Wow from Post Bubble City* (Tokyo: Inax Publishing, 2006)

Atelier Bow-Wow, *Graphic Anatomy – Atelier Bow Wow* (Tokyo: Toto Shuppan, 2007)

Atelier Bow-Wow, *Echo of Space, Space of Echo* (Tokyo: INAX Publishing, 2009)

Atelier Bow-Wow, *The Architectures of Atelier Bow-Wow: Behaviorology* (New York: Rizzoli, 2010)

Bestor, Th. C., *Neighborhood Tokyo* (Chicago: Stanford University Press, 1989)

Bestor, Th. C., Tsukiji, *The Fish Market at the Center of the World* (Berkeley and Los Angeles: University of California Press, 2004)

Bognar, B., *The New Japanese Architecture* (New York: Rizzoli, 1990)

Bognar, B., *World Cities: TOKYO* (London: Academic Editions, 1997)

Bognar, B., *Beyond the Bubble: The New Japanese Architecture* (London: Phaidon Press, 2008)

Buntrock, D., *Materials and Meaning in Contemporary Japanese Architecture. Tradition and Today* (London, New York: Routledge, 2010)

Chiba, M., Ishida, T., Sato, M., 'Small. Fragments of a Conversation', *The Japan Architect* 43 (2001), 4-9

Chiba, M., 'Can the City be Delineated by Means of Houses', *The Japan Architect* 34 (1999), 6-7

Chiba, M., *Rule of the Site* (Tokyo: TOTO Shuppan, 2006)

Cybriwsky, R., *Tokyo: The Changing Profile of an Urban Giant* (Boston: G.K. Hall & Company, 1991)

Cybriwsky, R., *Tokyo: The Shogun's City at the Twenty-First Century* (Seattle: Academy Press, 1998)

Davies, R. J., Ikeno, O., *The Japanese Mind: Understanding Contemporary Japanese Culture* (Tokyo: Tuttle Publishing, 2002)

Engel, H., *The Japanese House: A Tradition for Contemporary Architecture* (Tokyo: Charles E. Tuttle Company, 1964)

Engel, H., *Measure and Construction of the Japanese House* (Tokyo: Charles E. Tuttle Company (1985)

Fujimoto, S., *Primitive Future* (Tokyo: INAX Publishing, 2008)

Fujimori, T., 'Modernology and Research', *The Japan Architect* 71 (2008), 4-7

Fujimori, T., *Fujimori Terunobu Architecture* (Tokyo: TOTO Shuppan, 2007)

Futagawa, Y., 'Circumstances Surrounding Japanese Houses Today', *GA Houses* 100 (2007)
Hanada, Y., 'Seeing beyond Dichotomies', *The Japan Architect* 34 (1999), 16-18

Hasegawa, G., *Thinking, Making Architecture, Living* (Tokyo: INAX Publishing, 2011)

Hendry, J., *Understanding Japanese Society* (London: Routledge, 1995)

Herrigel, E., *Zen in the Art of Archery* (New York: Pantheon Books, Inc 1953)

Hirata, A., *Tangling* (Tokyo: INAX Publishing, 2011)

Igarashi, J., *The Construction of a State* (Tokyo: TOTO Shuppan, 2011)

Inui, K., *Episodes* (Tokyo: INAX Publishing, 2008)

Inoue, M., *Space in Japanese Architecture* (Tokyo: Weatherhill, 1985)

Ishido, T., Komaki, S. (eds)., *Contemporary Japanese Houses 1985-2005* (Tokyo: Toto Shuppan, 2005)

Ishigami, J., *Small Images* (Tokyo: INAX Publishing, 2008)

Ishigami, J., *Another Scale of Architecture* (Kyoto: Seigansha Art Publishing, 2010)

Ishi'i K., 'Urban Beauty in Tokyo', *The Japan Architect* April (1982) 60-61

Isozaki, A., *Japan-ness in Architecture* (London: The MIT Press, 2006)

Ito, T., 'Theoretical and Sensorial Architecture: Sou Fujimoto's Radical Experiments, *2G magazine* 50 (2009) 4-9

Ito, T., *Toyo Ito Recent Projects* (Tokyo: A.D.A. EDITA, 2008)

Jinnai, H., *Ethnic Tokyo* (Tokyo: Process Architecture Publishing Co., 1987)

Jinnai, H., 'Tokyo Then and Now: Keys to Japanese Urban Design', *Japan Echo* XIV (1987) 20-29

Jinnai, H., *Tokyo: A Spatial Anthropology* (Los Angeles: University Of California Press, 1995)

Kira, M., Terada, M. (eds), *Japan Towards Totalscape: Contemporary Japanese Architecture, Urban Design and Landscape* (Rotterdam: NAi Publishers, 2001)

Kitayama, K. , Tsukamoto, Y., Nishizawa, R., *Tokyo Metabolizing* (Tokyo: TOTO Shuppan, 2010)

Kojima, K., '"Black" and "White"', *The Japan Architect*, 61 (2006), 4-5

Kojima, K., Akamatsu, K., Sejima, K., Nishizawa, R., 'Works and Ideas of Cat', *The Japan Architect* 61 (2006), 122-126

Kuma, K, and Associates., *Studies in Organic* (Tokyo: TOTO Shuppan, 2009)

Kuma, K., 'Weak Architecture', *GA Architect* 19 (2005), 8-15

Kuma, K., Sato, J., Hirata, A., 'Beyond Deterministic Systems', *The Japan Architect* 83 (2011), 4-9

Kuroda, J., Kaijima, M., Tsukamoto, Y., *Made in Tokyo* (Tokyo: Kajima Institute Publishing Co, 2001)

Lafayette De Mente, B., *Japan's Cultural Code Words: 233 Key Terms That Explain the Attitudes and Behavior of the Japanese* (Tokyo: Tuttle Publishing, 2004)

Maki F., 'Japanese City Spaces and the Concept of Oku', *The Japan Architect* May (1979), 50-62

Maki, F., '50 Years Since Group Form', *The Japan Architect* 78 (2010), 4-7

Morse, E. S., *Japanese Homes And Their Surroundings* (Tokyo: Tuttle Publishing, 1972)

Nagayama, H., *Sketching* (Tokyo: Shinjuku Shobo, 2010)

Nakagawa, T., *The Japanese House: In Space, Memory, and Language* (Tokyo: International House of Japan, 2005)

Nango, Y., 'Research into the Research of Architects', *The Japan Architect* 71 (2008), 8-11

Nishizawa, R., Tsukamoto, Y., 'Discussing the Contemporary Urban Landscape', *The Japan Architect* 66 (2007), 10-17

Nishizawa, R., 'Creating Principles – Structure, Plan, Relationship, Landscape', *GA Architect* 18 (2005), 8-11

Nishizawa, R., Ishigami, J., 'Approach to Architecture', *The Japan Architect* 72 (2009), 4-11

Nishizawa, R., *Studies by the Office of Ryue Nishizawa* (Tokyo: INAX Publishing, 2009)

Nishizawa, T., *Taira Nishizawa Architects 1994-2004* (Tokyo: TOTO Shuppan, 2004)

Nitschke, G., 'Ma: The Japanese Sense Of "Place" in Old and New Architecture and Planning', *Architectural Design* March (1966), 117-130

Nitschke, G., *From Shinto to Ando: Studies in Architectural Anthropology in Japan* (London: Academic Editions, 1993)

Okada, E., Yamasaki, Y., *DEROLL* Commissions Series 1 (Kyoto: DEROLL, 2007)

Popham, P., 'Tokyo: Notes Towards Four Chapters', *Process Architecture* No 49 (1984), 30-31

Popham, P., *Tokyo: The City at the End of the World* (New York: Kodansha USA, 1985)

Richie, D., *A Lateral View: Essays on Contemporary Japan* (Tokyo: The Japan Times, 1991)

Richie, D., *A Tractate on Japanese Aesthetics* (Berkely: Stone Bridge Press, 2007)

Sand. J., *House and Home in Modern Japan: Architecture, Domestic Space and Bourgeois Culture 1880-1930* (Cambridge: Harvard University Press, 2003)

Sakamoto, K., Kitayama, K., Chiba, M., 'Explorations in Collectivity', *The Japan Architect* 49 (2003) 6-13

Sasaki, M., *Flux Structure* (Tokyo: TOTO Shuppan, 2005)

Sato, J., *Items in Jun Sato Structural Engineers* (Tokyo: INAX Publishing, 2010)

Seidensticker, E., *Low City, High City: Tokyo from Edo to the Earthquake: how the shogun's ancient capital became a great modern city, 1867-1923* (Cambridge: Harvard University Press, 1991)

Seidensticker, E., *Tokyo Rising: The City Since the Great Earthquake* (Cambridge: Harvard University Press, 1991)

Seike, K., *The Art Of Japanese Joinery* (Tokyo: Weatherhill, 1977)

Seike, K., Terry, C. S., *Contemporary Japanese Houses* (Tokyo: Kodansha Internatonal Ltd. 1964)

Shelton, B., *Learning From The Japanese City: West Meets East in Urban Design* (New York: Routledge, 1999)

Sejima, K., Nishizawa, R., *Kazuyo Sejima in Gifu* (Barcelona: Actar, 2003)

Sogabe, M., 'A New Form of Public Spiritedness', *The Japan Architect* 82 (2011), 10-13

Sorensen, A., *The Making Of Urban Japan* (London: Routledge Curzon, 2002)

Suzuki, A., *Do Android crows fly over the Skies of an Electronic Tokyo?: the Interactive Urban Landscape of Japan* (London: AA Publications, 2004)

Suzuki, H., 'Tokyo Has A Thousand Eyes', *The Japan Architect* (1982) 10-13

Suzuki, H., Kuma, K., 'A Return to Materials', *The Japan Architect* 38 (2000) 4-7

Tanizaki, J., *In Praise of Shadows* (New Haven: Leete's Island Books, 1977)

Taut, B., *Houses And People Of Japan* (Tokyo: The Sanseido Press, 1958)

Terry, C. S., *Contemporary Japanese Houses Volume 2* (Tokyo: Kodansha International Ltd. 1968)

Tsuzuki, K., *Tokyo: A Certain Style* (San Francisco: Chronicle Books, 1999)

Tsukamoto, Y., Fujimoto, S. 'Window, Interior, Exterior. On the Questions of What should decide Window Character', *The Japan Architect* 74 (2009), 8-15

Ueda, A., *The Inner Harmony of the Japanese House* (Tokyo: Kodansha International, 1990)

Ueda, A., *The Electric Geisha* (Tokyo: Kodansha International, 1994)

Waley, P., *Tokyo City of Stories* (Tokyo: Weatherhill, 1991)

Yamamoto, R., 'Thoughts On Tokyo Housing', *The Japan Architect* April (1982) 56-57

Yamamoto, R., Nakamura, H., Fujimura, R., *Modelling the Local Community Sphere* (Tokyo: Inax Publishers, 2010)

Yatsuka, H., 'The New Japanese Architecture' in Botond, B. (ed), *An ArchitectureFloating On The Sea Of Signs*, (New York: Rizzoli, 1990) 38-41

Yatsuka, H., 'The 1960 Tokyo Bay Project of Kenzo Tange', *Cities in Transition* (Rotterdam: 010 Publishers, 2001) 178-191

Yoshimura, Y., *Super Legal Buildings* (Tokyo: Shokokusha, 2006)

PHOTO CREDITS

Cover photo: Mitsutaka Kitamura
first published in Casa BRUTUS (February, 2010)

Atelier Bow-Wow: 96, 97,100-101,104,105

Daici Ano: 32-33, 36, 37,40-41, 168, 169, 172, 176-177, 180, 181, 184, 185, 188-189, 192, 193, 196, 197, 300, 301, 314, 316, 317

Ryota Atarashi: 200-201, 204, 205, 208-209

Iwan Baan: 0-1, 4-5, 6, 10-11, 56-57, 60-61, 64-65, 128-129, 132-133, 136, 137, 144-145, 148-149, 152-153, 229, 232-233, 306

Mitsumasa Fujitsuka: 44-45, 48, 49, 52, 53

Go Hasegawa & Associates: 224-225, 228

Sadao Hotta: 68-69, 72, 73, 76-77

Hiroshi Kikuchi Architects: 292

Katsuhiro Miyamoto & Associates: 121, 126

Mount Fuji Architects Studio: 296

Yuko Nagayama & Associates: 248-249

Ryuji Nakamura & Associates: 264-265

Masao Nishikawa: 84-85, 88, 89, 92-93, back cover

MUJI: 288 (top), 294, 295

Mitsuo Okamoto: 240 (bottom), 241

Yuki Omori: 318, 319

Takumi Ota: 8-9, 236-237, 240 (top), 244, 245, 302, 303

Tomohiro Sakashita: 108-109, 112, 113, 116, 117, 310, 311

Toshihiro Sobajima: 120, 298, 299, 305

Ken'ichi Suzuki: 312, 313

Koichi Torimura: 280

Toshiyuki Yano: 2-3, 7, 12-13, 156, 157, 160, 161, 164-165, 212-213, 216-217, 220-221

Toshiyuki Yano/ Nacása & Partners Inc.: 290, 291

Makoto Yoshida: 14-15, 16

Courtesy of Architecton: 308

Courtesy of Toyo Ito & Associates: 321

Courtesy of Hiroshi Sambuichi Architects: 309

ILLUSTRATION CREDITS

Ryuji Fujimura architects: 282

Daiwa House Industry Co., Ltd. : 288(bottom)

Riken Yamamoto & Field Shop: 287

Yasutaka Yoshimura Architects: 284, 285

Yuko Nagayama & Associates: 252

junya.ishigami + associates: 256-257, 260, 261,

Ryuji Nakamura & Associates: 270, 271

Aerial View of Tokyo

Threefold House in Kumamoto by Takao Shiotsuka Atelier

House N in Oita by Sou Fujimoto

Okurayama Apartments in Yokohama by Kazuyo Seijima & Associates

ZXY in Tokyo by NAF architect & design

Life in Spiral in Tokyo by Hideaki Takayanagi

Garden & House in Tokyo by Office of Ryue Nishizawa

Oshikamo in Toyota by Katsutoshi Sasaki

Reflection of Mineral in Tokyo by Atelier Tekuto

Lucky Drops in Tokyo by Atelier Tekuto

ACKNOWLEDGEMENTS

The author wishes to acknowledge the following individuals and institutions

Parts of the interviews that appear in this book have previously been published in MARK Magazine. Nuijsink is very grateful to the editors Arthur Wortmann and David Keuning for their continuous support and interest into the contemporary Japanese house and the young generation of Japanese architects.

Professor Manabu Chiba for guiding me during my years at The University of Tokyo and the Japanese government for the *Monbukagakusho* Scholarship

REVIEW COMMITTEE
Floris Alkemade, Jacob van Rijs (MVRDV), Arie Graafland

SPECIAL THANKS
Sachiko Ando, Daici Ano, Jun Aoki, Mari Aoki, Suguru Aoki, Shuhei Aoyama, Kanna Arita, Yasuko Arita, Rafael Balboa, Chiba Manabu-laboratory, Hideto Chijiwa, Setsuko Eguchi, Hiromi Fujii, Terunobu Fujimori, Takashi Fujino, Ryuji Fujimura, Teppei Fujiwara, Yoshie Furuya, David Glaettli, Shogo Hagiwara, Kayo Hasegawa, Masahiro Hashimoto, Megumi Hosaka, Takeshi Hosaka, Taro Igarashi, Hisashi Ikai, Mariko Inaba, Akihiro Ito, Toyo Ito, Shinichi Kawakatsu, Hitomi Kawasaki, Junko Kawauchi, Hiroshi Kato, Ryota Kidokoro, Eriko Kinoshita, Atsushi Kitagawara, Koen Klinkers, Miryon Ko, Kimika Komiya, Marieke Kums, Yuko Machida, Keisuke Maeda, Sakie Miyake, Kyoko Mishima, Yoshitaka Miyauchi, Keiko Motegi-Klinkers, Ai Kubota, Chie Nabeshima, Yuko Nagayama, Mami Nakada, Yusuke Nakada, Hiroshi Nakamura, Akio Nakasa, Jo Nagasaka, Taeko Nakatsubo, Hideyuki Nakayama, Tetsuya Nakazono, Marie Nishida, Chiharu Nishimura, Taira Nishizawa, Kenji Ogawa, Toshiya Ogino, Haruko Ogita, Eizo Okada, Mutsuko Ota, Takumi Ota, Miki Oyamada, Ineke van de Pol, Darko Radović, Iku Sakakibara, Jun.ichi Sampei, Jun Sato, Oki Sato, Edward Schuurmans, Jun Shibata, Naomi Shibata, Toshihiro Sobajima, Kazuhiro Sobue, Michiko Sumi, Seiji Tanaka, Makoto Takei, Kentaro Takeguchi, Kei Takeuchi, Aya Tatsuta, Naoki Terada, Takahara Tezuka, Yuriko Toki, Keiko Uchiyama, Satoru Umehara, Bas Valckx, Makiko Wakaki, Maaike Weijers, Suzuko Yamada, Asako Yamamoto, Yasuhiro Yamashita, Teruhiro Yanagihara, Miho Yanagisawa, Toshiyuki Yano, Makoto Yokomizo

CREDITS

This publication was partially made possible through the financial support from the Netherlands Architecture Fund, the Japan Foundation and the Suntory Foundation.

AUTHOR: Cathelijne Nuijsink
COPY EDITORS: Pierre Bouvier, D'Laine Camp
DESIGN: Studio Sander Boon, Amsterdam
PAPER: Maxioffset
LITHOGRAPHY AND PRINTING: Drukkerij van Gorcum
PUBLISHER: Marcel Witvoet, nai010 publishers, Rotterdam

nai010 publishers is an internationally orientated publisher specialized in developing, producing and distributing books on architecture, visual arts and related disciplines.
www.nai010.com

nai010 books are available internationally at selected bookstores and from the following distribution partners:

North, Central and South America – Artbook | D.A.P., New York, USA, dap@dapinc.com

Rest of the world – Idea Books, Amsterdam, the Netherlands, idea@ideabooks.nl

For general questions, please contact nai010 publishers directly at sales@nai010.com or visit our website www.nai010.com for further information.

Printed and bound in The Netherlands
Fifth printing 2025

ISBN 978-90-5662-850-5

サントリー文化財団
SUNTORY FOUNDATION

Stimuleringsfonds voor Architectuur
the Netherlands Architecture Fund

JAPANFOUNDATION

Cathelijne Nuijsink (1977, the Netherlands) is a young academic trained in design at the Design Academy in Eindhoven, the Netherlands, and in architecture at Delft University of Technology, the Netherlands and the University of Tokyo, Japan. From 2005 to 2011 she intensively interviewed Japanese architects as part of her research at the Manabu Chiba laboratory of the University of Tokyo, which resulted in the monograph *How to Make a Japanese House.* Nuijsink is currently continuing her studies of Japan as a PhD student at the University of Pennsylvania, Department of East Asian Languages and Civilizations in Philadelphia, USA.
www.cathelijnenuijsink.com